Deleuze and New Technology

Deleuze Connections

"It is not the elements or the sets which define the multiplicity. What defines it is the AND, as something which has its place between the elements or between the sets. AND, AND, AND – stammering.'

Gilles Deleuze and Claire Parnet, *Dialogues*

General Editor
Ian Buchanan

Editorial Advisory Board
Keith Ansell-Pearson
Rosi Braidotti
Claire Colebrook
Tom Conley
Gregg Lambert
Adrian Parr
Paul Patton
Patricia Pisters

Titles Available in the Series
Ian Buchanan and Claire Colebrook (eds), *Deleuze and Feminist Theory*
Ian Buchanan and John Marks (eds), *Deleuze and Literature*
Mark Bonta and John Protevi (eds), *Deleuze and Geophilosophy*
Ian Buchanan and Marcel Swiboda (eds), *Deleuze and Music*
Ian Buchanan and Gregg Lambert (eds), *Deleuze and Space*
Martin Fuglsang and Bent Meier Sørensen (eds), *Deleuze and the Social*
Ian Buchanan and Adrian Parr (eds), *Deleuze and the Contemporary World*
Constantin V. Boundas (ed.), *Deleuze and Philosophy*
Ian Buchanan and Nicholas Thoburn (eds), *Deleuze and Politics*
Chrysanthi Nigianni and Merl Storr (eds), *Deleuze and Queer Theory*
Jeffrey A. Bell and Claire Colebrook (eds), *Deleuze and History*
Laura Cull (ed.), *Deleuze and Performance*

Forthcoming Titles in the Series
Ian Buchanan and Laura Guillaume (eds), *Deleuze and the Body*
Stephen Zepke and Simon O'Sullivan (eds), *Deleuze and Contemporary Art*
Paul Patton and Simone Bignall (eds), *Deleuze and the Postcolonial*

Deleuze and New Technology

Edited by Mark Poster and David Savat

Edinburgh University Press

© in this edition Edinburgh University Press, 2009
© in the individual contributions is retained by the authors

Edinburgh University Press Ltd
22 George Square, Edinburgh

www.euppublishing.com

Typeset in 10.5/13 Sabon
by Servis Filmsetting Ltd, Stockport, Cheshire, and
printed and bound in Great Britain by
CPI Antony Rowe, Chippenham and Eastbourne

A CIP record for this book is available from the British Library

ISBN 978 0 7486 3336 4 (hardback)
ISBN 978 0 7486 3338 8 (paperback)

The right of the contributors
to be identified as authors of this work
has been asserted in accordance with
the Copyright, Designs and Patents Act 1988.

Contents

Acknowledgements

We are especially grateful to Carol Macdonald for her kind patience and support, as well as to Máiréad McElligott and Tim Clark. We also thank Michael Blanchard and Tauel Harper for their assistance, and a special thank you to Katinka.

Introduction:
Deleuze and New Technology

David Savat

Mark Poster closes this book with the observation that Deleuze never theorised new media, and, indeed, rarely made use of the term. As Poster points out, given France's experiment with Minitel this may be an important point to make in the context of a book entitled *Deleuze and New Technology*. Opinion on the usefulness of Deleuze's work with respect to theorising new technology diverges in this volume, ranging from scepticism about the use of Deleuze and Guattari's concept of the rhizome in theorisations of the Internet, to critiques of Deleuze's understanding of language as it concerns the idea of the concept, to explorations of how his work on an older technology such as film can offer valuable insights into new developments in neuroscience. As some contributors point out, since Deleuze died before the recent proliferation of new media it should come as no surprise that a large proportion of the essays in this book take as their starting point one of the few pieces in which Deleuze did engage specifically with new technology, namely his short essay entitled 'Postscript on the Societies of Control' (1992).

At the same time, Deleuze made obvious use of a concept of the machine throughout much of his work, and was at times directly engaged in considering specific technologies and the effect of their usage as a component or function within larger assemblages. In different ways Deleuze and Guattari's *Anti-Oedipus* (1983) and *A Thousand Plateaus* (1987) are most representative in this regard, as well as Deleuze's *Foucault* (1988), *Cinema 1: The Movement-Image* (1986), and *Cinema 2: The Time-Image* (1989), amongst others. In short, while Deleuze may not have devoted that much attention to so-called 'new' technology, and especially 'new' media – certainly less so and more negatively so than Guattari – his conceptualisation of technology and the machine, in both its material and its more abstract forms, is careful and considered, and plays a significant role in much of his work.

While Deleuze's, and Guattari's, concept of the machine is sympathetic to the concept of the machine as defined by Humberto Maturana and Francisco Varela, a much stronger influence comes by way of Karl Marx and, perhaps even more so, Lewis Mumford. Mumford's concept of the megamachine is particularly useful in coming to grips with Deleuze's conceptualisation of the machine, including his concept of the social machine (Ansell-Pearson 1999: 217). In explaining his reasons for treating specific forms of human collectivities as machines, and for viewing the military machine as the first such machine (Mumford 1994: 315), Mumford focuses precisely on the productive energies or capacities these machines enable, as well as the processes by which the energies of their diverse components – that is, the human components in Mumford's case – are harnessed into a coherent entity with a sense of unity or unicity (Guattari 1995) capable of producing such productive energy. Here Mumford states that:

> To call these collective entities machines is no idle play on words. If a machine be defined more or less in accord with the classic definition of Reuleaux, as a combination of resistant parts, each specialised in function, operating under human control, to transmit motion and to perform work, then the labor machine was a real machine: all the more because its component parts, though composed of human bone, nerve, and muscle, were reduced to their bare mechanical elements and rigidly restricted to the performance of their mechanical tasks. (Mumford 1994: 316)

And he goes on to state that the labour machine that built the pyramids in Ancient Egypt was

> a machine of a hundred thousand manpower, that is, the equivalent of ten thousand horsepower: a machine composed of a multitude of uniform, specialized, interchangeable, but functionally differentiated parts, rigorously marshalled together and coordinated in a process centrally organised and centrally directed: each part behaving as a mechanical component of the mechanised whole: unmoved by an internal impulse that would interfere with the working of the mechanism. (Mumford 1994: 318)

In other words, Mumford did not define the machine by its materiality but, like Varela, and like Deleuze and Guattari, by 'the set of inter-relations of its components independent of the components themselves' (Varela in Guattari 1995: 39). As Mumford explained: '[t]o understand the structure or performance of the human machine, one must do more than centre attention upon the point where it materialises' (Mumford 1994: 319).

What is critical therefore in the concept of the machine, as both Deleuze and Guattari employ it, is a consideration of the organisation of the variety of components in relation to each other that comprises any given machine. For that reason machines can and do exist on any scale and can be both material and immaterial, or as Mumford coined it, visible or invisible. Guattari's explanation of the concept of the machine in his *Chaosmosis* (1995) indicates its connection to a series of other concepts that he and Deleuze made use of, most notably the idea of the abstract machine, which forms a component in any machine. Indeed, Guattari explains that the abstract machine, as one component, is transversal to the other components of a machine, in such as way as to give them an existence, an 'efficiency', as Guattari terms it. As he further explains, it is in this manner that 'the different components are swept up and reshaped by a sort of dynamism' (Guattari 1995: 35). It is the resultant functional ensemble that Deleuze and Guattari describe as the machinic assemblage.

On this latter point Guattari stressed that the use of the word assemblage 'does not imply any notion of bond, passage, or anastomosis between its components', but, rather, that it is 'an assemblage of possible fields, of virtual as much as constituted elements' (Guattari 1995: 35). It is precisely for this reason that any technology, or machine, opens up a specific field of action, recognising that thought too is a form of action. At the same time, any technology or machine may close off certain forms of action (and thought) (Guattari 1992), or, as Mumford stated, support or enlarge the capacity for human expression (Mumford 1994: 310), as his example of the invention of containers should make clear enough.

For Deleuze and Guattari then, the key focus was on the assemblage as a collective machine and not, as William Bogard reminds the reader in this book, on the actual technical object. In this respect Deleuze's approach to thinking about machines and technology diverges from Heidegger's. Here, as Bogard points out in the opening chapter, it also becomes important to understand that for Deleuze and Guattari 'assemblages are passional, they are compositions of desire'. This is a point that a number of contributors also engage with, most notably Ian Cook, in his discussion of Internet addiction, and Ian Buchanan, in considering the Internet's body without organs.

In this context it is also crucial to recognise that for Deleuze any machine or technology is social before it is technical – again, a point that a number of contributors to this book make. As Deleuze states in his essay on societies of control, any technology or machine is an expression of a given social form, and is neither its cause nor its effect. Stated differently, machines form part of a given societal assemblage: '[t]ypes of machine are easily matched with each type of society – not that machines are determining, but because they express those social forms capable of generating them and using them' (Deleuze 1992: 6). In other words, contemporary machines express something about a given society today, in much the same way that machines such as the pyramids expressed something about the ancient Egyptians.

For Deleuze (1992), computers are the latest such technological evolution and, significantly, a further mutation of capitalism. So, if I were to attempt to define 'new technology' in the context of this book, it could begin with this as a starting point, recognising that most of the recent developments in genetic engineering, biotechnology, nanotechnology, surveillance techniques, medical technology, and so on, at some level have the digital computer as an essential component. It would therefore be tempting simply to define this new societal assemblage as 'the digital', though this itself produces a generalisation that a number of contributors to this book would be wary of. The digital societal assemblage has a complexity that goes well beyond the simplicity of increased control offered by Boolean logic and the binary digit, and the very term 'control', like the term 'digital', as Manovich (2001) has pointed out, needs unpacking. This book is in part a step towards that.

One important point to make here is that while Deleuze did not write much about the new technologies of the digital assemblage, he did draw attention to a number of key expressions of this assemblage, not all of which were necessarily as negative as is suggested in his 'societies of control' essay. One notable point, for example, also made by others such as Jameson (1991), is that the new technologies make a very different use of energy. Deleuze alluded to this in his essay on the societies of control, when he stated that while the disciplinary societies made use of machines that had the 'passive danger of entropy and the active danger of sabotage', in the societies of control the machines have the 'passive danger of jamming and [their] active danger is piracy' (1992: 6). He elaborates on this with the suggestion that 'disciplinary man was a discontinuous producer of energy, but the man of control is undulatory, in orbit, in a continuous network. Everywhere *surfing* has already replaced the older *sports*' (1992: 6).

This focus is important, since different uses of energy form part of ongoing processes of deterritorialisation and reterritorialisation in the ongoing mutation of capitalism. For example, one critical point in that mutation came with the invention of the steam engine, which enabled a very significant and literal deterritorialisation. As Marx observed:

> [n]ot till the invention of Watt's second and so-called double-acting steam-engine was a prime mover found which drew its own motive power from the consumption of coal and water, was entirely under man's control, was

mobile and a means of locomotion, was urban and not – like the water-wheel – rural, permitted production to be concentrated in towns instead of – like water-wheels – being scattered over the countryside and, finally, was of universal technical application, and little affected in its choice of residence by local circumstances. (Marx 1990: 499)

No longer reliant on muscle, wind and water power, one consequence was a further reterritorialisation:

> [i]n so far as machinery dispenses with muscular power, it becomes a means for employing workers of slight muscular strength, or whose bodily development is incomplete, but whose limbs are the more supple. The labour of women and children was therefore the first result of the capitalistic application of machinery! That mighty substitute for labour and for workers, the machine, was immediately transformed into a means for increasing the number of wage-labourers by enrolling, under the direct sway of capital, every member of the worker's family, without distinction of age or sex. (Marx 1990: 157)

With the machines of the so-called digital or information age comes a very different use of energy, and Deleuze sees a difference in approach not only in philosophy, but also a more general shift where action is more about being taken up in the motion of something else, like a wave, than about 'being the origin of an effort' (Deleuze 1995: 121). As Jameson pointed out, a further consequence is that

> It is immediately obvious that the technology of our own moment no longer possesses [the] same capacity for representation: not the turbine, nor even Sheeler's grain elevators or smokestacks, not the baroque elaboration of pipes and conveyor belts, nor even the streamlined profile of the railroad train – all vehicles of speed still concentrated at rest – but rather the computer, whose outer shell has no emblematic or visual power, or even the casings of the various media themselves, as with that home appliance called television which articulates nothing but rather implodes, carrying its flattened image surface within itself. (Jameson 1991: 36–7)

In other words, these are machines that express not motion and kinetic energy but, rather, a concern with very different reproductive processes (Jameson 1991). As Castells, following Lyotard (1984), explained, these are machines that engage in the 'action of knowledge upon knowledge' as their main source of productivity (Castells 1996: 16–17). With such a different use of energy come very different processes of deterritorialisation and reterritorialisation, some of which, depending on the assemblages they are part of, may be positive, and others more negative in their productions and manifestations – which is in great part what the variety of contributions in this book demonstrates.

The book is organised into two parts: 'Control' and 'Becoming'. The contributions in the first part tend to focus on Deleuze's idea of the societies of control and the politics surrounding new technologies, including possible strategies to resist new techniques of control enabled by those technologies. William Bogard, in the first chapter 'Deleuze and Machines', asks whether with Deleuze we actually have a politics of technology and of control societies, and suggests that care needs to be taken in pursuing that question. He points out that there is no universal form of control, nor a universal form of resistance. While the new abstract machines of control may be ruled by corporate capital, there is no necessary reason for that to be so. Bogard suggests that there can be experimentation with the abstract machine, pointing out that newly emerging networks create possibilities for people to have positive encounters with what the assemblage of control produces and encloses as its outside, the common and the multitude. On this Bogard makes the very important point that discipline also creates a potential for positive social encounters, as discipline is required in most transformative human activity, and urges that people likewise experiment with control networks, pointing out that resistance is not simply 'anti-control'. In this respect, Deleuze and Guattari's concept of the body without organs holds significant value, though, like Deleuze and Guattari, Bogard cautions against too rapid a deterritorialisation.

After offering a brief review of some of Deleuze and Guattari's concepts, Verena Conley's chapter, 'Of Rhizomes, Smooth Space, War Machines and New Media', engages with the question of how those concepts can be used in dealing with the impact of so-called new media today, especially given that Deleuze himself rarely engaged with such media. Like Bogard, Conley is concerned with the question of resistance against the new mechanisms of control, and argues that digital media, in spite of (some might argue, because of) the binary digit, offer creative and unprecedented possibilities. While, like Buchanan in his chapter, she is critical of the manner in which some people have made use of Deleuze and Guattari's concept of the rhizome in relation to new media (often mistakenly equating the rhizome with computer networks), she argues that Deleuze and Guattari's work is useful in exploring new technology because they made it very clear that much depends on how technologies are made use of. In short, it is a matter of questioning the larger assemblages of which new technologies will form a component.

If Bogard's and Conley's contributions offer a more general consideration of Deleuze and Guattari's work with respect to new technologies of control, the following chapters offer detailed explorations of control as a mode of power. David Savat, in his chapter 'Deleuze's Objectile', argues that while Deleuze suggested that the newer modulatory mode of power replaced the disciplinary mode of power identified by Foucault, the two modes of power can actually function at the same time, through the very same writing apparatus, producing effects that may be at times complimentary, and at times quite antagonistic. Here Savat makes use of Fourier's principle of superposition, as well as key ideas in Deleuze's *The Fold* (1993) regarding the objectile and the superject, to suggest that this twin production by the disciplinary machine and the new modulatory machine is central to the experience of dividuality as Deleuze identified it. Indeed, Savat argues that dividuality, and both the objectile and the superject, are useful concepts in coming to terms with a potentially new 'fluid politics', very different from the more 'solid politics' associated with the concept of the individual.

The experience of dividuality identified by Deleuze in his essay on the societies of control is further explored by Bent Meier Sorenson in his chapter 'How to Surf'. Here Sorenson offers a more detailed view of life in the society of control, and observes that if you have never been unemployed you have not really understood anything about modernity. It is precisely this condition of being 'unemployed' in the context of societies of control that Sorenson focuses his attention on. Like other contributors to the book, he also asks how people might 'resist', or more accurately and significantly, how people might 'surf the wave'. Here Sorenson, besides reminding the reader of Deleuze's debt to Franz Kafka, makes use of Deleuze and Guattari's concept of the body without organs to indicate that by connecting to what is established as the outside by the abstract machine of control people can potentially begin to establish more positive connections and productions.

In her chapter on the 'chemical cane', Abigail Bray focuses specifically on new technologies that form part of what Deleuze described as 'the fantastic pharmaceutical productions' that form part of the installation of societies of control. Much as Deleuze asked people to do, Bray, like Sorenson and Savat, offers a more detailed socio-technological study of emerging technologies and systems of control in their specificity, pointing out that the dis-ordered child is increasingly no longer punished but simply medicated. Here she draws attention not only to how people are identified as being 'at risk', but also to how those so identified are preemptively controlled by way of modifying the body at the molecular level with pharmaceutical technologies.

While Bray offers a detailed examination of a newly emerging biopolitics, as expressed in new medical technologies, Saul Newman in his chapter 'Politics in the Age of Control' focuses more explicitly on the political implications of such technologies. Newman, like Bray, Sorenson and Savat, identifies how a wide variety of new techniques of control immediately position people as subjects of risk and suspicion. Indeed, he points out how these techniques and technologies are increasingly aimed at identifying 'future risks', and that control is sought at both the global level of populations and at the infinitesimal level of people's biological substratum, the latter in many respects being the focus of Bray's chapter. Newman strongly advocates that we examine not simply the more subtle technologies that Deleuze notes in his essay on societies of control, but, more importantly, the entire panoply of control mechanisms, ranging from anti-terrorist measures to the policing of borders. In short, following Deleuze, Newman asks us to consider the assemblage as a whole. It is in this context that he questions the usefulness of so-called identity politics, but also asks whether it is possible to have a politics without identity, and considers the utility of Deleuze's idea of 'becoming-minor'.

Much like Bogard and Conley, Tauel Harper in his chapter 'Smash the Strata!' notes that Deleuze and Guattari's work contains clear suggestions that we ought not fear technology in any struggle against political oppression. This chapter also opens the second part of the book, on Becoming. According to Harper, Deleuze, like Guattari, is an ideal theorist for exploring the more political possibilities enabled by new technologies, pointing out that a technology is always part of an assemblage that contains the possibility of both emancipation and capture. Taking open-source programming as an example, Harper suggests that it is not a question of simply acquiescing to societies of control but, rather, that such programming involves experimentation with Deleuze and Guattari's rhizomatic formula n–1. After all, open-source programming, Harper argues, involves multitudes conspiring to produce a program that is never complete, that is always n–1.

Ian Buchanan, in his chapter 'Deleuze and the Internet', offers a critical view on how some of Deleuze and Guattari's concepts have been used, focusing mainly on their concept of the rhizome. Taking his cue from Deleuze's explanation that philosophy has the concepts it deserves according to how well it constructs its problems, Buchanan suggests that people should not start with the idea that the Internet might be a body without organs, or a rhizome, or anything else for that matter. Instead, he suggests that we first consider how a new assemblage like the Internet actually works, and only then begin to consider how to develop the appropriate concepts. In the process of constructing this argument Buchanan challenges the idea that the Internet is somehow expressive of a new kind of politics, and instead argues, using Google as his example, that it is simply another institution used by capitalism to extract surplus value from the economy. At the same time, Buchanan does not close off the possibility that the Internet, with some work, could become a global body without organs, but, like Harper, he warns the reader to take great care.

Where Newman and Harper indicate that a new politics is emerging, Eugene Thacker in his chapter 'Swarming' follows up on their argument in a different way to Buchanan. Thacker is specifically interested in the new forms of protest and organisation enabled by new technologies, and especially in the use of the idea of swarming as a form of multiplicity in relation to this. He investigates how a different politics, one not focused on the identity politics that Newman argues is finished, might be conceptualised. Thacker points out that 'swarms', whether they be biological, technological, or political, have no centre, which raises a number of political concerns. He suggests that swarms are a foe that is stripped of its 'faciality', and in that context asks what the shape of the ethical encounter might be. This is reminiscent of the question Deleuze posed in his essay on societies of control as to how one might fight a gas.

The new experiences of sensation enabled by digital technologies are to some extent explored by Ian Cook in his chapter 'The Body Without Organs and Internet Gaming Addiction'.[1] Cook, focusing mainly on First Person Shooter games, makes the point that these are highly immersive twitch games because they involve rapid body configuration and reconfiguration, as well as additional elements, such as sounds, that are enfolded in the games. Using Deleuze and Guattari's concept of the body without organs, Cook makes the point that Internet gaming addiction is a specific configuration of mechanic, organic and imaginative emergences which express a need to continuously reconfigure themselves. As Cook points out, in the context of these games it is not so much winning that is the point – that is, completing the game – but, rather, the actual joy experienced in playing the game. This is an experience that can only be produced by way of connection to the world of the game, or rather, to that assemblage.

Horst Ruthrof too is interested in sense and perception in his chapter 'Deleuze's Concept in the Information-Control Continuum'. Here Ruthrof specifically questions Deleuze and Guattari's argument concerning the philosophical concept as presented in their *What Is Philosophy?* While he is critical of Deleuze's concept, Ruthrof argues that it can be applied not only to philosophy but, indeed, to all language and perception. Here Ruthrof makes the point that when Deleuzian concepts are connected to habitual thought, they do not simply replace older concepts but, in fact, open up a different way of viewing a given discursive field. This, in part, is what some of the contributors to this book engage in, and Ruthrof in that respect offers one more well-considered response to the question 'why Deleuze and new technology?'

Patricia Pisters, in her chapter 'Illusionary Perception and Cinema', moves away more explicitly from digital or new media, to focus instead on new developments in the neurosciences. She makes the point that Deleuze was well aware of the transformation that the biology of the brain continues to undergo, and, indeed, that it is in this area, rather than psychoanalysis or linguistics, that philosophy should look for new concepts and principles, the main reason being that in using psychoanalysis or linguistics people apply ready-made concepts. In this respect Pisters, by way of Deleuze, expresses a concern similar to that of Buchanan and Ruthrof in their respective contributions. She makes the argument that Deleuze's cinema books, while dealing with the older technology of film, relate the brain and the screen in a very immanent way, and in doing so have a lot to offer when considering recent developments in neuroscience.

A different way of thinking about the new sensibilities offered by new technology is explored in several respects in Timothy Murray's chapter 'The Archival Events of New Medialised Art'. As Murray points out, what is at issue in considering the impact of digital technologies on the parameters of the artistic archive is the actual place of memory in the work of art itself, including its dependence on technology. Here Murray asks the reader to rethink the notion of technê, especially when the variety of digital media, ranging from various databases to wireless networks and other communications systems, merge into what he terms a 'new skin of fibrous event'. What is at issue for Murray is a very significant shift in art from a focus on perspective and projection, to one of experimentation with fold and surface.

The fact that this volume is divided into two separate parts, 'Control' and 'Becoming', does not negate the fact that there is significant overlap between the different contributions, both within each part and between them. One obvious reason for this is that the contributions deal with both new technologies and the assemblages they are a part of, and because the authors in one form or another engage with the work of Deleuze. At the same time, it is important recognise that the so-called 'new' technologies, and recent developments in multiple fields, are in many respects underpinned by the digital computer. As the variety of the following contributions should make clear, it is far too simplistic to characterise any so-called new age or society as one of control or as 'the digital age'. Understood more broadly and appropriately, new forms of control are perhaps better understood as new techniques, new ways of doing things. As stated above, and as a number of the contributors make clear, the resultant productions can be both negatively and positively experienced depending on the assemblages these new techniques form a part of. One clear aim identified by Deleuze is that a more detailed study of the new forms of control is required, and in many ways that is what the contributions to both parts of this book attempt to supply.

Deleuze's work is useful in a more critical consideration of new technologies in a number of different ways. As I suggested at the beginning, while Deleuze did not engage a great deal in thinking about so-called new technology, technology was in different ways, and on different levels, an important consideration in his work, not least in terms of the centrality it affords to the concept of the machine. At the same time, Deleuze was engaged in a style of, and approach to, thinking that is highly productive in its own right. It is in this context that the contributors to this book can be seen to be picking up Deleuze's arrows.

References

Ansell-Pearson, K. (1999), *Germinal Life: The Difference and Repetition of Deleuze*, London: Routledge.

Castells, M. (1996), *The Rise of the Network Society*, Oxford: Blackwell Publishers.

Deleuze, G. (1986), *Cinema 1: The Movement-Image*, trans. H. Tomlinson and B. Habberjam, London: Athlone Press.

Deleuze, G. (1988), *Foucault*, trans. Sean Hand, Minneapolis: University of Minnesota Press.

Deleuze, G. (1989), *Cinema 2: The Time-Image*, trans. H. Tomlinson and R. Galeta, London: Athlone Press.

Deleuze, G. (1992), 'Postscript on the Societies of Control', *October*, 59: 3–7.

Deleuze, G. (1993), *The Fold: Leibniz and the Baroque*, trans. T. Conley, Minneapolis: University of Minnesota Press.

Deleuze, G. (1995), *Negotiations*, trans. M. Joughin, New York: Columbia University Press.

Deleuze, G. and F. Guattari (1983), *Anti-Oedipus: Capitalism and Schizophrenia*, trans. R. Hurley, M. Seem and H. Lane, Minneapolis: University of Minnesota Press.

Deleuze, G. and F. Guattari (1987), *A Thousand Plateaus: Capitalism and Schizophrenia*, trans. B. Massumi, Minneapolis: University of Minnesota Press.

Guattari, F. (1995), *Chaosmosis: an Ethico-Aesthetic Paradigm*, trans. P. Bains and J. Pefanis, Bloomington: Indiana University Press.

Guattari, F. (1992), 'Regimes, Pathways, Subjects', in J. Crary, and S. Kwinter (eds), *Incorporations*, New York: Zone Books.

Jameson, F. (1991), *Postmodernism, or, the Cultural Logic of Late Capitalism*, London: Verso.

Lyotard, J. F. (1984), *The Postmodern Condition: A Report on Knowledge*, trans. G. Bennington and B. Massumi, Minneapolis: University of Minnesota Press.

Manovich, L. (2001), *The Language of New Media*, Cambridge, MA: MIT Press.
Marx, K. (1990), *Capital*, London: Penguin Books.
Mumford, L. (1994), 'The First Megamachine', in D. L. Miller (ed.), *The Lewis Mumford Reader*, Athens: University of Georgia Press.
Parisi, L. (2008), 'Technoecologies of Sensation', in B. Herzogenrath (ed.), *Deleuze/ Guattari & Ecology*, Hampshire: Palgrave Macmillan.

Note

1. For an excellent exploration of sensation in the new technological context see Luciana Parisi's 'Technoecologies of Sensation' (2008).

CONTROL

Chapter 1

Deleuze and Machines:
A Politics of Technology?

William Bogard

Assemblages

Deleuze is not so much interested in questioning technology, like Heidegger, as in articulating, along with Guattari, a problem about machines (Guattari 1990). Heidegger's questions lead him to an essence of technology, Enframing, or the potential to convert all of *Dasein* into 'standing reserve' (Heidegger 1977: 20). Deleuze and Guattari's problematisations of machines lead them, by contrast, to a concept of a multiplicity without an essence – or better, with a 'nomadic' essence[1] – a complex configuration of machinic and enunciative elements called an 'assemblage' (Deleuze and Guattari 1987; Deleuze and Parnet 1987; DeLanda 2006).[2] The problem of machines is not Heidegger's question of technology: Is there a possible escape from Enframing? Can technology save the world before it annihilates it? For Deleuze, there is neither an essential 'saving power' nor a nihilism of machines. Safety and danger are matters of experimenting with assemblages, with their compositional forms. Such experiments can either move us forward and add to our joy and connectedness, or send us into a black hole, but these are always historical problems relative to today. It is not a question of an essence of technology, but of what Deleuze and Guattari call an abstract machine, a machine immanent in assemblages that both integrates them and opens them to an outside, to counterforces that break them down. Understanding the production and counter-actualisation of assemblages by abstract machines is the key to understanding Deleuze's concept of 'societies of control', and his critique of the power of global information networks (Deleuze 1992).

According to Deleuze and Guattari, assemblages have a dual form: a 'form of content', that is, a machinic form composed of variably fixed matters and energetic components; and a 'form of expression' or 'enunciation' consisting of statements and articulated functions (Deleuze and

Guattari 1987: 504). A machine interrupts a flow of matter or energy, such as when an infant's mouth sucks her mother's milk in a mouth-breast assemblage, or a turnstile funnels a crowd through a gate. The form of the machine refers to the order in which components are selected and assembled, the 'vector' of the machine's assembly (more on this below) (Deleuze and Guattari 1987: 43). There are material machines and immaterial machines, technical machines and imaginary machines, desiring machines and abstract machines, machines inside machines inside still other machines, nested like fractals. Machines, in a word, are multiplicities. Guattari advocates viewing machines in their 'complex totality', in all their 'technological, social, semiological and axiological avatars', and resists attempts to assimilate them to mechanist or vitalist forms, or to any concept that would essentialise either them or the assemblages they compose (Guattari 1995: 34).[3]

Functions are forms of expression of assemblages; not simply what they do, but what they 'say' and 'mean'. Schools, it is said, function to educate students. But this is meaningless unless the function of education is seen as an interpretation of how the assemblage works – an interpretation that is conjoined to statements about knowledge and truth, power and desire, that is, to systems of signification and subjectivisation, in other words, to a whole social field. The meaning of education, to stay with this example, changes historically and does not depend on the content of the assemblage, which may be composed of very different machines at different times, different classroom arrangements, methods of examination, instruction rituals, student distributions, and so on. Whether any of these machines constitute 'education' machines is an historical and political question.

The two forms of the assemblage, content and expression, differ in nature – they are not in any kind of symbolic correspondence or linear relationship, yet they are in 'reciprocal presupposition' and can be abstracted from each other only in a relative way (Deleuze 1988: 33; Deleuze and Guattari 1987: 141). They are heterogeneous forms of a single assemblage, even if they emerge together at the same time. To complicate matters, each form is itself dual. Different assemblages have different contents, but within assemblages there are always multiple contents, from molar to molecular, that develop their own forms of expression. Assemblages like schools are multiplicities that integrate architectures to body parts to brain chemistry and everything in between. The same is true of expression – in assemblages a function or statement may have multiple forms of content. Content and expression are each double in their own right and within the same assemblage can multiply and divide indefinitely, in the manner of fractals, and for this reason there are always many intermediate forms of them.

In addition to dual forms, assemblages have dual vectors or faces. Deleuze and Guattari write:

> One vector [of an assemblage] is oriented toward the strata,[4] upon which it distributes territorialities, relative deterritorialisations, and reterritorialisations; the other is oriented toward the plane of consistency or destratification, upon which it conjugates processes of deterritorialisation, carrying them to the absolute of the earth. It is along its stratic vector that the assemblage differentiates a form of expression (from the standpoint of which it appears as a collective assemblage of enunciation) from a form of content (from the standpoint of which it appears as a machinic assemblage of bodies); it fits one form to the other, one manifestation to the other, placing them in reciprocal presupposition. But along its diagrammatic or destratified vector, it no longer has two sides; all it retains are traits of expression and content from which it extracts degrees of deterritorialisation that add together and cutting edges that conjugate. (Deleuze and Guattari 1987: 145)

It is this 'diagrammatic' or destratified vector of assemblages that most interests Deleuze and Guattari. This becomes for them the problem of the 'abstract machine', a deterritorialising machine immanent in the concrete assemblage. The abstract machine is a paradox. Despite its name, it exists only within concrete assemblages. It integrates the two forms of the assemblage, content and expression, and causes the assemblage to 'distribute territorialities, relative deterritorialisations, and reterritorialisations' (1987: 145). But at the same time the abstract machine opens the assemblage to its outside and is a force in its metamorphosis or counter-actualisation, in the same way, to cite a well-known example, the head of a hammer can be fused by heat into a molten mass (Guattari 1995: 35).[5] The hammer loses its form of content and expression, its territoriality; what remains are only the flowing informal 'traits' of its former condition. According to Deleuze, the abstract machine is 'like the immanent cause of the concrete assemblages that execute its relations' (Deleuze 1988: 37). But those relations are deterritorialised and deterritorialising. An assemblage, from the point of view of the abstract machine that it effectuates, works by breaking down or fleeing itself, by adding degrees of deterritorialisation along its edges, and by conjoining or mixing together deterritorialised elements at its border with the outside. It is in this sense that assemblages can be said to inhabit the surfaces of strata, between layers of strata, or between a stratum and its destratified milieu. Assemblages are multiplicities of interfaces.

Deleuze and Guattari ask what causes the integration or co-adaptation of the two forms, content and expression, of an assemblage. Foucault once inquired why imprisonment became the general form of punishment in modern societies (Foucault 1979). He was asking how a material practice, imprisonment or, more broadly, incarceration, and an abstract function, punishment, came to be conjoined – what produced them as an integrated assemblage, namely, the prison, with all its complex connections of bodies and statements? His answer was that an abstract machine (or diagram) called discipline produced and conjoined them. In *Discipline and Punish* (1979), Foucault discusses the relation between Panoptics as a system of visibility for displaying bodies and organising space, and penal law, the system of language for classifying crimes and punishments (Deleuze 1988: 32). Panoptics is a form of content that works by distributing light within a circular enclosure (the familiar design of Jeremy Bentham). Penal law is a form of expression that, along with normative theories in the human sciences, articulates the function of prisons in terms of statements about delinquency (in effect, producing delinquency as an object of knowledge and intervention). Discipline is a machine that integrates both forms – content and expression, the visible and the articulable – in an assemblage in which a central guard station monitors the confinement of multiple individuals. The assemblage renders its subject, the delinquent, simultaneously viewable and knowable, and imposes on it a regime of self-inspection and self-control. Discipline actualises many different assemblages beyond just the prison, however, and Foucault maintains that it becomes coextensive with the whole social field (Foucault 1979). The abstract formula of discipline, which to different degrees organises every modern social institution, is to 'impose order on a multiplicity' of bodies, through generalised techniques of individuation, such as examinations, normalising judgements and hierarchical observation (Deleuze 1988: 34; Foucault 1979: 170–94).

Control Societies

Like Foucault, Deleuze asks how the integration of a form of content and a form of expression is effectuated by an abstract machine. In a well-known essay, Deleuze writes that control is replacing discipline as an abstract machine that invests the entire social field today (Deleuze 1992). Although it is also a function of disciplinary assemblages, control as an abstract machine differs from discipline in many ways. In control societies, the form of content, the machinic form, is the distributed network, whose model supplants the Panopticon as a diagram of control.[6] Distributed networks deterritorialise the disciplinary assemblage. There is a shift from mastery over visible space to the integrated management of information, and control operates less through confinement than through the use of tracking systems that follow you, so to speak, out the door and into the open. What matters most in these assemblages is not that your body is visible – that is an already accomplished fact for the most part – but that your information is available and matches a certain pattern or profile. Matching information, in fact, becomes a precondition for visibility in control societies, for example, when your racial profile makes you a target of observation by the police (Bogard 1996).

The abstract machine of control no longer 'normalises' its object, as discipline does. Normative information rather is integrated into numerical codes. 'The numerical language of control', Deleuze writes, 'is made of codes that mark access to information, or reject it', for example, your passwords or DNA (Deleuze 1992: 5). Codes are the form of expression or enunciation in control societies; unlike norms, which demand prolonged training to instill, codes only require programming and activation.[7]

The socius, Deleuze and Guattari write in *Anti-Oedipus*, is basically an 'encoding machine': 'this is the social machine's supreme task . . . [to code] women and children, flows of herds and of seed, sperm flows, flows of shit, menstrual flows: nothing must escape coding' (Deleuze and Guattari 1983: 141–2). Immanent within the socius, however, are 'decoding' machines that carry it away and open it to the outside. Capital is such a machine. In an interesting analysis, Deleuze and Guattari note that the general business of the pre-capitalist social machine is to overcode flows of desire. Capital, however, decodes these codes and places them in flux (Marx understood this as Capital's destruction of the prior mode of production) (Deleuze and Guattari 1983). Decoded desire and the desire for decoding exist in all societies, even pre-capitalist ones, but capital turns them into axioms and ends of production. This does not mean codes do not exist in capitalist societies. In fact they proliferate even more – in the way, for example, fashion codes proliferate through their continuous decoding, or decoded DNA can be recoded. Capital does not aim to make codes extinct but to produce fluid codes that adapt to its changing technical means of control. It does not decode the socius to eliminate social codes, but to re-engineer them. The following extended passage from *Anti-Oedipus* is relevant here:

In defining pre-capitalist regimes by a surplus value of code, and capitalism by a generalised decoding that converted this surplus value of code into a surplus value of flux, we were presenting things in a summary fashion, we were still acting as though the matter were settled once and for all, at the dawn of a capitalism that had lost all code value. This is not the case, however. On the one hand, codes continue to exist – even as an archaism – but they assume a function that is perfectly contemporary and adapted to the situation within personified capital (the capitalist, the worker, the merchant, the banker). But on the other hand, and more profoundly, every technical machine presupposes flows of a particular type: flows of code that are both interior and exterior to the machine, forming the elements of a technology and even a science. It is these flows of code that find themselves encasted, coded, or overcoded in the pre-capitalist societies in such a way that they never achieve any independence (the blacksmith, the astronomer). But the decoding of flows in capitalism has freed, deterritorialised, and decoded the flows of code just as it has the others – to such a degree that the automatic machine has always increasingly internalised them in its body or its structure as a field of forces. (Deleuze and Guattari 1983: 232–3)

This, however, only describes capital's decoding function in relation to pre-capitalist societies. We must consider how decoding works in the movement from disciplinary to control societies. In disciplinary societies, capital takes a code of enclosure originally designed for prisons and adapts it to factories, schools, homes and other sites of production. The code of enclosure in disciplinary societies is the panoptic formula of 'seeing without being seen' (Deleuze 1988: 32). It encapsulates the control of visibility that Foucault describes in such detail in *Discipline and Punish* and formulates a method for the production of individuals (Foucault 1979: 198–9). In control societies, capital decodes the panoptic code of enclosure, which is no longer sufficient to model flows of information across networks.[8]

Thanks to Foucault, we are all familiar with the Panopticon, an abstract machine that itself decoded prior figures of enclosure like the dungeon. The Panopticon is a system of 'light' rather than darkness, a model of enclosure that produces knowledge rather than conceals brutality and pain. The individual in disciplinary society is a product of systematic training in which punishment breaks its ties to torture (although torture is not abolished) and becomes a process of continuous observation and sorting of bodies. The latter is still 'punishment' because the whole point of panoptic enclosure is not to abolish punishment but to make it gentle, a practice of self-control (Foucault 1979: 104). Because it is so efficient, this model is generalised to every space that can be organised under capitalist production: factories, schools, homes, all become enclosures for producing self-controlled individuals. These enclosures are bound together serially, so when you leave one space, you must enter another, like links of a binding chain. This is disciplinary society.

In control societies, all this shifts into another register. Panoptic space is decoded by capital, and enclosure develops a very different meaning and mechanism. Control societies experiment with the limits of panoptic enclosure and the serial connection of spaces. These are organised by a model not of visibility, but of communication over distributed networks. Distributed networks are relatively deterritorialised in the sense that they are not bound by location, but are not totally free either. Instead, they have logins and passwords that allow or restrict access to them (Lyotard 1984). Instead of enclosing you, your body, they enclose your information. Your information does not flow serially between discrete spaces of control but is redistributed simultaneously and selectively across multiple networks, each protected by slightly modified codes, effecting a continuous modulation of control independent of location. 'Visibility' does not organise these redistributions; codes do, in the sense that the passage of information within and between distributions entails having the right code.

How does all this qualify as 'decoding'? Postmodern capital continuously decodes these codes, since networks are always in flux and information threatens to leak in and out. Decoding codes is a means of managing distributions of information for which panoptic enclosure is too rigid; it is easier simply to modify the instructions for accessing and routing data as the network grows and changes. In one sense, control societies are just disciplinary societies in a radically decoded form. Capital's project today is to engineer the disciplines directly into our DNA, which after all is just coded information. The final frontier in this project is to transform the socius into a distributed bio-network, whose relations nano-technologies can adjust in real time, all in the name of power and money.

Decode and deterritorialise enclosure, make it flow. Deleuze remarks at the end of his essay that, in control societies, the corporation, not the prison, becomes the model of every organisation (Deleuze 1992: 7). Corporate capital breaks down walls in order to deconstruct every desire, every social relation, percept, affect and concept, indeed the entirety of life on the planet. Deleuze is not referring to the centralised, stratified, hierarchical corporation of the past. The postmodern corporation is a distributed network. Global business, global labour, global exploitation, all operate under the new imperatives of fluidity and 'flexibility'.

But what has really changed with control society is not just the institutional model that organises it, but its machinic form. Deleuze says that disciplinary societies 'mold individuals', while control societies 'modulate dividuals' (Deleuze 1992: 4). The difference between a mold and a modulation is that the former is a rigid enclosure, the latter a fluid format, one that changes with the content to be formatted. Modulation is like editing the parameters of a piece of music live, as it plays, or as it is being recorded (for example, varying its tempo, velocity, attack, reverberation, and so on). Modulation is not intended to produce an individual, which would be equivalent to making a fixed recording. Instead, the format itself is opened to variation in real time. In society, this is a difference between the production of fixed and variable controls, between, as Deleuze says, schooling and perpetual training or, alluding to Kafka and the mechanisms of punishment, between apparent acquittal and the indefinite postponement of one's trial. An individual is an extended unit; it has a number, like the prisoner in a cell, or the labourer on an assembly line. A dividual, on the other hand, is a variation in an intensive parameter (mood, temper, pace, climate, velocity, and so on). Performance elements, large and small, are informated, tracked and stored in the database, and results fed back to make fine adjustments in the codes that govern them as they unfold – a continuous 'deformation' of differences substitutes for the rigid form of the individual.

There is nothing mysterious about the idea of 'dividuals' in control societies. They are products of new 'dividing practices', ones that distribute information rather than bodies, and that use networks rather than physical enclosures to separate and distribute functions. Are dividuals 'subjects'? Not in Foucault's sense of disciplined, normalised subjects. They are not self-controlled but 'controlled in advance', through simulation and modelling, more designed than docile (Bogard 1996). Dividuals are database constructions, derived from rich, highly textured information on ranges of individuals that can be recombined in endless ways for whatever purposes. They are the abstract digital products of data-mining technologies and search engines and computer profiling, and they are the profiled digital targets of advertising, insurance schemes and opinion polls. A dividual is a data distribution open to precise modulation, stripped down to whatever information construct is required for a specific intervention, task or transaction. Increasingly, postmodern subjectivity is defined by interaction with information meshes and the fractal dividuals they produce. When you use an ATM machine, or access your work environment via your home computer, you are interacting with your dividual self. Likewise, when a database is mined for information on your buying habits, leisure habits, reading habits, communication habits, and so on, you are transformed into a dividual. All aspects of life converted to information, databanks, digital samples: this is control society.

Deleuze: A Politics of Technology?

> The socio-technological study of the mechanisms of control, grasped at their inception, would have to be categorical and to describe what is already in the process of substitution for the disciplinary sites of enclosure, whose crisis is everywhere proclaimed. It may be that older methods, borrowed from the former societies of sovereignty, will return to the fore, but with the necessary modifications. What counts is that we are at the beginning of something. (Deleuze 1992: 7)

Does Deleuze have a 'politics of technology'? We have seen that he is more focused on the problem of machines than technologies, and in particular on abstract machines that integrate the form of content and expression in assemblages. He also understands that abstract machines break down assemblages and open them to the outside. Although discipline is an abstract machine taken over by capital and its socio-technical mechanisms of control in the nineteenth century, there is no necessary historical alignment between them. Discipline in a society organised along non-capitalist, non-technical lines would take very different and, perhaps, far more positive forms. It is not discipline per se that is the issue, but how as an abstract machine it conjoins a socio-technical assemblage (for example, capitalist means of production) and a deterritorialised, decoded environment (for example, non-capitalist modes of consumption). There is still much to understand about how discipline creates the potential for positive social encounters, rather than the exploitative relations and destroyed communities and traditions of capitalist societies. Some form of discipline, after all, is required in art and sports, in love and play, as in most transformative human activity. How does it open this activity to an outside that it does not immediately objectify and subjectify, as capital does, but encounters in a positive, joyful and loving way?

For Deleuze, there is no reason to despair at the beginning of control societies, if we understand how control assemblages open to their outside. Because these kinds of societies are new, it is impossible to predict their future; they may even bring back mechanisms of the past if they can be upgraded for present conditions (dungeons can make a comeback!). The first step to conceptualising this is to understand that control is not just a function of 'technical' machines. Like Foucault, Deleuze views technologies as social before they are 'technical'. So-called technological 'lineages' – tools and their associated techniques – are not linear progressions, but depend on 'human technologies' that vary with non-linear shifts in demographics, working conditions, climate and seasons, and so on. Deleuze gives the example of the burrowing stick, the hoe and the plow, whose evolution is not simply technical or rational but 'refer[s] to collective machines that vary with the density of the population and the time of the fallow' (Deleuze 1988: 40). He cites Braudel's dictum that the tool is a consequence and not a cause (Braudel 1979: 128). All this merely reasserts that the real problem is the assemblage, as a collective machine, not the technical object.

But Deleuze does not stop at a recognition of the social or human side of assemblages. He and Guattari write that 'assemblages are passional, they are compositions of desire' (Deleuze and Guattari 1987: 399).[9] Ultimately, they have a side that is neither technical, nor social, nor human, but simply the intensive energy of becoming-different of the assemblage itself. The desiring assemblage is selected in turn by an abstract machine that operates immanently within it and is itself a force of desire – the prison is selected as a socio-technical mechanism by the disciplinary diagram, just as the phalanx assemblage of the hoplite armies is selected by the abstract machine of feudalism, and the network assemblage is chosen by the abstract machine of control (Deleuze 1988: 40; Deleuze and Guattari 1987: 398–400). This latter machine, of course, is ruled today by corporate capital, but there is no necessary reason why this must the case. To grasp why, we need to understand more clearly how control connects to an outside.

We have seen that all assemblages have a territorialised side that faces the strata (fixed forms and contents), as well as a deterritorialised side facing the outside. The abstract machine both integrates the dual form of the assemblage and connects it to the outside. Here we return to the example of enclosure in disciplinary societies and ask: what is it that the assemblage encloses? Precisely, it encloses the outside. Deleuze writes that Foucault, because he studied the ways social institutions confined people, is sometimes misread as a philosopher of confinement. But he notes that 'Foucault always considered confinement a secondary element derived from a primary function that was very different in each case' (Deleuze 1988: 42). The models of confinement for delinquents, madmen, plague victims, children, sexual deviants, and so on, were all very different, as were the actual technologies for confining them (for example, the madman's confinement was a kind of 'exile' and he was treated as a leper, while delinquents were partitioned off like plague victims). Foucault made an important distinction between how an assemblage encloses something in an interior sense, that is, how it locks people up in cells, behind walls or bars, and how it encloses its outside, how it encircles, so to speak, what it first excludes, then brings it back inside for examination, correction, punishment, and so on. Prisons may confine delinquents in cells, but delinquency itself is really already the prison's outside, as madness is the outside of the asylum, the deterritorialised, decoded space that the assemblage surrounds, captures and immobilises. When Foucault says prison assemblages produce delinquency, he is referring not just to the inmates who are already housed there, but to the incarceration, by disciplinary societies, of anything they can label and come to know as different, dangerous, perverse, that is, as material to be moulded to a norm. Disciplinary societies always find new dangers to mitigate, new perversions to treat, new threats from the unruly populations that exist outside their doors. They stumble across the abnormal everywhere, at ever earlier ages in a person's life, in smaller parts of the body, in every unexpected turn of events.

The enclosure of the outside in disciplinary societies is an important clue to how enclosure functions in control societies. But what is control society's outside, and how is it enclosed? Networks expand by adding nodes – typically this means linking to another computer – or by increasing the number of connections to each node. In control societies, the expansion of network connections is selective and distributions of networks develop – some nodes are confined to specific networks and cannot access others without the proper passwords. Blocking a connection is not quite like locking up a prisoner, however, since no physical confinement of nodes is necessary, just the denial of access to a network. Like in Foucault, confinement is secondary to a primary function of exclusion that takes different forms in disciplinary and control societies.

What do control societies exclude? In an interesting argument that draws on Deleuze and Guattari, Hardt and Negri suggest that networks produce a new 'common', and that this common takes the form of the 'multitude' (Hardt and Negri 2004: xi–xviii). It is the common and the multitude that today constitute the outside of the distributed network, what the abstract machine of control simultaneously produces and excludes, what it encloses yet what escapes it at every turn. The new 'common', as Hardt and Negri (2004: xv) describe it, refers to the hegemony of 'immaterial production' in the postmodern global organisation of labour.

For Hardt and Negri, information networks increasingly order all sectors of production in the global economy – manufacturing, agriculture and services. They are not saying that production today has somehow become immaterial, but rather that immaterial forces structure and connect very different spheres of production, that these forces have become hegemonic 'in qualitative terms and have imposed a tendency on other forms of labor and society itself', hence the term 'common' (Hardt and Negri 2004: 109). Just as 150 years ago, economic and social production were organised by the 'industrial model', and all forms of labour had to industrialise even though industry in itself accounted for only a small proportion of global output, today production is structured by the information sector of the economy despite its size relative to global production as a whole. Immaterial production is the production of ideas, knowledge, communication, affects and social relations, and today 'labor and society have to informationalise, become intelligent, become communicative, and become affective' (Hardt and Negri 2004: 109).[10]

Ultimately, immaterial production is geared not just to the manufacture of goods or services. Hardt and Negri recognise that the problem of the information common involves not only class and labour issues but the control of life in all its complexity. They borrow Foucault's concept of 'biopower' to name the form of sovereignty that today rules over the new common (Foucault 1978; Hardt and Negri 2004: 18–25).[11] Biopower is the negative form of the common. It is a way of life that threatens the planet with destruction and death (war, ecological catastrophe, the annihilation of species). It is not just technical production, however. Hardt and Negri describe the global context of biopower as a permanent state of civil war, governed by exceptionalism and unilateralism in global politics and economics, high-intensity police actions, preemptive strikes, and of course network control. The dominant climate of the new common is fear and greed, accompanied by the need for security (or the absence of risk) (Beck 1992, 1999). In postmodernity, the need for security replaces defence as the moral justification for global police interventions of all kinds, in military matters to be sure, but also in economic, political and cultural affairs, in matters of health, sexuality, education, entertainment, and so on. 'War' and policing become the frameworks through which all problems are recognised and addressed, both in the relations of states to other states, but also of states to their own populations. In fact, when it comes to the multiplicity of wars in postmodernity, the old categories of international or intra-national conflict no longer apply. The regime of biopower, like the modern system of penality, has no walls and is truly a planetary form of sovereignty and a totalising form of immaterial enclosure; it dismantles the old oppositions between public and private spheres, erases the economic and political boundaries between states, and aims at the absolute elimination of risk in advance through 'total information awareness'.[12] Biopower is network control of the common, of the production of life itself.

The new common, however, also has liberatory and democratic potentials, which Hardt and Negri locate in what they term 'biopolitical production', the production of the 'multitude' (which for them has replaced industrial labour as the postmodern force of revolutionary change) (Hardt and Negri 2004). Biopolitical production is not biopower, but it is not the opposite of biopower either. Both engage the production of life and social relations in their entirety, but in very different ways. Hardt and Negri write: 'Biopower stands above society, transcendent, as a sovereign authority and imposes its order. Biopolitical production, in contrast, is immanent in society and creates social relations and forms through collaborative forms of labor' (Hardt and Negri 2004: 94–5). Biopower is the new form of Empire, whereas biopolitical production is the new form of resistance to Empire. Both are effects of changes in the organisation of production brought about by the advent of information networks and control societies. In arguments reminiscent of Marx, that the development of the means of global communication create the potential for the revolutionary organisation of labour, Hardt and Negri show how global information systems have not only destabilised traditional forms of private property and cut across class divisions, but have also cut across race, gender and other hierarchies, producing a common 'poverty' from which new forms of democratic participation and social creativity can emerge. It is as if biopower, the system of sovereign control supported by global networks and the culture of war and fear, had produced the very communicative and geopolitical conditions necessary for the development of a shared humanity.

Hardt and Negri are quick to point out, however, that their use of the term 'common' does not imply any sameness of elements. Nor is the common some transcendent identity standing over society. Rather it consists of singularities whose differences constitute a heterogeneous multiplicity capable of spontaneous organisation and the power to deconstruct the global sovereign regime of biopower (Hardt and Negri 2004: 128–9). The new common, in other words, is a force of deterritorialisation immanent in networks, an 'outside' resistant to the control systems that produce it. Today, despite (and because of) differences of class, race, gender, nation, occupation, language, religion, age, and so on, new and singular forms of resistance are arising grounded in the common subjection of the global population to the imperatives of biopower, and the common impoverishment of life subjected to network control.

Hardt and Negri's concept of a common composed of heterogeneous singularities owes much to Deleuze and Guattari's idea that the abstract machine, control, is actualised in a multiplicity of concrete assemblages that are simultaneously social, political, aesthetic, economic, linguistic, technical and diagrammatic. Networks are not uniform or homogeneous. Control, as well as resistance to control, functions in a multiplicity of ways on a multiplicity of planes. In this sense, Deleuze does not have a 'politics' of control societies, if that implies a unitary concept or critique of them. A politics cannot be separated from an ethics, an aesthetics, a technics, and so on. The problem rather is the multiplicity of assemblages and the abstractness of control – one must map the latter's effects within very different concrete assemblages; in this case, within very different kinds of networks (for example, communications networks, commercial networks, social networks, bio-networks, and so on). Nothing privileges political over aesthetic, technical or other forms of resistance to network control. The use of networks in art, network practices like file-sharing, hacking, encryption, the use of proxies for anonymity, podcasting, denial of service attacks, open-source application development, along with more traditional methods like refusal to use networks, unplugging, and so on – there are many ways to resist information control.

More importantly, resistance is not just anti-control. Networks have liberatory and democratic potentials that function immanently within control (Bogard 2006). Networks are not the property of corporations or the state. Information, to use a well-known phrase, 'wants to be free'. Passwords and codes, the very tools control assemblages use to restrict access to information, are also means of escaping these assemblages and levelling the information playing field (the firewall on your computer is an example). The point is that resistance, though common, is always specific and immanent within a concrete assemblage. Just as there is no universal form of control, there is no universal mode of resistance to control, only experimentation with the abstract machine and the possibilities networks create for us to have positive encounters with the outside, with the common – encounters that are joyful, create solidarity, abandon hierarchies and denounce power, that generate lines of flight and multiply connections beyond what the network can dominate. Those potentials are real, but the network police and control society enclose the common and bring it inside their radar, into their databases and tracking and bio-tech systems, just as disciplinary society brought the delinquent it saw everywhere outside into its machinery of visibility, examination and manipulation.

For Deleuze, the abstract machine of control is intrinsically neither nihilistic nor redemptive. He does not ask, with Heidegger, if, somewhere in the essence of technology, we might discover a 'saving power' of revealing or opening that resonates in the nature of *Dasein* (to the extent that *Dasein*'s essence is revealing). Concepts of the outside or the common, like those of machines and assemblages, which define them as multiplicities, resist the temptation to essentialise this problem. There is indeed a problem regarding the 'safety' of machines in Deleuze, but it has to do with how we experiment with them. Experiments with control networks involve how they connect with the common. This question is very close to Deleuze and Guattari's problem of how you make yourself a 'body without organs', for the common consists only of unformed matters and flows (Deleuze and Guattari 1987: 149). Like all experiments that connect an assemblage to an outside, that destratify and deterritorialise an assemblage, there is a danger of being propelled into a black hole. Experiments with control networks, like those in finding your body without organs, require caution – you must not deterritorialise too rapidly or you might not find your way back. There are many cautionary examples. Artists and scientists who experiment with becoming-cyborgs, with neural interfaces and digital implants, and so on, take great risks with the body. Hackers who experiment with bringing down networks may also release the violence they contain (the B movie *War Games* depicted a young man whose network hacking nearly started a third world war). And, of course, the biggest danger of all comes from corporate and state experiments with control assemblages that really do threaten the annihilation of the species and the planet. Deleuze never questions Heidegger's concern with the threats from technology, only his ability to grasp assemblages as multiplicities. Because control societies are just beginning, our knowledge of them is only categorical. No one can predict the direction that control society, embedded in a multiplicity of concrete assemblages, will take. Certainly, the corporate/state war machine will attempt to create and use networks to its own advantage. The abstract machine, however, is our clue – it is what is breaking down the old disciplinary assemblage and substituting a new one, the assemblage of information nodes we call the network. The problem today is how the abstract machine of control breaks down the network, 'fuses' it like the parts of a hammer, and deterritorialises and decodes an already thoroughly deterritorialised and decoded milieu.

References

Beck, U. (1992), *Risk Society: Towards a New Modernity*, Newbury Park, CA: Sage Publications.
Beck, U. (1999), *World Risk Society*, Malden, MA: Polity Press.

Bogard, W. (1996), *The Simulation of Surveillance: Hyper-Control in Telematic Societies*, New York: Cambridge University Press.

Bogard, W. (2006), 'Surveillance Assemblages and Lines of Flight', in David Lyon (ed.), *Theorising Surveillance: The Panopticon and Beyond*, Cullompton, UK: Willan Publishing.

Braudel, F. (1979), *Civilisation Matérielle, Economie et Capitalisme: XVe-XVIIIe Siècle*, Paris: A. Colin.

DeLanda, M. (2002), *Intensive Science and Virtual Philosophy*, New York: Continuum.

DeLanda, M. (2006), *A New Philosophy of Society: Assemblage Theory and Social Complexity*, New York: Continuum.

Deleuze, G. (1988), *Foucault*, trans. Sean Hand, Minneapolis: University of Minnesota Press.

Deleuze, G. (1992), 'Postscript on the Societies of Control', *October*, 59: 3–7.

Deleuze, G. and F. Guattari (1983), *Anti-Oedipus: Capitalism and Schizophrenia*, trans. R. Hurley, M. Seem and H. Lane, Minneapolis: University of Minnesota Press.

Deleuze, G. and F. Guattari (1987), *A Thousand Plateaus: Capitalism and Schizophrenia*, trans. B. Massumi, Minneapolis: University of Minnesota Press.

Deleuze, G. and C. Parnet (1987), *Dialogues*, trans. H. Tomlinson and B. Habberjam, New York: Columbia University Press.

Foucault, M. (1978), *The History of Sexuality: An Introduction*, trans. R. Hurley, New York: Pantheon Books.

Foucault, M. (1979), *Discipline and Punish: The Birth of the Prison*, trans. Alan Sheridan, New York: Vintage Books.

Guattari, F. (1990), 'On Machines', *Journal of Philosophy and the Visual Arts*, 6: 8–17.

Guattari, F. (1995), *Chaosmosis: an Ethico-Aesthetic Paradigm*, trans. P. Bains and J. Pefanis, Bloomington, IN: Indiana University Press.

Hardt, M. and A. Negri (2004), *Multitude: War and Democracy in the Age of Empire*, New York: The Penguin Press.

Heidegger, M. (1977), *The Question Concerning Technology, and Other Essays*, trans. W. Lovitt, New York: Harper & Row.

Lyotard, J. F. (1984), *The Postmodern Condition: a Report on Knowledge*, trans. G. Bennington and B. Massumi, Minneapolis: University of Minnesota Press.

Notes

1. A nomadic essence is not a Platonic universal or unity, but an essence immanent to becoming and actualised only within concrete historical conditions. Deleuze never denies essences, only their transcendence.
2. 'What is an assemblage? It is a multiplicity which is made up of many heterogeneous terms and which establishes liasions, relations between them, across ages, sexes and reigns – different natures. Thus, the assemblage's only unity is that of co-functioning: it is symbiosis, a 'sympathy'. It is never filiations which are important, but alliances, alloys; these are not successions, lines of descent, but contagions, epidemics, the wind' (Deleuze and Parnet 1987: 69). Assemblages can be anything from chemical bonds to cultural patterns. Assemblages in their machinic form, above all, are 'compositions of desire' (Deleuze and Guattari 1987: 399). Note also Manuel DeLanda's (2006) important contribution to this subject in relation to the micro–macro problem in sociology.
3. The difference between a machine and an assemblage is not a difference between the one and the many, or part and whole, but between two different multiplicities.

Every machine is already an assemblage, and it always enters into other assemblages with other machines. The concept of a machinic assemblage as a multiplicity is prior to the one/many or part/whole distinction (DeLanda 2002; Deleuze and Guattari 1987).

4. '[Strata] consist of giving form to matters, of imprisoning intensities or locking singularities into systems of resonance and redundancy, of producing upon the body of the earth molecules large and small and organising them into molar aggregates. Strata are acts of capture, they are like "black holes" or occlusions striving to seize whatever comes within their reach. They operate by coding and territorialisation upon the earth; they proceed simultaneously by code and by territoriality' (Deleuze and Guattari 1987: 40).

5. The destratified vector is asymmetric to its stratified vector. Guattari says that a hammer whose head and handle have been separated is still a hammer, although in 'mutilated' form. That is, the parts are still stratified, and only relatively deterritorialised. If the head is melted down, however, it deterritorialises absolutely and becomes a flow a metal, no longer an assemblage. But flows organise themselves spontaneously as machines, as flows interrupt other flows, and new strata and assemblages inevitably re-emerge (reterritorialisation).

6. Written at a time before a wider appreciation of its role in the critique of information systems, Deleuze uses the concept of a 'network' only once in his essay on control societies. Still, he gets his point across effectively: 'the disciplinary man was a discontinuous producer of energy, but the man of control is undulatory, in orbit, in a continuous network. Everywhere surfing has already replaced the older sports' (Deleuze 1992: 5).

7. All codes are basically repetitions. Encrypted language, for example, is based on some rule for repeating a translation operation, from one character or set of characters into another. Other examples are the conversion of money into goods or statuses into ranks. To decode a code means to discover its rule(s) of repetition. Breaking codes is an old strategy of power, but global networks and electronics have generalised its practice. Code-breaking has counter-strategic potentials as well, as hackers, info-junkies, pirates and spammers have known for a long time (Bogard 2006).

8. Enclosure is the act of surrounding or marking off something, a 'dividing practice', as Foucault calls it. Enclosures are things like boundaries, borders, limits and obstacles, and they need not always be physical. Disciplinary societies do emphasise physical enclosure, specifically, the confinement of the material body, but they also enclose thought, for example, through the imposition of interpretive codes and rules of signification.

9. 'Desire has nothing to do with a natural or spontaneous determination; there is no desire but assembling, assembled, desire. The rationality, the efficiency of an assemblage does not exist . . . without the desires that constitute it as much as it constitutes them' (Deleuze and Guattari 1987: 399).

10. Affective labour is labour that produces feelings of comfort, security, excitement and so on. We can see this labour in the work of service workers, care providers, and other occupations where the 'pro-social' attitude and character of employees are qualifications for work.

11. The foundation of biopower today is the surveillance and simulation of life processes. The control of information organises, among many other things, genetic science, food science, the medicalisation of culture, and the social distribution of risk.

12. The name of a once secret plan of the US Defense Department to create a universal database that would have supposedly thwarted the plans of terrorists and enhanced 'homeland security'.

Chapter 2

Of Rhizomes, Smooth Space, War Machines and New Media

Verena Andermatt Conley

Throughout their writings, Deleuze and Guattari seem obsessed with machines and technologies. Deleuze makes clear that machines are always a part of a collective assemblage and in that way can be understood to express the social forms that give birth to them. Historically, if the energetic machine expressed the disciplinary bourgeois society of the eighteenth and nineteenth centuries, computers, electronic and cybernetic machines express today what Deleuze calls the society of control. The latter cannot be separated from a shift in capitalism from speculation and accumulation towards circulation, the abstract and often dizzying process of the buying and selling of products in which the importance of marketing exceeds that of the commodities themselves. Deleuze declares provocatively that our society is no longer simply one of inclusions, exclusions or enclosure but one of undulation and continuous formation. Digital technologies that enable and accelerate circulation are part of a global networked society that has no outer border or limit.

Deleuze and Guattari's writings include a range of concepts, among them the concepts of the rhizome, smooth space and the war machine. They are often said to make possible a productive analysis of the cultural and social impact of digital technologies and new media. I will briefly review these concepts as they developed in the post-1968 context before asking how we might use them to deal with the social and cultural significance of new media today. Can the rhizome and the war machine help us resist – if resistance is either warranted or possible – new mechanisms of control that are put in place? Can they help further creativity and transformation? Can they enable the opening of new spaces?

Unlike those French thinkers who follow a Heideggerian blueprint, Deleuze and Guattari do not condemn technologies that supersede their earlier or seemingly outmoded avatars as being dehumanising. In fact, they are keenly interested in 'becomings' both between humans and machines and in computer-assisted subjectivities (Deleuze and Guattari 1987: 5). At stake at once is the reorienting of the controlling function that, according to them, technology has in today's capitalist societies, and an undoing of the deleterious effects of those societies seemingly inherent binary oppositions. *Grosso modo*, the computer and most digital technology route their information along ever-bifurcating paths. Logic would have it that the binary opposition at each bifurcation point would belong to the classical metaphysical order of oppositional logic, that order which philosophers affiliated with the ferment of 1968 undertook to deconstruct. As did Deleuze and Guattari: they proposed to displace a hierarchical Western thought that they associate – perhaps somewhat infelicitously in today's ecological context – with the rooted tree. Nature, they claim, runs ahead of human thought. They turn to botany and to Eastern philosophy, where the rhizome is defined as a grass or a kind of 'subterranean stem' that can take on very diverse forms, 'from ramified surface extension in all directions to concretion into bulbs and tubers' (Deleuze and Guattari 1987: 6–7). Rhizomes are made of lines, not points. Without beginning or end, they connect from a *milieu*, not a given place, but a middle, a median space and a complex environment. While the tree always grows into the same form, rhizomes are constantly changing. They are part of a multiplicity that is never a one (n–1). They thrive on alliances and heterogeneous connections that replace the ubiquitous either/or with *and*. Addition replaces opposition.

It comes as no surprise then that readers have connected the rhizome with computers and the concept of a network associated with them. Like the rhizome, networks have no centre and no enclosing borders. Deleuze and Guattari introduce the rhizome as a concept for new ways of thinking that would displace arborescent, hierarchical thought based on either/or. The rhizome 'includes the best and the worst, potato and couchgrass or the weed' (Deleuze and Guattari 1987: 7). It can lead to flourishing or runaway conditions. It never exists alone. Trees, centres, points and hierarchies form in the rhizome at the same time that they are being undone in an incessant movement of deterritorialisation and reterritorialisation. Unlike the tree that promotes a fixed, static presence of itself ('from little acorns great acorns grow'), the rhizome with its delicate and adventitious filigree is in constant movement. The rhizome is flat and asymmetrical, part of a *chaosmosis*, a chaotic osmosis of varied and variable connections rather than an ordered cosmos. It clearly has some proximity to the concept of network that has gained such momentum today, which makes Deleuze and Guattari's thought seemingly so productive for an analysis of contemporary societies defined by the electronic circulation of information.

However, in spite of this obvious proximity between the rhizome and digital networks or between smooth, unstriated space and raw information, no equivalence between them can be discerned. While networks facilitate ongoing horizontal connections, they also enable the reconstitution of centres and are not free from arborescent thought. For Deleuze and Guattari, the latter would, in fact, be especially prevalent in a computerised world functioning according to the binary digit that they criticise harshly:

> Arborescent systems are hierarchical systems with centers of significance and subjectification, central automata like organised memories. In the corresponding models, an element only receives information from a higher unit, and only receives a subjective affection along pre-established paths. This is evident in current problems in information science and computer science, which still cling to the oldest modes of thought in that they grant all power to a memory or central organ. (Deleuze and Guattari 1987: 16)

They make a clear distinction between computers and the rhizome. Computers that run according to pre-established pathways are co-opted by a science based on binary oppositions and mainly arborescent, hierarchical thinking that does not engage or encourage creativity. In terms of their mechanical functioning, computers are not rhizomatic. It is important not to fall into the trap of a *false* multiplicity or of a science based on binary oppositions and hierarchical thinking. To make a rhizome, one has to make connections outside pre-established paths, from the 'middle, where things pick up speed', something that computers and, by extension, information science, cannot and will not do. Rhizomes are not hierarchical or part of binary systems. As singular or collective assemblages, they can proliferate through connections that lead to becomings. They can also solidify and grow into trees. It is not a question, then, of equating the computer networks with the rhizome but of thinking rhizomatically *from* and *with the help of* computers and electronic media. In doing so the user exceeds their inherent binary structures. At stake is the optimal use of digital technology to produce networks that function like rhizomes.

By means of the rhizome Deleuze and Guattari develop the concept of smooth space that undoes the striated space of the state and the war machine (Deleuze and Guattari 1987: 351–423). They show how in the thirteenth century, in the steppes of Asia, nomads invented a war machine to combat the state from outside of its perimeters. In the era immediately post-1968, they find it productive to lift a dynamic process from the Asian war machine and associate it with tribes, bands and guerilla warfare, all part of a generalised becoming-minoritarian that would combat the state from areas outside of its control. But smooth space – like the rhizome – can carry a positive or negative valence. By 1980 the nomadic war machine that combats the state in order to open space and make becoming possible has, so Deleuze and Guattari declare, also been appropriated by capitalism and by what is not quite the 'state' any more. Acknowledging their debt to Paul Virilio, the philosopher and the psychoanalyst show how, over time, the military-industrial complex (a term coined by Dwight Eisenhower after 1954, at the time of the Cold War) appropriated the nomadic war machine and created its own smooth spaces on the sea and in the air (Deleuze and Guattari 1987: 418).

By way of reference to Virilio, Deleuze and Guattari insist that society must be analysed in terms of today's conditions, that is, at the time of *A Thousand Plateaus*, the conditions of the military-industrial complex. In his more recent writings, however, Virilio declares that the military-industrial complex has been transformed into a *military-informational* complex that even further exceeds the limits of the former state in a globalised world. In *The Information Bomb* (2000) Virilio argues that real bombs have been replaced by information. A primarily economic war is waged by controlling people's minds through technologies that generate and circulate information. Since the end of the twentieth century, any cultural and social analysis has to be done in view of the military-informational complex.

How then can we displace Deleuze and Guattari's concepts of rhizome, smooth space and the war machine, elaborated specifically in response to the post-1968 conditions of the military-industrial complex, into our moment? Can we take the rhizome as a form of creative resistance to the more controlling aspects of electronic media? Are rhizomes and the nomadic war machine that Deleuze and Guattari encounter in the late 1960s, in the context of theoretical revolutions and a generalised becoming-minoritarian, still productive in today's military-informational smooth space? Can we use them to analyse today's digital societies where, after the sea and the air, capitalism has appropriated information to create *false smooth spaces* in order to control the circulation of people and of goods?

Numerous critics have argued that new media do not become widely used until after 1995, and even as late as 2000, when computing and digital technologies replace older forms of resemblance with similitude (Rodowick 2001: 203). Deleuze and Guattari both passed away on the threshold of the proliferation of new media. In retrospect, we can say that they were in many ways prescient or at least keenly attuned to the first signs of the massive transformations underway. They did not, however, experience the full impact of new media, and thus we may wonder how they would have progressively deterritorialised themselves in relation to their post-1968 pronouncements. In their later texts, there may be some indications. Here Deleuze and Guattari speculate that to create is to resist. Accordingly, to open up new spaces, they invest their energies less in the new media than in literature, music and painting.[1] Deleuze's two-volume study of cinema, published in France in 1983 and 1985, deals mainly with older celluloid and not with digitally constituted images. In the last pages of the second volume, Deleuze briefly anticipates new media in connection with what he calls the new and old components of the image. In a discussion about the separation of image and sound tracks, he declares that digital imagery favours such separation even more than its analogue counterpart (Deleuze 1989: 265–8).

Only in their very last works, published between 1989 and 1992, do Deleuze and Guattari address more openly new media, especially in connection with their cultural and social impact. Sensing an 'epistemological shift' having wide-ranging consequences, Deleuze disinters and effectively popularises the term *societies of control*, first coined by William Burroughs in a very different context (Deleuze 1995: 178). These societies are made possible with new media. They are one with globalisation insofar as the latter is defined as a worldwide circulation of electronic information. Institutions defined by structures of inclusion and exclusion are progressively replaced with a ubiquitous mechanism of control by way of incessant feedback, polling and marketing. Without relinquishing the force or conviction of their earlier pronouncements, Deleuze and Guattari seem to be less contentious when writing about digital communication in relation to these societies of control. With the onset of new media, they note both an extension and an intensification of capitalism. When people are homogenised and their desires controlled, possibilities of resistance are, they claim, if not rendered impossible, at least strongly diminished.

It is of importance, then, to invent ways of thinking that would enable people to break with the onslaught of information. In order to do so, they need to escape the narcosis into which capital-controlled economies have put them. In an interview with Deleuze, Toni Negri notes that in his later texts – especially *Foucault* (1986) and *Le Pli* (1988) – Deleuze seems to pay more attention to processes of subjectivation in an era of false smooth spaces and generalised homogenisation under the impact of marketing (Deleuze 1995: 175). To counteract the weakening of creative resistance Deleuze insists on the processes of subjectivation already discussed in *A Thousand Plateaus*. In addition to channeling people's desires, societies of control base their strategies on the accelerated circulation of information and the selling of products that now lay claim to the arts. Deleuze seems rather pessimistic about the emergence of new singular and collective assemblages. The emergence of new voices – like those of the proletariat or those of the Third World in 1968 and its aftermath – is no longer possible in a global world of advertising where all values are calibrated under the sign of money. Because of money, speech, for Deleuze, is rotten to the core: 'Maybe speech and communication have been corrupted (*pourries*). They're thoroughly permeated by money – and not by accident but by their very nature. We've got to hijack speech. Creating has always been something different from communicating' (Deleuze 1995: 175).

These words reflect a change from 1968 when 'the capture of speech' seemed to be at the heart of the revolution, when rhizomes, smooth spaces and war machines were linked to vigorous cultures of shanty towns and a generalised becoming-minoritarian. For Deleuze, in global societies of control that function by virtue of new media, it is impossible to capture speech. In an information society, cognitive skills replace a more psycho-analytic concept of fraying (*frayage*), reflexes replace reflection and acquisition replaces creation. The making of creative connections and the opening of passages becomes more difficult. It is not so much the digital technologies themselves but how they are implemented in the new society that leads to oppression and arborescent thinking – though, for Deleuze, it seems to become increasingly difficult to separate the two.

How then, faced with the new mechanisms of control, can creative resistance be marshalled in a society of control that optimises a seamless, smooth circulation of information? Just as 'sabotage' – the insertion of workers' wooden clogs (*sabots*) in the factory machines brought the latter to a complete standstill – so the introduction of viruses into computers, Deleuze suggests, would act as an interruptor. Viruses, however, may shut down computer networks indiscriminately, including those that attempt to create 'good' smooth spaces. One possible way to elude control, Deleuze suggests, would be the creation of *vacuoles* of non-communication or circuit breakers at the level of micropolitics (Deleuze 1995: 175). While Deleuze recognises both the increasing difficulty of resistance and a weakening of a generalised becoming- minoritarian, he restates the necessity not only of making rhizomes and lines, but also of having continued recourse to the war machine in a nascent digital era, primarily to dispel dominant values that, for him, are associated with capitalism and marketing.

Guattari, for his part, insists less on an interruption than on a progressive sliding of values, that is, on what he calls an ongoing transformation of sensibility, desire and intelligence. In *The Three Ecologies* (2000) and *Chaosmosis* (1995), published in France in 1989 and 1992 respectively, Guattari denounces not so much the new as the *mass* media – especially television and film – and insists, somewhat surprisingly at first, on the importance of reconstructing the subject. The media have, writes Guattari, echoing Deleuze, reduced everything to sameness: consumers worldwide have the same imaginary; their sensorial reality is composed of the same pabulum of images. To bring about transformations, homogeneous subjectivities produced by mass media have to be replaced by processes of subjectivation similar to those written about in earlier works. Spaces have to be opened up through singular and collective resistance, which for Guattari continues to go through a politics of aesthetics and of ethics. Singular and group subjects can be affected from the inside. As Guattari describes it: 'something is detached and starts to work for itself just as it can work for you if you can "agglomerate" yourself to such a process' (Guattari 1995: 132–3). Such a re-questioning also concerns institutional domains, such as the family, the school or the state. Subjects can be affected from the outside too. Guattari reminds those who are in a position to intervene in others' psyches – be it in the domains of architecture, education, fashion, food or urbanism – of their ethical responsibility. Guattari prefers these forms of resistance and intervention to the kind of strict militancy that in his view remains tainted by memories of Communist Party loyalty.

Guattari takes great pains to distinguish between the vitamin-fed pseudo-creation that is part of the capitalist system and another creativity that leads to the opening of new spaces (Guattari 1995: 132). When privileging the creation of mental territories that are not tied to a land or limited by pre-existing boundaries, he praises computer-assisted subjectivities. Continuing to advocate the importance of lines and mutations, Guattari makes reference to rhizomes and war machines but now also, with a nod to Ilya Prigogine and Isabelle Stengers, to complexity theory, that is, to the making of connections in systems that are always off centre, in movement and on the threshold of bifurcating. Of importance in a world of increasing homogeneity is to make possible the emergence of new forms – even of mutations – that is, of new singular and collective assemblages. To resist dominant arborescent thought imposed by the media in the guise of a false smooth space of information, Guattari continues to advocate deterritorialisation through creative resistance, that is, through all the arts that include computers in what he calls a *machinic heterogenesis* that does not, as in the era of the Cold War, introduce an alternative but rather a progressive shift in values that may lead to an eventual mutation.

For Deleuze resistance is in the opening of vacuoles and the interruption of the flow of communication. Guattari sees transformation coming from a sliding of values that leads to bifurcation. For both the philosopher and the psychoanalyst, digital media offer possibilities of creation. However, the intensification of global capitalism that Deleuze describes as 'an extraordinary generator of both wealth and misery' (Deleuze 1995: 172), and with which new media are increasingly intertwined, makes resistance ever more difficult. With the onset of a digital world there is an obsession with communication that, for Deleuze and Guattari, enables the spread of advertising and marketing. Resistance, as it was known in the 1960s, has definitely been weakened. Creatively fashioned war machines have largely been appropriated by dominant systems. The desire for social experimentation at the basis of Marxism has been replaced by that of accelerated speculation. Since 1989, when Guattari wrote *The Three Ecologies* on the heels of the collapse of the Soviet Union, we can say that globalisation has done away with opposition to capitalism. Deleuze already noted that the latter's competitive values had been interiorised following the introduction of competitive salaries or what he calls 'a deeper level of modulation into all wages' (Deleuze 1995: 179). To denounce capitalism, Guattari draws an analogy between fish killed by polluted waters and the symbolically dead humans killed by Donald Trump's evacuation plans in New York City and Atlantic City (Guattari 2000: 43). A contemporary reader familiar with the recent popular show on NBC, *The Apprentice*, will most likely fail to understand the logic. As Etienne Balibar (2004) would have it, at this point there is no organised resistance to globalisation. In fact, Balibar criticises Deleuze and Guattari's very notion of smooth space that he sees playing too easily into the hands of global capitalism. He argues instead for a kind of performative resistance through speech acts of sorts that, by introducing a slight negative, would continually reformulate dominant discourse.

This suggestion is, however, not so far as Balibar would like to think from what Deleuze and Guattari themselves are advocating through their concepts of mapping and continuous deterritorialisation and reterritorialisation. While decrying new media for making possible unprecedented forms of social control, Guattari especially sees them as offering novel possibilities. Deleuze declares that the state of things in a society of control is neither better nor worse when he writes: 'It's not a question of asking whether the old or new system is harsher or more bearable, because there's a conflict in each between the ways they free and enslave us' (Deleuze 1995: 178). In spite of the binary digit that leads to centres and hierarchies, the philosopher and the analyst continue to assert that it is not the new media themselves but the use to which they are put in today's societies that leads to closures and openings. For them, it is the intensification of capitalism and the appropriation of the media by a dominant elite that produce zombie-like subjects and prevent people from thinking creatively. It is also a matter of scale. Marketing and an unprecedented fetishising of money aim at controlling the imaginary and doing away with the desire for resistance and emancipation.

Let us then come back once more to the rhizome, smooth space and the war machine in today's context. Over a decade ago Deleuze, more so than Guattari, felt that communication and capitalism facilitated by new media make resistance much more difficult to countenance. Guattari pushes for awareness and a breaking out of our current soporific state towards creative resistance. He calls for new sensibilities and new desires. Today, however, with the proliferation of new media unknown to Deleuze and Guattari, we can argue that people are far from being simply controlled. In fact, digital technologies may help people become creatively resistant in unprecedented ways. If the machines put in place new centres and hierarchies, if they follow pre-established pathways, they also make top-down communication and the structures associated with it, if not impossible, then at least increasingly difficult. As Deleuze and Guattari never ceased to write, the rhizome can be good and bad. The enemy can appropriate smooth spaces and the war machine. However, with the propagation of new media we are witnessing simultaneously a proliferation of creativity and resistances. Crucial here is the *distribution* of new media and more equal *accessibility* to it, in order to, in modified Foucauldian terms, spread knowledge and dilute power.

Increasingly, people all over the globe have access to cheap machines – especially videocams and webcams – that enable them to be creative and to resist power by exposing it, while inventing new ways of writing and producing images. If new technology is productive in this kind of digital 'capture' in the first world, it is also important in the Third World where machines are used as tools of resistance against various forms of local and global oppression. Even if no organised, worldwide resistance is available, there are now not only more sites of power but also many more pockets of creative resistance. We can say that, today, fifteen years after the publication of Guattari's essay, the creation of new sensibilities, desires and intelligence is everywhere in the making precisely *with* the help of new media.

While new media may have brought about closures through the homogenisation of subjects and created new social inequalities, they also defy complete control and make possible new alliances at an ever faster rate. Where there is email, no tyranny is possible, the late Michel de Certeau wrote already in *The Capture of Speech* (1997).[2] The absolute secrecy upon which power depended has become impossible. Any 'power elite' is now also part of a universal *chaosmosis*. It is often more the desire for control by the media or a new power elite that is taken for reality. The social milieus are not dominated, controlled top down or even manipulated by the media, as Adorno (2001) had it in relation to old media, or as even Deleuze and Guattari seem to intimate. New media bring about sameness through marketing and advertising, but they also enable an unprecedented – even if at times limited – creativity. The relative accessibility and affordability of a variety of new media help produce awareness and enable novel social groupings that bring about entirely different ways of being and acting as singular subjects or groups in the world. These novel ways of being and acting, of connecting and creating, help us to rethink or even go beyond institutions such as the nation-state decried by Deleuze and Guattari. Rejecting old structures of inclusion and exclusion, people connect rhizomatically; opening spaces and constructing war machines when rallying around causes on their computers or mobile phones. Once again, as Deleuze and Guattari repeatedly insist, rhizomes and war machines may be good or bad. They can be used by 'militants', a power elite or terrorists to make connections all over the globe.

Deleuze and Guattari anticipated new computer-assisted subjectivities that become more prevalent every day. Drawing on their concept of the rhizome, Bruno Latour notes that while in cold societies kinship structures are rigid and the individual has a set identity and is firmly entrenched in place, in hot societies, like our own, identities are no longer stable. Identities often emanate from new media; they emerge temporarily at the intersection of many lines (Latour and Hernant 1998: 72). Far from being dehumanising, these transformations open up new spaces for people. Deleuze and Guattari had repeatedly shown how in the disciplinary societies rigid social structures linked to the dominant powers led to the Oedipal imprisonment of the subject. The undoing of a constraining symbolic order under the impact of new media and the creation of abstract territories (music, film) carries further the kind of liberation Baudrillard (1983, 1996) had analysed in relation to objects and consumerism. With the withering of traditional orders, spatial constraints are loosened and people are free to invent their own. If there is homogenisation, there is also unprecedented rhizomatic activity and even an increased recourse to qualified war machines that continue to alter the smooth spaces of the military-informational complex.

What is true for the subject also works for the group. In 2001 David Rodowick speculated briefly about the future of public space on the Internet;[3] several years later, public space in new media is much more developed (Anderson et al. 2006; Poster 2006). There are ever growing numbers of websites on YouTube, MySpace, Facebook and elsewhere that create mental territories dealing with myriad topics from the personal to the political. People who visit the sites are often creatively resistant and even if they rarely oppose capitalism proper, they nevertheless expose its abuses and scandals in business and government. If new media operating on binary digits can lead to the creation of centres of power, they also facilitate deterritorialisations and reterritorialisations much more readily and quickly than old media. People who visit the sites do so motivated by a common desire more than by hierarchical party allegiances.

We have used the concept of new media to encompass computers, mobile phones, webcams, videocams and CDs. With the help of Deleuze and Guattari's often prescient pronouncements, we have tried to review current instances of domination and control but also locate where there might be a continued possibility of escape. The digital world includes new forms of oppression – infantilisation and control of the subject and the creation of new inequalities – but also forms of liberation (freedom to connect and open up new spaces). It is the functions to which the machines are put in a given regime that determine which forms of control come into play. If new media readily lead to oppression and exploitation, the inverse also holds true. In the global, digital world, the scales have changed, including those of resistance. In addition, since the post-1968 era when Deleuze and Guattari developed their concepts, resistance is directed less against global capitalism in the name of socialism or communism than against specific abuses, be they political, economic, cultural or, increasingly, ecological. The capitalism that Deleuze and Guattari designated as the main culprit to be resisted has been displaced by the ubiquitous catchwords of democracy and human rights. The question today is less one of opposing capitalism than of creating democracy. Like smooth space, the new concept can be used as a form of resistance or appropriated by dominant powers. As Derrida wrote in 2003, the term 'democracy' is often bandied around as a cliché. In itself, democracy is not a perfect system, but it is one of the few whose structure allows itself to be continually perfected (Derrida 2003: 133).

New media can lead to the worst, such as the construction of the military- informational complex armed with its pseudo-rhizomes, deceptive smooth spaces and false war machines, but also to the best, that is, to an unprecedented rhizomatic creativity and the opening up of new spaces. If not all creative works bring about change, some do. Some works create supple lines – even lines of flight – that recompose singular and collective assemblages. Dispelling the perceived cultural and social threat of digital media and globalisation, Michel Frodon, the director of *Cahiers du cinéma*, draws on Deleuze and Guattari's work to suggest that when people create, they do not know if they play the social game in their niche or if they actually work to destroy these niches, and produce and put in circulation differences that cannot be assimilated by the dominant state of the world. There are, he claims, no direct answers, only myriad experimentations (Frodon 2006: 183).

After the creatively fashioned rhizomes and fabled war machines of the 1960s that helped students, women and colonised people emancipate themselves, their more digitally powered counterparts can still enable people to occupy time and space in novel ways. It is up to us to obtain and learn how to use the technological wherewithal necessary to resist the dominant strategies creatively and to experiment with myriad rhizomatic connections.

References

Adorno, T. (2001), *The Culture Industry: Essays on Mass Culture*, New York and London: Routledge.

Anderson, J. W., J. Dean and G. Lovink (eds) (2006), *Reformatting Politics: Information Technology and Global Civil Society*, London and New York: Routledge.

Balibar, E. (2004), *We, the People of Europe? Reflections on Transnational Citizenship*, trans. J. Swenson, Princeton: Princeton University Press.

Baudrillard, J. (1983), *Simulations*, trans. P. Foss, P. Patton and P. Beitchman, New York: Semiotext(e).

Baudrillard, J. (1996), *System of Objects*, trans. J. Benedict, New York: Verso.

Bogue, R. (2003a), *Deleuze on Literature*, London and New York: Routledge.

Bogue, R. (2003b), *Deleuze on Music, Painting, and the Arts*, London and New York: Routledge.

De Certeau, M. (1997), *The Capture of Speech*, trans. T. Conley, Minneapolis: University of Minnesota Press.

Deleuze, G. (1986), *Foucault*, Paris: Les Editions de Minuit.

Deleuze, G. (1988), *Le Pli: Leibniz et le Baroque*, Paris: Les Editions de Minuit.

Deleuze, G. (1989), *Cinema 2: The Time-Image*, trans. H. Tomlinson and R. Galeta, Minneapolis: University of Minnesota Press.

Deleuze, G. (1995), *Negotiations*, trans. M. Joughin, New York: Columbia University Press.

Deleuze, G. (2005), *Cinema 1: The Movement-Image*, trans. H. Tomlinson and B. Habberjam, New York: Continuum.

Deleuze, G. and F. Guattari (1987), *A Thousand Plateaus*, trans. B. Massumi, Minneapolis: University of Minnesota Press.

Derrida, J. (2003), *Voyous: Deux Essais sur la Raison*, Paris: Galilée.

Frodon, J-M. (2006), *L'art du Cinéma dans le Monde Contemporain à l'âge du Numérique et de la Mondialisation*, Paris: Cahiers du cinéma.

Fruin, N. W. and N. Montfort (2003), *The New Media Reader*, Cambridge, MA: MIT Press.

Guattari, F. (1995), *Chaosmosis*, trans. P. Bains and J. Pefanis, Bloomington: Indiana University Press.

Guattari, F. (2000), *The Three Ecologies*, trans. G. Genosko, London: Athlone Press.

Latour, B. and E. Hernant (1998), *Paris: Ville invisible*, Paris: La Découverte.

Poster, M. (2006), *Cyberdemocracy and the Public Sphere*, Durham: Duke University Press.

Rodowick, D. (2001), *Reading the Figural, or, Philosophy After the New Media*, Durham: Duke University Press.

Virilio, P. (2000), *The Information Bomb*, trans. C. Turner, London: Verso.

Notes

1. See Bogue 2003a: 170–3 especially; and Bogue 2003b: 187–90.
2. The original of this text appeared in 1994, as part of a collection of essays reaching back to 1968.
3. See the concluding pages of *Reading the Figural, or, Philosophy After the New Media* (Rodowick 2001).

Chapter 3

Deleuze's Objectile: From Discipline to Modulation

David Savat

Deleuze's short essay 'Postscript on the Societies of Control' (1992) has received much attention, in large part I think more for what it doesn't state than for what it does. Here I want to explore further some of Deleuze's suggestions in that essay. More specifically I'm interested in the product he suggests is produced by the new modulatory mode of power that replaces the disciplinary mode and its associated production of the individual. This product he refers to as the 'dividual'. I'm also interested in delineating some of the possible mechanisms, instruments and techniques by which that production might occur, since Deleuze does not elaborate on these. I will not be focusing here on the important question, perhaps more inspired by Guattari, as to how one might construct and maintain an existence or sense of unicity in this newly emerging machinic and societal ensemble. That question, I argue, concerns the broader politics surrounding the emergence of the new modulatory mode of power, in relation to which Deleuze's concept of the superject might be more usefully explored. As part of that process, however, a consideration of the modulatory mode of power, and its production of the objectile, is a first step.

The Amplification of Discipline

The use of databases is, for obvious reasons, a key issue when examining newly emerging forms of social control. This is not only because databases constitute very efficient information observation and recording machines but, crucially, because being digital technologies they have a tremendous capacity for convergence and symbiosis. One could well argue that all digital technologies are in some way of the database form, and that they are the dominant cultural form of information societies (Lyotard 1984; Manovich 2001). Indeed, when it comes to an examination of Foucault's disciplinary mode of power, and against any premature announcement of its demise, databases have very much come to constitute the writing apparatus underlying that mode of power. As others have so clearly demonstrated (Poster 1990), digital technologies, principally in the form of the database, have amplified the disciplinary mode of power, leaving essentially intact all its mechanisms, instruments and techniques, the combined operation of which is exemplified in the assemblage that is Bentham's Panopticon. In other words, discipline, a machine singularly focused on producing the useful individual, can still be observed operating today, and, rather than nearing its demise, does so in ever more aspects of our lives.

Foucault's disciplinary machine operates by way of making things visible. As a mode of power it is a 'political anatomy of detail' (Foucault 1979: 139). It is by way of this production of detail that out of a body it creates a useful force, otherwise known as that reality we call 'the individual'. As Foucault explained, this individual is standardised to the degree that all individuals, ideally, have four key features: they are cellular, organic, genetic and, most importantly, combinatory. Likewise, the machine that produces bodies in the form of a specific force is composed of four key mechanisms or parts, each of which in turn consists of several techniques or processes. First, the *distribution of individuals in space* (Foucault 1979: 141), which is part of making spaces functional; second, *the control of activity* (151–2), which essentially breaks up activities into constituent parts and arranges them in the most efficient or effective manner; third, *the organisation of geneses*, which is the machinery that, amongst other things, organises the training of individuals into temporal segments, guaranteeing both standardisation amongst them as well as differentiating each and every individual's abilities (158); fourth, the *composition of forces* (162), which is what organises the overall operation of all mechanisms and techniques, resulting in the body becoming 'constituted as a part of a multi-segmentary machine' (164).

Crucial for Foucault is that this machine or mode of power regards individuals 'both as object and as instruments of its exercise' (Foucault 1979: 170), and does so in an exceedingly simple and modest manner. This, Foucault argued, is thanks to the use of three simple instruments: hierarchical observation, normalising judgement, and the examination – the latter being the combination of the former two. These three instruments most clearly exemplify how the disciplinary mode of power is a political anatomy of detail. For the purposes of my argument here, it is in the use of these instruments that the function and importance of the actual material writing apparatus become clear.

The use of databases constitutes a major amplification of discipline (Mehta and Darrier 1998; Poster 1990) because by increasing the writing apparatus through which discipline operates one increases visibility and therefore the field of power. This is manifested not only in the greater level of detail by and through which an individual is known, but also in the increasing degree to which an individual's life is subject to a disciplinary gaze, especially as people's working and social lives increasingly occur by way of digital networks. The use of digital technologies amplifies the disciplinary machine's writing apparatus both by enabling a greater depth and breadth of detail about a person's life to be recorded, and because that information can subsequently be easily linked up to a variety of databases, much of this process being automated.

The key thing to recognise is that the increase in visibility, in terms of the reality that can be recorded about an individual's life, does not in itself destroy or nullify the four disciplinary mechanisms Foucault described. These continue to operate, but what we have with the use of databases and digital networks is an amplification or intensification of the field of force that is produced or effected. The network or power of writing by which discipline operates is both expanded and intensified without necessarily destroying any of the four disciplinary mechanisms. Any destruction of any part of the machine would result in the disciplinary machine grinding to a halt in its production of useful forces, that is, individuals. As I will argue further on, this continued production of individuality is actually an essential component of Deleuze's 'dividual'.

The Emergence of Modulation

The amplification of the disciplinary mode of power through the use of databases has produced a range of effects over the past couple of decades that, while disciplinary in origin, are increasingly non-disciplinary in character. One of the first effects to have been observed is that with the use of databases both the role of the expert and the status of knowledge have been altered (Castel 1991; Lyotard 1984). Knowledge is increasingly held not by experts but produced by way of databases or so-called 'expert-systems'. One consequence is that the actual expert or practitioner becomes increasingly subordinate to the administrators of such systems. In short, the administrator becomes the actual decision-maker, without necessarily needing any extensive knowledge concerning what or who they actually administer (Castel 1991).

This changing function of the expert also indicates a shift in the relationship between the observer and the subjects being observed. With the digitisation of the material writing apparatus the relation of immediacy that exists in the disciplinary mode of power between the expert as observer and the subject as observed ceases to exist because much of the observation and recording of a subject's behaviour is increasingly automated. In fact, much of this observation and recording is actually done by the subject itself (Poster 1990), without the subject necessarily needing to be aware of it. In other words, the subject is increasingly no longer required to be present so to speak (Castel 1991; Virilio 1986, 1991). Significantly, it is the disappearance of this relation of immediacy that reflects the operation of a form of intervention that is not disciplinary in character.

Observation in the context of discipline is focused on the internal state of individuals, and is part of a form of intervention that, by way of care, reward, punishment and, crucially, awareness of being observed, aims to make individuals adopt a specific form of behaviour. One of the forms of observation that emerges through the use of databases is instead focused on a series of factors that are more external to, or rather that are outward manifestations *of*, the individual (Colwell 1996: 215). This happens as part of a process that aims to anticipate any deviant behaviour, with a view to preventing that behaviour from arising in the first place (Castel 1991; Virilio 1986; Feeley and Simon 1992). As Virilio has pointed out:

> If in these tests someone is still listening for a confession, it is evident that this confession is no longer the story of a crime by its author. This was completed notably by the mapping of heavy crime zones in urban planning systems, and beyond this by the 'criminostat' (computer-aided visualisation of statistical fields) currently being tested by the police. We could imagine that at this level the gaps and hazards inherent in the ordering of materials should disappear, since with computers they could make the accusing discourse perfectly coherent, or at least approaching coherence, having to do both with the name of the subject and that of the object. At that point, they could do totally without the confession of the accused, who would be less informed about his own crime than the computer, and who, no longer being the one who knows 'the truth', would have nothing left to confess. (Virilio 1986: 154–6)

In short, the newly emerging mode of observation is pattern recognition. With the emergence of pattern recognition the aim of observation is to preempt a subject's behaviour, that is, to try to anticipate its actions before they occur (Bogard 1996; Castel 1991). The focus of observation in such a context is on the sort of external patterns that any person might generate rather than on the internal state of a given subject. It quite literally is a mode of observation that sees before the event (Bogard 1996). It is, in other words, simulation. It can be seen in the profiling of individuals and populations, genetic screening, facial recognition software, computer modelling, risk analysis, and so on. While it certainly can be used as part of a disciplinary schema, and like it operates by way of strict and detailed categorisation, it has elements that are distinctly not disciplinary in character.

This new mode of observation or visibility, unlike Foucault's instrument of hierarchical observation, cannot have a coercive function. In the first instance this is because in the context of being on a digital network – something which in so-called information societies is unavoidable – people aren't necessarily aware of the fact that most of their actions while on that network are being observed and recorded. The awareness of being observed, even when in fact one is not, is of course essential to the operation of discipline, but in the context of forms of observation like pattern recognition it matters not whether individuals are aware of being observed or not. More to the point, there isn't necessarily a mode of behaviour or 'mould' to follow or adhere to. Consequently, neither is there a gratification–punishment mechanism in place. After all, it is a mode of observation that sees before the event, before the behaviour actually occurs. Indeed, even were there such a mould, this mode of observation does not require awareness of it on a person's part. It simply doesn't matter either way, the reason being that a person will generate a given pattern, and actions will be anticipated according to the categories that person is deemed to fit. In short, while there is constant modulation or adjustment there is no model to adhere to. As Baudrillard stated, claiming the panoptic gaze had ended: 'There is no longer any imperative of submission to the model, or to the gaze "YOU are the model!" "YOU are the majority!"' (Baudrillard 1994: 29).

The emergence of a mode of observation that requires no compliance can also be characterised as content or risk analysis. It is precisely this sort of insidious social control that movies such as *Gattaca* (1997) and *Minority Report* (2002) explore, and it is precisely this aspect of control societies that Deleuze laments. The moment when a person's weaknesses and strengths, likely diseases and resistances, likely failures and desires can be predicted, is effectively the moment one can order those persons in advance (Bogard 1996, Castel 1991). The new forms of observation, because they are 'observation before the fact' (Bogard 1996: 27), not only constitute people as already a norm or model but, as a consequence, also enable them to be programmed in advance. As Castel (1991: 295–6) pointed out:

More the projection of an order than an imposition of order on the given, this way of thinking is no longer obsessed with discipline; it is obsessed with efficiency. Its chief artisan is no longer the practitioner on the ground, who intervenes in order to fill a gap or prevent one from appearing, but the administrator who plans out trajectories and sees to it that human profiles match up to them. The extreme image here would be one of a system of prevention perfect enough to dispense with both repression and assistance, thanks to its capability to forward-plan social trajectories from a 'scientific' evaluation of individual abilities. This is of course only an extreme possibility, what one might call a myth, but it is a myth whose logic is already at work in the most recent decisions taken in the name of the prevention of risks.

Nearing two decades on and living with the 'war on terror' and its legitimation in the form of a similar 'prevention of risks', it is a logic that seems only to increase.

As Deleuze suggests in his essay, it is significant that in the context of living in such a control society it matters little where one is – 'we are in the midst of a general breakdown of all sites of confinement' (Deleuze 1995: 178). Virilio terms this a 'deregulation of the management of space' (Virilio 1991: 16). More to the point, in the context of digital technologies it is not so much that the new forms of observation are not hierarchical, external and detached from the specific space or site being observed, but rather that they are the actual site or scene itself – as Bogard suggests 'it is perhaps not really a "gaze" at all, but a kind of "informated touch", since the whole environment is transparent and hyperperceptual' (Bogard 1996: 76–7). After all, in the context of using digital technologies any action one performs is always already almost instantaneously also an observation and recording as one always already writes or constitutes oneself as code.

It is for this reason that there is also a deregulation of disciplinary time. More precisely, time ceases to be organised in a linear manner having successive elements. In the context of becoming part of a digital network, like the Internet, one is always potentially available for work, play, advice or help. Perhaps more precisely, it is not so much that one is always potentially available, which would be more in keeping with a Heideggerian reading (Heidegger 1977), as that one is never quite finished. It is perhaps in this sense that, while the disciplinary machine distributes bodies in space, the modulatory machine, to borrow Virilio's phrase, 'populates time' (Virilio 1991: 120).

At this stage I want to reiterate that, unlike Deleuze, I do not see the disciplinary machine coming to an end. As indicated earlier, I maintain that today the effects of the disciplinary machine are amplified, leaving its four key mechanisms intact. At the same time, Deleuze argued there was a new machine emerging, a new mode of power. As argued above, one can see this in the form of newly emerging forms of observation aiming to anticipate behaviour. Before exploring what exactly this emerging machine produces it will be useful to delineate the mechanisms and instruments enabling this new mode of power to operate.

Mechanisms of Modulation

As indicated above, the new forms of observation, unlike those associated with discipline's hierarchical observation, do not focus on bodies and their individual behaviour as such. Indeed, they do not operate in any spatial sense because there is no construction of useful space at all (there may be a construction of useful time, but this is a different matter). Rather than operating in any perspectival space, the new forms of observation always project on a screen (Bogard 1996: 21). Stated differently, they tend to focus on the recognition of patterns of code. A first mechanism of modulation, then, is *the recognition of patterns*.

Significantly, if this mechanism does not operate spatially, in the way discipline might, then the behaviour of subjects and, indeed, what might come to be constituted as a 'subject' in the first place, take on a very different character as well. Deleuze alludes to this character in his essay when he notes a shift from the factory form of organisation, to which discipline belongs, to that of the corporation, to which the new form of control belongs. He describes the corporation as being 'gaseous' (Deleuze 1992: 4), that is, as fluid. This is significant, because if one can conceive of the corporation as fluid in character, then its actions must take on the character of a fluid as well. Indeed, many have argued that in the context of new or digital media the so-called subject becomes fluid. The key problem here, though, is that most continue to use words to describe the actions of these entities as if they are the actions of entities with a solid form, that is, individuals.

Fluids and solids behave differently from one another. They are differently situated in a spatial and, therefore, temporal sense. Most notably, in describing the behaviour of fluids or flows, concepts of 'force' and 'mass' cease to have any use, unless, of course, the fluids are contained. It is for this reason that one ought not to describe and conceptualise the behaviour of such flows using the more or less standard Newtonian language with which modern political thought has usefully described and conceptualised politics. Indeed, using such a conceptual imagery or toolset, one would be hard-pressed to understand fluids other than as lacking force, and any situation that lacks recognisable forms as being anything but turbulent, that is, chaotic, even if full of potential.

Discipline, as Foucault argues, constructs useful forces out of docile bodies. These forces are called individuals and they are obviously of a solid form, that is, they have a shape that they are able to maintain, otherwise they would not be able to exert 'force'. In part this is achieved through observation and by coercing or moulding bodies into a specific form. As Deleuze suggests, however, in the context of the newly emerging form of control the mould is dispensed with and replaced more by something resembling a sieve, effecting a constant modulation (Deleuze 1992: 4). Stated differently, where discipline controls activity by way of forcing individuals to adopt a specific form or mould, a stable shape that these individuals must then actively work at maintaining, the new form of control anticipates activity, and often as part of an aggregate or group. This is expressed, for example, in the emergence of a new penology (Feeley and Simon 1992), as well as in an increased use of strategies of risk management (Rose 1999: 236–7). For this reason one may refer to a second mechanism of the new mode of power as *the anticipation of activity*.

A third mechanism might reasonably concern the construction and organisation of time. Where the disciplinary mode aimed to break time up into clearly delineated segments, with each segment constituting a clear and distinct period of specific training punctuated by the examination, in the modulatory mode of power, or modulation for short, all of a person's time effectively constitutes one segment. In this context all of a person's time is potentially useful time and subject to different and simultaneous forms of training, none of which have a clear end point. Deleuze refers to this as a shift from 'apparent acquittal' to 'endless postponement' (Deleuze 1992: 179). Where in discipline the mechanism that organises time is referred to as the organisation of geneses, in the context of modulation and its construction of time it may be referred to as the *organisation of antitheses*.

While it may be possible to try to conceptualise this in terms of a given fluid consisting of various flow-lines at any one time, perhaps another way, in keeping more with the digital technology theme, is to think of time in terms of the construction of memory. Where discipline organises time, and therefore the subject, in the form of what might be a serial file, modulation stores it more in the manner of a random access file. The former stores data serially, so that in order to access data the whole code needs to be read from beginning to end, while the latter enables any piece of data to be accessed at any point in time without having to go through the whole code from beginning to end (Sinclair 1997: 357). As Colwell explains, 'it is a different form of repetition' (1996: 212).[1]

As with Foucault's disciplinary mode of power it is necessary to assume that Deleuze's modulatory mode of power might also have a fourth mechanism that combines or connects the other three into a fully functioning machine. After all, if components are not connected, not related to one another in some way, one won't have a machine (Guattari 1995). As argued above, the new forms of observation associated with the modulatory mode of power appear not to be aimed at the production and composition of useful forces, that is, individuals as such. Indeed, the internal state of a subject, as pointed out above, does not appear to be a central concern in these new modes of observation. This reflects a major shift in the operation of power. The shift is one from a situation in which forces are composed and arranged in relation to each other to a situation which is more of an attempt to control turbulence. While discipline attempts to construct and unify forces spatially in a mechanical manner, modulation attempts, by way of calculation, to anticipate the emergence of patterns of flow or energy within a turbulent system (DeLanda 1991, Parisi and Terranova 2000). As discussed above, once something is anticipated it can be ordered or programmed for in advance, and it is for this reason that the fourth mechanism could be referred to as *the programming of flows*.

Instruments of Modulation

Like the disciplinary mode of power, the modulatory mode may have a number of instruments by which it operates. Where discipline makes use of hierarchical observation, modulation tends to make use of the instruments of computer modelling or *simulation* (Bogard 1996). It should also be noted that observation in the context of discipline is hierarchical and has a centre. In the context of modulation observation is very much flatter than a pyramidal structure and has no centre as such, in part because any action performed by way of digital networks is simultaneously an observation and recording, and potentially available anywhere on the network.[2] In other words, it matters not 'where' one is connected, so long as one is connected.[3]

A second instrument, I would argue, is *categorical sorting*. While there are certainly norms and categories in place, these do not appear to have a gratification–punishment mechanism attached to them, as is the case with discipline. Rather, modulation in part consists of a more or less infinite comparative process that determines which norms, profiles or categories you are. As indicated above, the new modes of observation do not have an obvious norm or model associated with them in terms of determining how to adjust one's behaviour. It is more a matter of determining what norm you are and for the control to continuously adjust itself with respect to the patterns that are generated.

The third instrument, which Deleuze views as significant, is the test or *the sample* (Deleuze 1992: 179–80). This replaces the examination. Crucially, samples require no awareness, and, to the extent that one may be aware of being sampled, there is, again, never a clear model in place to adhere to. Samples or tests are important for determining the pattern of behaviour one exemplifies, which is why, for Deleuze, marketing may well be a key form of social control today as it relies strongly on samples to determine patterns of consumption.[4]

A Machine for Making Objectiles

Comparing the two machines with each other suggests that each of them produces a very different reality. Discipline's basic aim is to make useful forces out of docile bodies, and the construction of a unique and individual identity is central to that product. That is the reality it produces and it is this reality that constitutes the individual. It aims to produce specific forms of behaviour, specific outward manifestations. Modulation, on the other hand, has no interest in the actual production of such outward manifestations. Instead, it is solely interested in the patterns of code that are generated – in part because it is interested in predicting rather than producing specific forms of behaviour, and in part because, depending on the code that is generated, a given pattern is allowed or enabled to continue or not. Of course, in the context of digital networks, one need never be aware of how one is excluded or enabled differently from others, whereas in discipline that awareness of exclusion (and inclusion) is important.[5] It is for this reason that Deleuze contrasts discipline's mould with modulation's sieve, 'whose mesh varies from one point to another' (Deleuze 1992: 178–9).

Discipline, in short, is aimed at the production of something that has form and substance. It produces objects that can be moved, combined and separated, while still maintaining their same basic structured form. They are standardised objects that have both substance and essence, and much of discipline's energies, including the subject's own energies, are aimed at revealing, or rather producing, this internal essence, that is, identity. The fact that the objects are standardised in terms of form and function is precisely why they are useful. After all, mass standardisation is the tremendous advantage the factory form of organisation creates. Modulation, however, neither produces such an object nor aims towards such a production. Rather, modulation is a constant, varying production process, which has neither a clear beginning nor end. In short, modulation's product is not so much a form as a flow, and in that respect its product is of an entirely different status.

Deleuze explored the idea of a change in the status of the object in *The Fold* (1993). This changed status he referred to as the 'objectile', which

> refers neither to the beginnings of the industrial era nor to the idea of the standard that still upheld a semblance of essence and imposed a law of constancy ('The object produced by and for the masses'), but to our current state of things, where fluctuation of the norm replaces the permanence of a law; where the object assumes a place in a continuum by variation . . . The new status of the object no longer refers its condition to a spatial mould – in other words, to a relation of form-matter – but to a temporal modulation that implies as much the beginnings of a continuous variation of matter as a continuous development of form. (Deleuze 1993: 19)

Given that the objectile here refers both to a continuous variation of matter as well as a continuous development of form, it suggests that to the extent that there is a product it is fluid – that is, it is best understood as flow, as process. If we accept that Deleuze's modulatory mode of power exemplifies such a production of objectiles, then we can understand the products of the machine, that is, both the form of control and the dividual, somewhat better.

In this respect, in the context of modulatory power the concept of identity ceases to have much use because identity, as 'absolute sameness' or a 'continuous unchanging property throughout existence' (NSOED 1997), is simply not what this machine produces or aims to produce. Indeed, it produces its total opposite. It does not make distinct, relatively stable entities of standardised form and substance, that is, subjects as individuals, as objects with an essence. Instead, it produces objectiles. The objectile has no essence, it is, rather, an event (Deleuze 1993: 19). Deleuze also argues that just as we have a transformation in the status of the object, from essence to event, so we have a transformation from subject to superject (Deleuze 1993).

The Aim of Production

Discipline and modulation, then, produce two very different sets of effects. The disciplinary machine is intensely interested in subjects as individuals. It concerns itself with the well-being of the individual to the extent that it enables it to be a useful force. In that respect it 'cares' for the individual.[6] The modulatory machine, however, has no such concern. It does not have this concern because individuals literally do not exist, or rather, it does not have the machinery to even recognise such entities; after all, it recognises and produces events, not essences. This, however, ought not to be understood as a 'lack' on the part of modulation, the reason being that modulation has a very different interest.

Discipline's function is to produce an entity or object of well-defined form. Modulation, on the other hand, much like Leibniz's mathematics, 'assumes variation as its objective'.[7] As Deleuze points out, the consequence of assuming variation as the objective itself is not only that 'the notion of function tends to be extracted, but [that] the notion of objective also changes and becomes functional'. It may well be then, that the aim of the modulatory machine is not 'defined by an essential form' (Deleuze 1993: 18) but that it 'reaches a pure functionality, as if declining a family of curves, framed by parameters inseparable from a series of possible declensions or from a surface of variable curvature that it is itself describing' (Deleuze 1993: 19). To phrase that differently, while the function of discipline is to produce an object as efficiently as possible, the function or aim of modulatory power may well be pure functionality.[8]

Deleuze conceptualised and described this difference of function as an increase in the level and degree of control in society. While this may be one element that it is important to consider in any broader digitisation of politics, it implies that 'control' sits on a single continuum, within which one either has more or less control. This is perhaps only part of the story, which is why 'control' may be a somewhat problematic term in the sense that it increasingly lacks precision.

In the context of the disciplinary mode, control, certainly initially, is something people actively experience. Ideally individuals learn to impose that control upon themselves as part of a process of regulating their own behaviour. Control in this context is intensive and something that is experienced, in great part because having a sense or imagined awareness of being observed is critical to its operation. In the context of modulation, control is experienced entirely differently. One is not made into a 'good individual'. Whether one makes oneself such or not is an irrelevancy – in fact, it doesn't even register since the modulatory machine simply does not contain a connection amongst components capable of even recognising it.[9]

Modulation is about the anticipation of events. Indeed, it is the very anticipation of events that, properly speaking, is what constitutes the actual objectile. As Deleuze explains, the objectile is 'the trace of the same line' (Deleuze 1993: 19). The objectile is not something that is made or controlled in the way that an object is made or controlled. Modulation is about recognising the generation of flow, a pattern of code on the machinic level if you like, and then anticipating the likely continuation or outcome of that pattern. It is for that reason that the objectile, produced by the modulatory machine, is that very anticipation of the event. From such a perspective modulatory power is engaged in the continuous anticipation of events in what it perceives as a turbulent system. It matters not whether any given flow constitutes a given identity because the objectile as such, that is, the actual product of modulatory power, is not controlled as such. Rather, objectiles are prepared for in advance.[10] The development of such advance preparation can be seen in how different advertising is generated depending on how one makes use of the World Wide Web and what patterns of code that usage generates. It is suggested that mobile phone technology will adopt a similar approach where, depending on your geographical location and your anticipated individual tastes, different targeted advertisements may appear by way of your phone.[11]

In such a situation control is experienced entirely differently than it is with disciplinary power. Instead of you actively adjusting your behaviour in order to conform to one or another norm, it is now the environment that adjusts to you, and does so in advance. This occurs not only in your interactions with digital machines but also at the level of genetic coding for example. Your 'faults' can increasingly be anticipated and, in order to prevent them from occurring, your genetic code may well come to be adjusted. In effect, your very genetic code becomes the control environment.

In a context where one is always already programmed for in advance, 'control' comes to be so subtle that it may well present itself in the form of 'choice'.[12] In such a situation, 'control emerges as an immanent process of rechannelling of turbulent flows' (Parisi and Terranova 2000), a process one may well not even experience as 'control'. More significantly, as I've indicated before, in such a context politics becomes increasingly concerned with the performativity of the system, or rather, with arranging flows in such a manner as to be most functional. Politics is then not about the projection of the 'good life', as Habermas (1971) argued, but with the avoidance of risk (Beck 1992), that is, the identification of potential factors affecting the performativity of the system. In other words, politics comes to be about the 'management of flows', or rather, the management of turbulence (Parisi and Terranova 2000). In that respect, a politics of fluids may well be emerging.[13]

The Principle of Superposition

There is one other issue that requires explanation. In his 'Postscript', Deleuze held the view that the disciplinary mode of power comes to an end and that modulation replaces it. But that is too rash a statement. Indeed, while Foucault may have stated something similar, he also recognised that the emergence of the disciplinary mode of power itself 'hasn't replaced all the others, but infiltrates the others, sometimes undermining them, serving as an intermediary between them, extending them, linking them' (Foucault 1979: 216). Again, when discussing governmentality as a mode of power, Foucault (1991) similarly argued that it operated concurrently with discipline.

Taking into account work which argues strongly that discipline, rather than being dismantled is, in fact, being strengthened (Boyne 2000, Mehta and Darrier 1998, Poster 1990, 1995), Deleuze's position in his short essay is a difficult one to maintain. At the same time, Deleuze, along with others, has identified the emergence of a mode of power that produces effects of power that are clearly not disciplinary in character. Important to note here is that both modes function by way of the same digitised writing apparatus – the database – and that both continue to produce their respective effects by way of that very same writing apparatus.

On the one hand, then, we have a machine that aims to produce a stable standardised object, an object of a specific and stable form. On the other hand, we have a machine that produces flow, that is, it constantly postpones or disperses identity.[14] If there is, then, an antagonism produced by way of the simultaneous operation of the two machines, this does not necessarily mean that one cancels out the other, nor that one necessarily overrides the other. Indeed, it is this very antagonism produced by way of the two modes of power operating at the same time, often by way of the same writing apparatus, that constitutes Deleuze's dividual (Colwell 1996). The operation of discipline is thus just as important to the overall effect and experience of dividuality as is the operation of modulation. In other words, the dividual is not the effect solely of the modulatory mode of power, which it would be if the disciplinary mode had come to an end. Rather, the dividual is precisely the effect and experience of on the one hand constantly being made into a subject, and on the other, of constantly being made, no doubt at varying speeds, into a superject, into an objectile. Stated differently, dividuality is the effect and experience of on the one hand being made into a form, an essence, a solid state, and on the other hand being made into a flow, an event, a fluid or formless state. Dividuality is precisely the experience of being neither this nor that, while at the same time perhaps being both at the same time.

Fourier's principle of superposition explains that 'a wave function describing the resulting motion . . . where a wave combines with a reflected wave, is obtained by adding the two wave functions for the two separate waves' (Sears et al. 1987: 499). This can be expressed by way of the following equation: $y(x, t) = y_1(x, t) + y_2(x, t)$ (Halliday and Resnick 1988: 403). What this principle explains is how at least two different sets of phenomena can coincide as independent influences on one and the same system. Stated differently, it provides a model of how two waves, each with an amplitude and frequency different from the other, can travel through one another and appear as one, yet still retain the effects and characteristics that are unique to each of them.

Discipline and modulation could be seen to behave similarly, in that both can function through one and the same database or profile, while simultaneously producing entirely different effects. They have, in other words, something resembling a different amplitude and frequency to one another, both of which, however, affect the same surface,[15] and at times by way of the same instrument. The resultant effect of power may or may not be harmonious. Indeed, as Foucault intimated, while power may be an orchestra, it is hardly ever well conducted, if at all (Foucault 1991: 103). And indeed, as Deleuze makes clear, it is during moments of unharmony in production that one may be able to fold the force, as it were. This, then, raises Deleuze's political and ethical question of how one exists or even maintains a form of existence despite the 'diversity of components of subjectivation' that pass through one as part of any assemblage and larger societal ensemble (Guattari 1995). It is a question that is in many respects central to his short essay. Deleuze's concept of the objectile, and more importantly its partner concept of the superject, may well be of use here in developing the necessary understanding of a digital being's sensibility, as part of the process of beginning to answer that more important political and ethical question.

References

Bailey, J. (1996), *Afterthought: The Computer Challenge to Human Intelligence*, New York: Basic Books.

Baudrillard, J. (1994), *Simulacra and Simulation*, trans. S. F. Glaser, Ann Arbor: The University of Michigan Press.

Beck, U. (1992), *Risk Society: Towards a New Modernity*, London: Sage.

Bogard, W. (1996), *The Simulation of Surveillance: Hypercontrol in Telematic Societies*, Cambridge: Cambridge University Press.

Boyne, R. (2000), 'Post-Panopticism', *Economy and Society*, 29 (2): 285–307.

Castel, R. (1991), 'From Dangerousness to Risk', in G. Burchell, C. Gordon and P. Miller (eds), *The Foucault Effect: Studies in Governmentality*, London: Harvester Wheatsheaf.

Colwell, C. (1996), 'Discipline and Control: Butler and Deleuze on Individuality and Dividuality', *Philosophy Today*, 40 (1): 211–16.

DeLanda, M. (1991), *War in the Age of Intelligent Machines*, New York: Zone Books.

Deleuze, G. (1992), 'Postscript on the Societies of Control', *October*, 59: 3–7.

Deleuze, G. (1993), *The Fold: Leibniz and the Baroque*, trans. T. Conley, Minneapolis: University of Minnesota Press.

Deleuze, G. (1995), *Negotiations*, trans. M. Joughin, New York: Columbia University Press.

Feeley, M. and J. Simon (1992), 'The New Penology: Notes on the Emerging Strategy of Corrections and its Implications', *Criminology*, 30 (4): 449–74.

Foucault, M. (1979), *Discipline and Punish: The Birth of the Prison*, trans. A. Sheridan, Harmondsworth: Penguin Books.

Foucault, M. (1991), 'Governmentality', in G. Burchell, C. Gordon, and P. Miller (eds), *The Foucault Effect: Studies in Governmentality*, London: Harvester Wheatsheaf.

Gattaca, film, directed by A. Niccol, USA: Columbia Pictures, 1997.

Guattari, F. (1995), *Chaosmosis: an Ethico-Aesthetic Paradigm*, trans. P. Bains and J. Pefanis, Bloomington, IN: Indiana University Press.

Habermas, J. (1971), *Toward a Rational Society: Student Protest, Science, and Politics*, trans. J. J. Shapiro, London: Heinemann Educational.

Halliday, D. and R. Resnick (1988), *Fundamentals of Physics*, New York: John Wiley & Sons.

Hardt, M. and A. Negri (2001), *Empire*, London: Harvard University Press.

Heidegger, M. (1977), *The Question Concerning Technology, and Other Essays*, trans. W. Lovitt, New York: Harper & Row.

Lyotard, J. F. (1984), *The Postmodern Condition: A Report on Knowledge*, trans. G. Bennington and B. Massumi, Minneapolis: University of Minnesota Press.

Manovich, L. (2001), *The Language of New Media*, Cambridge, MA: MIT Press.

Mehta, M. D. and E. Darrier (1998), 'Virtual Control and Disciplining on the Internet: Electronic Governmentality in the New Wired World', *Information Society*, 14 (2): 107–16.

Minority Report, film, directed by S. Spielberg, USA: 20th Century Fox, 2002.

Negroponte, N. (1995), *Being Digital*, Rydalmere: Hodder & Stoughton.

NSOED (1997), *New Shorter Oxford English Dictionary*, Oxford: Oxford University Press.

Parisi, L. and T. Terranova (2000), 'Heat-Death: Emergence and Control in Genetic Engineering and Artificial Life', *CTheory*, A084; http://www.ctheory.net/text_file.asp?pick=127

Poster, M. (1990), *The Mode of Information: Poststructuralism and Social Context*, Cambridge: Polity Press.

Poster, M. (1995), *The Second Media Age*, Cambridge: Polity Press.

Rose, N. (1999), *Powers of Freedom: Reframing Political Thought*, Cambridge: Cambridge University Press.

Sears, F. W., M. W. Zemansky and H. D. Young (1987), *University Physics*, Reading: Addison-Wesley Publishing Company.

Sinclair, I. R. (1997), *Collins Dictionary of Personal Computing*, Glasgow: HarperCollins Publishers.

Virilio, P. (1991), *The Lost Dimension*, trans. D. Moshenberg, New York: Semiotext(e).

Virilio, P. (1986), *Speed and Politics: An Essay on Dromology*, trans. M. Polizzoti. New York: Semiotext(e).

Notes

1. See Colwell on this point: 'From an electronically discursive standpoint, dividuals are constructed in databanks, each aspect of the person assembled in separate computer files, each file available for a different purpose, the parameters of each file organised around that purpose. This is quite different from Foucault's conception of the creation of an individual via the construction of a file that assembles the entire genealogic history of a person in order to make h/er an object for scientific study and intervention' (Colwell 1996: 212).
2. Here I do not want to suggest that this network is a rhizome, but rather that it is perhaps more usefully unserstood as a fluid. The notion of the fluid may also be worth exploring in terms of the temporal aspect of networks and any action that is constituted by way of them, in that a fluid always flows and never moves, the latter being a quality of solid forms. Fluids, while they do not move, are never at rest since otherwise they would become solid. Note also how gases and liquids, while both fluid, flow at different speeds. In terms of exploring ideas of differential speed, especially as it concerns political action in the context of networks, the concept of the flowline may well be productive here. Caution needs to be taken, however, not to think of action in the context of the network as fluid in the sense that one may have a flow of an aggregate of solids, like sand in a network of pipes, which is sometimes used to critique the use of the concept of the fluid in relation to networks. The network as a whole is fluid, in a similar sense to how a gas may occupy a room. In that respect it matters not 'where' the gas is, since it occupies the entire scene so to speak.
3. Of course, differences in the quality of that connection have political consequences as well as consequences for the effectiveness of the operations of both discipline and modulation.
4. The company Claritas, as well as the Nielsen Company of which it forms a part, is one such company, providing a useful example of an organisation engaging in such activity.
5. Indeed, digital environments and networks can easily give people access to the same environment but, depending on their behaviour, that environment can be made to adjust itself automatically and differently depending on the patterns generated. A simpler example of this is the way that, depending on your past web-surfing behaviour, a website may throw up different links, or different adverts. In this case it is not you who are required to change your behaviour to suit the environment, rather the environment now adjusts its behaviour as part of a process of preempting you.
6. Only in the sense, of course, that it cares about it in terms of it being productive, which, amongst other things, requires healthy individuals.
7. Here I leave aside any questions regarding Leibniz's contribution to the development of digital technologies as they currently operate.
8. Lyotard notably observed that the use of databases, because they exteriorise knowledge, express a shift in the production of knowledge away from a concern with the production of truth to a concern with making systems more efficient. As Habermas observed much earlier, in such a context, insofar as government action is directed towards the economic system's stability and growth, politics now takes on a peculiarly negative character. For it is oriented towards the elimination of dysfunctions and the avoidance of risks that threaten the system: not, in other

words, towards the *realisation of practical goals* but towards the *solution of technical problems* (Habermas 1971: 102–3).

9. The disciplinary machine certainly does contain such a connection amongst components, which is why I think it is a mistake to think of discipline as having been replaced.

10. A more simple example of this would be the use of wizards in software applications such as Microsoft Word, which, albeit crudely, aim to anticipate what form of help the user may require or will need. See also Negroponte (1995: 164–5). Manovich (2001), especially in his first chapter discussing modularity, is also useful, as is Bogard (1996) on the algorithm. Bailey (1996: 148) explains that such forms of anticipation are also developed in the form of financial investment applications that aim to predict the emergence of profitable trade opportunities in the global financial market. Such opportunities, according to Bailey, sometimes emerge only for a few minutes.

11. In once scene in the movie *Minority Report* (2002), the main character walks though a busy area, and as he proceeds the advertising in the street adjusts itself to his anticipated tastes and interests. Similar ideas are explored in movies like *Gattaca* (2002) – where a person's genetic code is read in order to determine what work, and life, they are best suited to – as well as in novels such as *Interface* by Neil Stephenson and Frederick George.

12. Negroponte's *Being Digital* (1995) represents such a view well.

13. How such a politics might connect to a politics of solids, and what sort of boundary-layer might eventuate between them, is a different matter.

14. The choice of the verb 'disperses' rather than 'fragments' is deliberate.

15. It is perhaps this surface that constitutes the boundary-layer.

Chapter 4

How to Surf: Technologies at Work in the Societies of Control

Bent Meier Sorensen

'So, I was thinking I could use a partner.'

'I don't know anything about being a detective.'

'There's nothing to it. But this being the nineties, you can't just walk up to a guy and smack him in the face. You gotta say something cool first.'

'Like, "I'll be back!"'

'Yeah, only better than that. Like, if you're gonna hit him with a surf-board you'll say. . .'

'Surf's up, pal!'

'Yeah. Something like that.'

The Last Boy Scout (1991)

If *Anti-Oedipus* should have been called *Introduction to a Non-Fascist Life*, as Foucault suggested in his preface, then perhaps *A Thousand Plateaus* should have been called *How to Surf*. After all, as Deleuze puts it:

> we've gone from one animal to the other, from moles to snakes, not just in the system we live under but in the way we live and in our relations with other people too. Disciplinary man produced energy in discrete amounts, while control man undulates, moving among a continuous range of different orbits. *Surfing* has taken over from all the old *sports*. (Deleuze 1995: 180)

In chapter six of *A Thousand Plateaus*, Deleuze and Guattari offer 'the experiment' as a method for producing intensity and change; they teach us how to ride the waves of desire on the plane of consistency or, as they put it, 'to make ourselves a body without organs' with which to touch the plane of immanence. The body without organs 'is not a notion or a concept but a practice, a set of practices' (Deleuze and Guattari 1987: 149–50) and *A Thousand Plateaus* is not a theory but a handbook. Making a body without organs is an experiment that *you* carry out, 'scurrying like a vermin . . . running like a lunatic. . .' (150), in a word, surfing. On the beach before dawn, groping around, almost sleepwalking, the mission is clear: 'find your body without organs' (151). This isn't going to be easy; it's not the nineties any more.

On page 161, however, Deleuze and Guattari calmly explain 'how it should be done'. First: 'Lodge yourself on a stratum'. This is their version of nomadism: the nomad is not the flâneur or the restless tourist. The nomad is, on the contrary, *'he who does not move'* (Deleuze and Guattari 1987: 381). Lodging yourself on a stratum means experiencing its dangers, it implies solidarity: it may take place in the streets, or it may take place through an experiment with the conceptual apparatus of struggle. It's a bit like being displaced and transfigured in the upheavals of '68 and then meeting a political psychologist called Félix, if you know what I mean. Lodged on the stratum, you should 'experiment with the opportunities it offers' (Deleuze and Guattari 1987: 161). Even in the most severely deterritorialised and captive stratum, even in the deadly boredom of outsourced industrial labour, even, as we shall see, in the army of the *un*employed, there is an 'imperceptible extra', attested by the desire it releases (Deleuze and Guattari 1984). Then, when you have established your 'advantageous place on [the stratum]', you start to 'find potential movements of deterritorialization, possible lines of flight' (Deleuze and Guattari 1987: 161). Now it's more like making love: you must go through the experience. Your movements only make sense if you are sensitive to the movements of the other(s). Or it's like coming face to face with A. N. Whitehead's processual God, which Deleuze, in a sense, is always seeking: a God that is himself recreated through the very act of creating. *When you surf, you are less interested in the changes in the wave than in changing yourself.* If you want your body without organs, you can't just map the lines of flight in passing them; you have to 'experience them, produce flow conjunctions here and there, try out continuums of intensities, segment by segment' (Deleuze and Guattari 1987: 161). It's a do-it-yourself job.

Step two: 'we are in a social formation' (Deleuze and Guattari 1987: 161). No matter what neoclassical economics and Nike want you to believe, you are not an individual. Rather, you are a host of 'dividuals' (Deleuze 1994: 258), effected by the social conjunction as an event. Given this collective premise, you must examine the formation and 'see how it is stratified for us and in us and at the place where we are; then descend from the strata to the deeper assemblage' (Deleuze and Guattari 1987: 161). Stratification occurs simultaneously in us and around us: the Hegelianism at the Humboldt University was, and is, much less dangerous than the perpetual Hegelian striation of our brains.[1] The former comes as 'science' while the latter is ready-made as 'education' (you simply 'install' it in the museum). We are always judging the peer and the pupil; it's 'go' or 'no go', never 'go with us' (Deleuze and Guattari 1987: 177). However, even if striation is true in its effect, it is not the ultimate truth about you and your situation. There is a deeper assemblage and this is what constitutes your crisis, as well as your way out. The assemblage is a material meshwork that links bodies and signs in the charged interstice between the strata and the body without organs, that is, between habits and stability and the intense whirlwind of molecules that surf the plane of consistency, drawing the plane of immanence. Having now sensed your current, empirical assemblage, you must also sense *the event* of this assemblage; you must sense what may enable it to change.

Thus, step three: 'gently tip the assemblage, making it pass over to the side of the plane of consistency' (Deleuze and Guattari 1987: 161). Schizoanalysis insists that you tip it *gently*; 'You don't do it with a sledgehammer, you use a very fine file' (160). This is the empirical part: count the connections in the assemblage, find its rhythm, listen to its refrain. As the senses stay alert, you look for the insignificant but important detail where the refrain might become deterritorialised and connect anew with an outside. It is here, when you see the plane at the horizon that 'the [body without organs] reveals itself for what it is: connection of desires, conjunction of flows, continuum of intensities'. You have finally 'constructed your own little machine, ready when needed to be plugged into other collective machines' (161). Keep this machine ready for later.

In 1977, Michel Foucault suggested that political philosophy must detach itself from the problem of sovereignty and the problems of law and prohibition. 'We need to cut off the King's head', as he famously put it (Foucault 1980: 121). Late in his life, Deleuze sensed the emergence of a stratification that seemed to proceed from a radicalisation of this suggestion, and which would eventually reconfigure the disciplinary societies that Foucault analysed. Deleuze termed this new stratification 'the societies of control' (Deleuze 1995). In this formation, your identity is not dependent on your narrative as a subject, whether of sovereignty or of discipline, whether as citizen, consumer or family man. Rather, your self is to be abstracted from databanks, registers, tests and focus group interviews, and the data is to be personalised in the 'security' of passwords that you memorise. You will be asked to carry out this abstraction yourself. The ultimate test of 'being human' is not the question of whether you are currently in or have ever been in prison, gone to school, or been in the army. The ultimate test is: do you currently have a paid job and which paid jobs have you had? The decisive technologies of our age are the technologies of the labour market where a decoded flow of labour joins up with a decoded flow of capital (Deleuze and Guattari 1984: 33). Some of these technologies are no more complicated than a folded piece of paper, a pamphlet.

We are going to have a look at one of these pamphlets (you don't read pamphlets, of course, you look at them. This look can be compared to an earlier one, see Sorensen [2004]). And you are going to plug your little machine into this pamphlet. It belongs to the actualised world, and, as it happens, it is also a function of your memory: it is what everyone gets at some point in life. It is a folder you receive when you have become unemployed, and it carries the lyrical title: *To Be Available* (Direktoratet for Arbejdsløshedsforsikring 1999). If you think you've never received this folder because, say, you have 'never been unemployed', you haven't understood anything about modernity. Modernity is exactly this experience. It is a vague feeling of always being a little bit unemployed, sometimes as a faint but haunting shadow behind your back, sometimes as a death sentence from the (Un)employment Office. It is Deleuze himself who in the 'Postscript on Control Societies' directs us to the work of Franz Kafka. Imagine yourself in the position of K. in *The Trial* as he loiters in front of the gates that lead into the Law: 'No one else could ever be admitted here, since this gate was made only for you.' This gate, this pamphlet, this wave . . .

The front page offers a picture of an umbrella that provides shelter from what could be the rain, an umbrella under which the unemployed can seek protection (Figure 4.1).

The picture is ambiguous:[2] if what hits the umbrella is indeed rain, it seems to be directed from a source, and seems to be aimed directly at the person holding the umbrella. The situation converges in a tautological statement of a double bind: the threat and the relief originate at the same source 'outside' the pictogram. Even if this seems to be an especially paranoid interpretation, it will not be the last production of double binds to be found in the folder; in fact, the discourse of Human Resource Management (HRM) – the stratum *par excellence* in the societies of control – is characterised precisely by ambiguity and double binds (Legge 1999).

This peripheral and extreme site, this folder, is exactly the place where the powers that produce subjectivity must be traced and analysed: not as powers in their central and sovereign positions, but, as Foucault points out, powers in 'the multiple forms of subjugation that have a place and function within the social organism' (Foucault 1980: 92). It calls for the analysis of power at its extremities, not the hand of power, but its

Om at
stå til
rådighed

Arbejdsdirektoratet
Februar 2003

Figure 4.1 (Source: Direktoratet for Arbejdsløshedsforsikring)

cuticles, its ragged and insignificant trivialities, a folder in its outmost folds, easily deconstructed, of course, but also a thin sheet of paper easily reproduced and dispersed. It is power confronted *prima facie*, 'on its face', in its cosmetic details where it directly intersects with and sometimes intercepts the ontological production of life.

The folder works by producing new folds in which the unemployed must reconstruct themselves while without a job. As an ordering device, the folder is a refrain, and a reconstruction of the refrain of the folder might create a war machine, possibly motivating a new refrain recreating the assemblage of client-AND-the folder. In the patently difficult eleventh chapter of *A Thousand Plateaus*, Deleuze and Guattari conceive 'the refrain' as a force ordering the socius, labelling its three aspects injection, inscription and interception (Deleuze and Guattari 1987: 311–12).

Injection is the initiation of a quasi-stable situation that connects the client temporarily to a territory following a local tactic of survival: the client's day-to-day combat, 'my stretch of sidewalk' (Deleuze and Guattari 1987: 321), my wave. This is followed by the dominant function of the refrain, dominant in the sense of a redundancy and rhythm necessary for the creation and maintenance of the assemblage altogether, namely the inscription of a geomorphic territory implying more systematic and time-consuming efforts. It's like how I keep trying to think of cool things to say about waves. Accordingly, by way of rules and habits, the inscription process creates a home by drawing a circle and perpetually organising a space that operates with an inside/outside distinction, especially as member and non-member of the organisation, inside or outside the waged labour force. Finally, the refrain (occasionally) intercepts and creates a way out when deterritorialised by creative forces: music, art, philosophy, or simply *the outside*. The refrain, however, has a tendency to segment and rigidify, to become a habit, morphing into what in human resource management is known as 'organisational culture'.

The Refrain of Organising

We habitually call life outside the waged labour force 'unemployment'. This habit constructs, quite literally, a negative difference, pointing out what the person in question is not, namely, employed. The word employed itself dates back to the fifteenth century and stems from Middle French *emploier*, from Latin *implicare*, to enfold, involve, implicate, from *in-* + *plicare*, to fold. From this it follows that, at least since the fifteenth century, being 'un-employed' has denoted the situation of *not being folded at all*. Of course this is not true. On the contrary, 'to be' implies a multiplicity of folds; it implies, in Deleuze's baroque vision, nothing but folds (Deleuze 1993). What our habitual denotation shows, rather, is how a certain, stratified fold, *le emploier*, has become the signifier and subjectifier of capitalism, a social imaginary that 'channels our desire so that desire desires its own repression' (Carter and Jackson 2004: 112).

The unemployed find themselves in the midst of a dangerous field of forces, a battlefield, a crisis and a threshold. In *A Thousand Plateaus*, Deleuze and Guattari conceive of this field, this assemblage, as the already sketched intermezzo of, on the one hand, the plane of immanence (or consistency) and, on the other, the plane of organisation (Deleuze and Guattari 1987: 265).[3] This pitches multiplicity against unity and posits 'a pluralism of organisation (based on enfoldedness, relational connections and becoming) against a pluralism of order (based on positions, interests and governmentality)' (Thanem and Linstead 2006: 42). The plane of immanence is drawn by a 'war machine', that is, by a surfboard: by a creative critique that strives to become a thought of the outside. To reach this limit, one needs to recreate the body without organs of any given assemblage, which means reaching the assemblage's full expression *as desire*. It is in this sense that the plane of immanence can be seen as the composition of *all* Bodies without Organs. Moreover, the body without organs is, as already indicated, an inevitable exercise or a perpetual experimentation: it is the limit of making things happen; it is the movement within the practice of counter-actualisation.

The assemblage of being (which contains but cannot confine a multiple and coexisting assemblage of *becoming*) is thus situated between the organised stratifications and its specific (if not specified) body without organs, letting the concept of the assemblage itself replace and reconfigure the staple sociological and philosophical concern of the relationship between the human and its world (Buchanan 2000: 120). The assemblage and the territory are the two main components in Deleuze and Guattari's 'social ontology' (DeLanda 2002). The assemblage becomes territorial on account of a mixture of chaos, organisation and change. However, 'these are not three successive moments in an evolution. They are three aspects of a single thing, the Refrain (*ritournelle*)' (Deleuze and Guattari 1987: 312).

As we move along the folder, scurrying like an unemployed, the conditions the client has to live up to in order to receive her unemployment benefits become specified. They range from the imperative that 'the client must be registered at the Employment Office' to the imperative that 'the client must have an individual plan of action'. We are moving from the injecting function of the refrain towards its inscribing function: it now inscribes onto the assemblage the codes that the client must adhere to in order to enter into the resource-distribution system itself. As such it works as a relay that organises inclusion and exclusion. The refrain is in other words *machinic*, and machines are what move through the assemblage when it undergoes deterritorialisation, and variations and mutations are drawn from it: '*Machines are always singular keys that open or close an assemblage, a territory*' (Deleuze and Guattari 1987: 333–4, emphasis in original). Social analysis implies the diagrammatisation of the two internal limits any assemblage has, two limits to be found within any concrete, empirical practice: the system of strata and the plane of immanence. Creative as it is, the refrain may also, as indicated, stratify and rigidify and drop the assemblage into a black hole: the national anthem that makes us feel and cry, kill and die. Such a hole is the face.

How About I Rearrange Your Face?

'The abstract machine crops up when you least expect it . . .' – right in your face (Deleuze and Guattari 1987: 168). Overstating, even shouting, the folder has equipped itself with small comic-like pictures within the text:

"How about the two of us just sit down and make ourselves a plan of action?"

"Oh? Fine. Then you just won't get any unemployment benefits."

Figure 4.2 (Source: Direktoratet for Arbejdsløshedsforsikring)

At first, what is decisive about the pictures is their ability to *produce faces*. In fact, Legge's above-mentioned analysis makes her conclude that the entire HRM discourse is a 'language of representation [that] appears, Janus-like, to produce two faces: the positive and the negative' (Legge 1999: 255). Specifically, the pictures in the folder produce the precise emotional and facial expressions that are needed to convey the significations of the folder altogether. Deleuze and Guattari argue that

> [a] language is always embedded in the faces that announce its statements and ballast them in relation to the signifiers in progress and the subjects concerned. Choices are guided by faces, elements are organised around faces: a common grammar is never separable from a facial education. The face is a veritable megaphone. (Deleuze and Guattari 1987: 179)

The textual content of the folder cannot be separated from the passion and emotions produced by its visuals. It is, on the whole, 'absurd to believe that language as such can convey a message' (Deleuze and Guattari 1987: 179); after all: 'language is made not to be believed but to be obeyed, and to compel obedience' (Deleuze and Guattari 1987: 76). One will find precisely *two* pictures in the folder: they create the only possible emotional expressions, and judge them according to doxa. In the first picture there are only persons indexed as women, with exposed and expressed emotions, the feminine here signifying that which has *and expresses* emotions: the young unemployed woman is crying while the older Employment Supervisor is comforting her. No surprise here: women's bodies are 'historically associated with wetness and fluidity, with flux and change, with fecundity and uncontrollable cycles of nature, with mood swings and passions' (Linstead 2000: 31). On top of that, the Supervisor furnishes the situation with an encouraging smile; a light bend of the neck signals a will to get down to eye-level with the younger woman, in order to control the double contingency of their uncontrollable mood swings.

In the second picture, meanwhile, the young man has either not been offered a seat or has elected to stand. Eye-level is, in any case, exactly what he refuses to level himself *down* to. Not only is the relation between the two characters one of no physical contact, the actual physical expression is that of conflict and refusal. Instead of a soft jumper, the young man is wearing what could be a leather jacket, jeans, a leather belt, and, to complete the picture of a miscreant, something as criminal as a ponytail. Even here, emotions are strong, but they are not expressed, they seem rather to be transformed into closure and action, namely that of self-containment and mutual rejection. The Supervisor is dressed according to the graveness of the subject matter: more precisely as a judge, reigning over the resources of the Unemployment Insurance Fund. The young man is silent, quiet and upright, a potential provocation to the case worker, if not to the entire unemployment insurance system.

In his, as it were, 'aberrant' introduction to Félix Guattari, Gary Genosko notes that capitalistic facialisation works exactly through such types of binaries when it sets up and exploits the 'two poles of the reassuring face and [the] face of anguish' (Genosko 2002: 48). This is the model of the welfare state as an inscriber of a particular refrain where direct and cognitively reasonable orders or commands are superseded by the inscription of an *emotional* rather than a *rational* code. Here it is less a matter of doing the right thing than of subscribing to the right emotional state, letting concepts like emotional intelligence become the abstract machine of the day (Goleman 1995, 2003). This jibes all too nicely with Elton Mayo's description of the employee as 'irrational, non-logical and sentimental', and therefore in need of counselling to address basic deviances (Townley 1999: 290).

To sum up, we have on the one hand the client's desiring machines: all the connections she makes and is made up of, in mind, body and social life. On the other hand there are the machines of social production or the social machines, namely all the connections that the system of production-consumption compels her to produce (Holland 1999). It is the faciality of the folder that attunes the desiring machines to the social machines. With faciality, the distinctive features of face and body are used to serve a specific mode of diagrammatisation that deterritorialises whole constellations of desiring machines and connects them to production machines (Guattari 1984: 162). Now, Deleuze and Guattari urge us to venture much further in order to learn, by detailed experimentation, 'what a subject's desiring-machines are, how they work, with what synthesis, what bursts of energy in the machine, what constituent misfires, with what flows, what chains, and what becomings in each case' (Deleuze and Guattari 1984: 338).

Immanence is a matter of combining the material at hand: the body without organs, as mentioned, is not a concept, but a set of practices: a practice of connectivity and heterogeneity, a *rhizomatic practice*, since 'any point of a rhizome can be connected to anything other, and must be' (Deleuze and Guattari 1987: 7 – here describing the programme of perpetual rhizome production, which I will try and adhere to in the following).

How to Deface Your Body

Think of a rhizome as a body without a face. After all, is it surprising that Foucault, who emphasised the indignity of speaking for others (Foucault 1977: 209), also wrote 'in order to have no face' (Foucault 1972: 17)? The adequacy of combining the bodies that comprise reality by the addition, subtraction and recombination of different rhizomes, stems from the fact that, as Slavoj Žižek argues, there not only remains 'an immaterial excess over the material reality of multiple bodies but that this excess is immanent to the level of the bodies themselves' (Žižek 2003: 113). The mistake was to give this excess a name, a value, in short, a face. Spinoza long ago framed this ethical dynamism of a Deleuzian social analysis in the (in)famous sentence that points towards the political: 'For indeed, no one has yet determined what the body can do, that is, experience has not yet taught anyone what the body can do' (Spinoza 1996: III P 2S). No one had yet taught the body to surf. Even today, despite our postmodern conditioning, perhaps because of it, we are not beyond our anger, our sense of injustice; we never left politics (Jones 2003).

In the following minor machinic experiment, the bodies of the folder are recombined in order to express this virtual (but real) excess, this burst of energy in the machine. Consider the new rhizome that the pictures from the folder comprise below (no totalities here: always some couchgrass, some of a rhizome [Deleuze and Guattari 1987: 9]). The face of the crying woman has been replaced with the face of the miscreant, while her body is situated where he formerly stood:

Figure 4.3 (Source: Direktoratet for Arbejdsløshedsforsikring)

Most strikingly, it becomes evident that the crying face *betrayed* the rest of the girl's body, ascribing it only a negative sign. While the body carries a crying face, or rather, while the crying face organises the body, it signifies what the body can do, which in the case of the crying girl is: nothing. The girl's body seems almost not able to carry the burden of the crying face. By contrast, in the above rhizome, the face of the young man evokes defiance if not refractoriness: the body is bored at worst, but it is above all not decomposed, not in need of comfort. It hides its anger yet shows its strength.

In the next rhizome the woman's crying face has been placed on the man's body, maintaining his gesture of rejection:

Figure 4.4 (Source: Direktoratet for Arbejdsløshedsforsikring)

The gesture notwithstanding, the crying face completely reterritorialises the strength exposed by the body itself, so that the solitary composure of the body now expresses a reaching out for help, confirming that the face is connected directly to the dominant signifier, the despot of meaning. The face universalises the significations of power and gains immediate control over individuals, connecting them to a decoded flux of work, be it, as here, non-work or the exhausting work of being 'available' for a decoded, that is, an arbitrary and undefined, labour market. The face is a modern tattooing of the body. Immanent to this tattoo a viral becoming explodes: man shall become the skin of the earth: 'Dermic power rises: the becoming of man-as-skin' (Cache 1995: 73).

To be human in this system is to have a profile on the Internet . . . or wherever, it's the same old story. But to think that what matters are your unique characteristics would be a blurring of the fact that your profile is relevant only insofar as it is able to unlock the code of the releasing habitus, like a key to what works under present conditions (Guattari 1984: 161). The resources of the client are constructed as such sedimentations, sedimentations that have been punched out of the plane of immanence, of thought and practice, that is, the plane of production, and that subsequently have been meticulously shaped so as to fit the lock. Here it is a face that will fit the lock, just as it is the case in uncountable passage points in modern society: in the passport, in Internet dating bureaus, in fashion, in more and more job areas. To counter-actualise the imploding refrain of the face further, to deterritorialise it, one needs to expand the zones of subjectivation, the zones of subjective experimentation. This experimentation will comprise the remainder of the analysis.

A Surfer's Paradise: Re-zoning the Subject

In the left picture in Figure 4.2 the two women, with their arms and body composure, together comprise a circle operating on the plane of the folder (O), whereas, in the right picture, the young man's arm and upright spirit produces a line towards the outside (–). A subtle distinction, I admit, but for your benefit Deleuze has made a drawing that enables such a produced circle (O) and a produced line (–) to be resituated in their ontological topography as real partakers in the production of subjectivity:

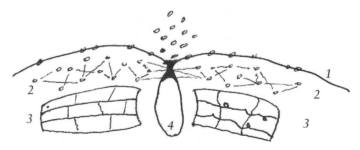

Figure 4.5 (Source: Deleuze 1988. By kind permission of Continuum International Publishing Group.)

In this composition of subjectivation 1 is the line of the outside; 2 are strategic zones; 3 are the strata; and 4 is the fold, or the zone of subjectivation (Deleuze 1988: 120).[4] The circle (O) that is expressed in the folder is the fold itself (marked '4' in the picture), but as a fold it is invalidated in a certain sense, since it has been cut off from its outside. The strata have moved in on it. The line (–) in the folder is found as one of the virtual dotted lines that pass the strategic zones between the strata and the outside. It is a smooth space between the strategic lines drawn in the system of unemployment between permanent supplementary benefit (a jungle) and full employment (a civilised life).

The fold is the liminal possibility for freedom, the only one. The fold is a diagram of forces (Rose 1996: 188), and, at least ontologically, is the way in which one creates an inside by folding the outside *into* an inside (Deleuze 1988: 96–7). There is no way out other than the folding of the outside. Hence, to produce what Deleuze and Guattari refer to as a new subjectivity or, perhaps more pompously, 'a people to come', is to fold the outside into an inside. The strata, on the other side, are the cartographies of common sense as expressed for instance in the waged labour system. The strategic zones are creative zones of metamorphosis, wherein the war machines move: so the question is how one situates oneself between the stratum of the visible and the stratum of the expressible, still working with the line of flight towards the outside. Below, Deleuze's drawing has been directly applied to the pictures in the folder (that's right: we are just plugging one machine into another!):

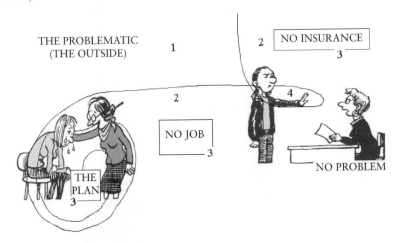

Figure 4.6 (Source: Direktoratet for Arbejdsløshedsforsikring)

In this model, the self appears as a fold of the outside, and a self is always a mixture between a closed circle (O) and a line (–). Again, 1 is the line of the outside; 2 are strategic zones; 3 are the strata; and 4 is the fold, or the zone of subjectivation. One observes that the left picture expresses a reduction of the strategic zones, intersecting in 'the plan' of action (which you create jointly with the Employment Officer) as the defining stratum. Contrary to the striated space controlled by the labour market, the strategic zones are smooth spaces, where one moves as cleverly as possible, keeping an eye out for the details that could connect to an outside (Deleuze 1988: 474). Often, though, the strata have engulfed them. The strata themselves, 'no insurance – no job', have closed in – both from the right and from the left – on the zone of subjectivation, thereby *cutting its connection to the outside*. The fold – now not a fold but a circle (O), namely the circle in the left picture – is entirely defined by the strata: resentment and defeat.

The right picture, conversely, maintains a line towards the outside, which is not yet confined. Moreover, the line of the outside sets a limit between 'the problematic' and what is considered 'no problem' (the solution every problem deserves according to common sense [Deleuze 1994: 159]). Turning every problematic into (no) problem is the strategy of all apparatuses of capture (Deleuze 1988: 424). But to believe in the future one does not need a face and an interior, one needs masks and an exterior (no circles, only lines of escape).

The paranoid machine – a version of which is the machine of faciality – blocks connections and ties all connections to the Father (the judging Supervisor in the right picture) and the desire for the Mother (the comforting Supervisor in the left picture). Let's bring them together. In the rhizome below, Neurosis meets Judgement:

Figure 4.7 (Source: Direktoratet for Arbejdsløshedsforsikring)

As could be expected: *nothing happens* – except, perhaps, titters from the audience? Neurosis and Judgement is Narcissus and the Mirror: there were no resources behind the comforting words, nor any authority behind the statement of the case. And even worse: if you happen to be a civil servant, you appear to have precisely these two possibilities: the comforting aunt or the judge, both tired and tiring. These abstractions hardly fit the concrete practice of being a public servant. But they jibe nicely with the abstractions inherent in the neo-liberal ideology currently in high regard throughout the world, in which the *real* free and productive individual is the private entrepreneur.

Leaving, then, the plane of organisation, moving towards the plane of immanence, one sees the free 'bachelor machine' (in the right picture) as it enters into composition with the sister, the maid and the whore, maybe the vampire, always towards an outside: 'in each case [the bachelor machine] augment[s] the connections of desire on the plane of immanence' (Deleuze and Guattari 1986: 63). The bachelor machine is characteristic of Kafka's artistic machine, serving a role as a transversal connector in the social field, establishing, as it were, a way out:

Figure 4.8 (Source: Direktoratet for Arbejdsløshedsforsikring)

Here the two possibilities are finally brought together. It appears that when the machine of faciality is intercepted and recombined, it can break down and become viral and productive (ten Bos and Kaulingfreks 2002: 9). The bachelor now functions as an agent of pure production that both comforts *and* dignifies, indicating a region of relative calm, a protected area, yet it also aerates the situation with a draught from a radical outside, an exterior beyond measure. As it turns out, the gesture the man performs makes the girl raise her head. Are you here to fight or to surf?

In the Teeth of HRM

As noted above, postmodern political theory arguably begins with the decapitation of the king, that is, by looking beyond the sovereignty of the state in our attempts to understand power (Foucault 1977: 121). Our reading of the folder is an explosion of a detail that can take us beyond the now somewhat too familiar headiness (headlessness?) of postmodernism, certainly a good way beyond Derridean deconstruction. Deleuze and Guattari show how a portrait photo, that is, the coagulated expression of the machines of faciality, should really be attacked: 'the goal is to obtain a blowup of the "photo," an exaggeration of it to the point of absurdity' (Deleuze and Guattari 1986: 10). By way of this absurdity, the aim has been to show that by plugging machines together they break down in decisive ways. We trace lines within the folder itself, issued by the Labour Directorate, that testifies to a becoming of a minor language: *surfing* accomplishes the deconstruction of the reactionary *juxtapostion* of the two pictures, in which the striating ideology lies. The ideology is not in the right or the left picture, but in their division of the subject. This minor language then rises up exactly where the refrain is deterritorialised and takes up its third function, that of interception and a line of flight, a line towards the outside. Hence, the two pictures become imperceptible and create a zone of indiscernibility in which they enter into viral proliferation; there is no longer left or right, but a becoming where left and right prove to be indistinguishable and something new is produced.

This novelty, then, has a number of implications for the conceptual construction of human resources as a process and production of different intercepting refrains, rather than as fixed sediments and layers, data to be mined and numbers to be calculated in tests and assessments: in the majority of the human resource management literature the concept of human resources appears as little more than a reterritorialisation of the human on the code of industrial economics. The very concept of resources is essentially connected to natural resources, that is, the raw material excavated from the ground. These latter are to a greater and greater extent exploited to their global limits: natural resources are scarce; what resources *are* available are only what is already *there*, since they became sedimented in pre-historic time. This counts also, *mutatis mutandis*, for the human resource. What is at play here is, quite literally, a *naturalisation* of a social fact that was originally itself deducted or cut off from the flow of natural fact: since natural resources amount to what is already there and are hence always already scarce, this is also the case for human resources. Counter-actualising this naturalisation will be to insist on the constructed nature of this social fact, since, in Holland's formulation, 'scarcity is not merely socially managed, but is socially fabricated in order to found and secure social organisation in various forms' (Holland 1999: 5). This conceptualisation further insists on the idea that societies, no matter what their circumstances may be, have always been in a surplus of production *in toto*. The full body of the social is a luminous body without organs, overflowing with desire. This idea stems from Georges Bataille and it defers the question of scarcity and the exploitable human resource to where the schism really should be approached, namely as a *political* problematic. This problematic focuses on how social organisation revolves around, and resolves itself in, the determination of *distribution*: the where, how and for whom the surplus shall in fact be actualised.

Meanwhile, this naturalised conceptualisation of resources finds itself imported directly and largely unaltered into the HRM discourse, with its preoccupation with the calibration of supply and demand, as well as with the optimal utilisation of human resources (Werther and Davis 1985: 168). It is a conceptualisation that is a strategic reduction of earlier uses of the word resource: it stems from Old French *resourdre*, relieve, to rise again, from *re-surgere*, to lift up again, as in resurrection; as such the concept is more in line with re-creation than it is with exploitation, more in line with surfing than with digging. A resource appears as a virtual multiplicity with no determinate actualisation, and it can never be fully exhausted. Rather than a layered and measurable sediment, it is an event of indefinite transmutation; it is an act and a direction, an event and a way out.

The umbrella on the cover shields us from the rain. But rain, if you hold it right, is a wave; and an umbrella, as a thousand cartoons have taught us, can be used as a makeshift surfboard. The somewhat flimsy *époque* of postmodernism, the familiar beach of the nineties, where theory could thrive only in rather closed circles, was of little use to us. The urge for more management and further 'liberalisations' would drive the area of work and organisation towards data mining and other sophisticated surveillance technologies. This urge forces both managers and employees into the passive role of mere technology *consumers*, leaving the field condemned to perpetual management commodity fetishism, that is, a 'fetishisation of the "techknowledgy" commodity' as Steffen Böhm succinctly puts it (Böhm 2002: 333)[5]. Altogether the decapitation of the king begat increased discipline which ultimately begat the society of control. Inventive academics must now speak with each other, experiment with *their own* becoming-available, that is, experiment with the material at hand and enter into a dangerous crisis with a virtual excess; they must experiment with the body without organs, where a new fragility, which is to say, a new ethics might appear. If the theory of human resource management, that is, the technology that controls our working life, lacks such an ethics, it is because it has for too long been ruled by the face. Perhaps we do not need to decapitate this king but to . . . surf's up! . . . smash him in the face with a surfboard.

References

Böhm, S. G. (2002), 'Movements of Theory and Practice', *Ephemera: Theory and Politics in Organization*, 2 (4): 328–51.

Buchanan, I. (2000), *Deleuzism: A Metacommentary*, Edinburgh: Edinburgh University Press.

Cache, B. (1995), *Earth Moves: The Furnishing of Territories*, Cambridge, MA: MIT Press.

Carter, P. and N. Jackson (2004), 'Gilles Deleuze and Félix Guattari', in S. Linstead (ed.), *Organization Theory and Postmodern Thought*, London: Sage.

DeLanda, M. (2002), *Intensive Science and Virtual Philosophy*, London: Continuum.

Deleuze, G. (1988), *Foucault*, trans. S. Hand, Minneapolis: University of Minnesota Press.

Deleuze, G. (1993), *The Fold: Leibniz and the Baroque*, trans. T. Conley, Minneapolis: University of Minnesota Press.

Deleuze, G. (1994), *Difference and Repetition*, trans. P. Patton, New York: Columbia University Press.

Deleuze, G. (1995), 'Postscript on Control Societies', in G. Deleuze (ed.) *Negotiations*, trans. M. Joughin, New York: Columbia University Press.

Deleuze, G. and F. Guattari (1984), *Anti-Oedipus*, trans. R. Hurley, M. Seem and H. Lane, London: Athlone Press.

Deleuze, G. and F. Guattari (1986), *Kafka: Toward a Minor Literature*, trans. D. Polin, Minneapolis: University of Minnesota Press.

Deleuze, G. and F. Guattari (1987), *A Thousand Plateaus*, trans. B. Massumi, Minneapolis: University of Minnesota Press.

Direktoratet for Arbejdsløshedsforsikring (1999), *Om at stå til rådighed* (*To Be Available* [author's translation]), Copenhagen: Direktoratet for Arbejdsløshedsforsikring.

Foucault, M. (1972), *The Archaeology of Knowledge*, trans. A. M. Sheridan, New York: Pantheon.

Foucault, M. (1977), 'Intellectuals and Power', in *Language, Counter-Memory, Practice: Selected Essays and Interviews*, trans. D. F. Bouchard and S. Simon, Ithaca: Cornell University Press.

Foucault, M. (1980), *Power/Knowledge: Selected Interviews and Other Writings, 1972–1977*, New York: Pantheon Books.

Foucault, M. (1984), 'Introduction to a Non-Fascist Life', in G. Deleuze and F. Guattari, *Anti-Oedipus*, trans. R. Hurley, M. Seem and H. Lane, London: Athlone Press.

Genosko, G. (2002), *Félix Guattari. An Aberrant Introduction*, London: Continuum.

Goleman, D. (1995), *Emotional Intelligence*, New York: Bantam Books.

Goleman, D. (2003), *Destructive Emotions: How Can We Overcome Them? A Scientific Collaboration with the Dalai Lama*, New York: Bantam Books.

Guattari, F. (1984), *Molecular Revolution: Psychiatry and Politics*, trans. R. Sheed, Harmondsworth: Penguin Books.

Holland, E. W. (1999), *Deleuze and Guattari's Anti-Oedipus: Introduction to Schizoanalysis*, New York: Routledge.

Jones, C. (2003), 'Theory after the Postmodern Condition', *Organization*, 10 (3): 503–25.

Legge, K. (1999), 'Representing People at Work', *Organization*, 6 (2): 247–64.

Linstead, S. (2000), 'Dangerous Fluids and the Organisation-without-Organs', in J. Hassard, R. Holliday and H. Willmot (eds), *Body and Organization*, Sage: London.

Massumi, B. (1992), *A User's Guide to Capitalism and Schizophrenia*, Cambridge, MA: MIT Press.

Rose, N. (1996), *Inventing Our Selves: Psychology, Power and Personhood*, Cambridge: Cambridge University Press.

Sorensen, B. M. (2004), 'Defacing the Corporate Body. Or, Why HRM Needs a Kick in the Teeth', *Tamara: Journal of Critical Postmodern Organization Science*, 3 (4): 7–23.

Sorensen, B. M. (2005), 'Immaculate Defecation. Gilles Deleuze and Félix Guattari in Organization Theory', in C. Jones and R. Munro (eds), *Contemporary Organization Theory*, Oxford: Blackwell.

Spinoza, B. (1996), *Ethics*, trans. E. Curley, London: Penguin Books.

ten Bos, R. and R. Kaulingfreks (2002), 'Life Between Faces', *Ephemera: Theory and Politics in Organization*, 2 (1): 6–27.

Thanem, T. and S. Linstead (2006), 'The Trembling Organisation: Order, Change and the Philosophy of the Virtual', in M. Fuglsang and B. M. Sorensen (eds), *Deleuze and the Social*, Edinburgh: Edinburgh University Press.

The Last Boy Scout, film, directed by T. Scott. USA: Warner Bros Picture and Geffen Pictures, 1991.

Townley, B. (1999), 'Nietzsche, Competencies and Übermensch: Reflections on Human and Inhuman Resource Management', *Organization*, 6 (2): 285–305.

Weiskopf, R. (2002), 'Deconstructing "The Iron Cage" – Towards an Aesthetic of Folding', *Consumption, Markets and Culture*, 5 (1): 79–98.

Weiskopf, R. and B. Loacker (2006), '"A Snake's Coils Are Even More Intricate Than a Mole's Burrow." Individualisation and Subjectification in Post-disciplinary Regimes of Work', *Management Revue*, 17 (4): 395–419.

Werther, W. B. and K. Davis (1985), *Personnel Management and Human Resources*, New York: McGraw-Hill.

Žižek, S. (2003), *Organs Without Bodies: On Deleuze and Consequences*, New York: Routledge.

Notes

1. On this see Massumi (1992), page 4 onwards.
2. The observant reader will note the year 2003 on the front, different from the year 1999 in the references for the pamphlet. The thing is, the pamphlet continues to be published, also in 2007.
3. For a further elaboration see Sorensen (2005).
4. In what can be seen as an extension of this line of thought, Richard Weiskopf invests in his 'aesthetic' analysis of the Weberian iron cage the same Deleuzian figure as an expression of organisation *per se*, namely as a (contested) multiplicity (Weiskopf 2002).
5. For a different but very promising analysis of the new HRM discourse in terms of a shift from disciplinarity to control, see Weiskopf and Loacker (2006).

Chapter 5

Chemical-Control™®: From the Cane to the Pill

Abigail Bray

> The pill is a commodity *par excellence* – truly 'consumed', genuinely mate-
> rial and measurable, utterly standard, and infinitely repeatable. It also
> adheres to the bureaucratic norms of reliability and efficiency and infinite
> substitutability. This amounts to the actuarialisation and financialisation of
> the sick mind. (Miller and Ledger 2002: 28)

As is well known, the opening of Foucault's *Discipline and Punish*
(Foucault 1979) contrasts the public dismemberment of Damiens the
regicide in 1757 with the docile and regimented bodies of children in
Mettray some eighty years later as a stark illustration of the transition
from the societies of sovereignty to the disciplinary societies. 'In the normalization of the power of normalization, in the arrangement of a
power-knowledge over individuals, Mettray and its school marked a
new era' (Foucault 1991: 237). Foucault reads this dramatic shift as
central to the emergence of the disciplinary power of Western capitalism
that requires docile bodies in order to maximise profit. The children in
Mettray are subjected to a continuous regimen of discipline and punishment, moulded by a 'network of permanent observation', examined by
experts, defined, categorised, pathologised, improved, trained and,
above all, *reformed* (Foucault 1991: 236). In tracing the genealogy of
this new form of political anatomy Foucault describes how these technologies of biopower emerge through

> a multiplicity of often minor processes, of different origin and scattered
> location, which overlap, repeat, or imitate one another, support one
> another, distinguish themselves from one another according to their domain
> of application, converge, and gradually produce the blueprint of a general
> method. (Foucault 1991: 182)

This blueprint for a general method also constitutes a *diagram* of
biopower, a continually mutating strategy of territorialisation that seeks

to accelerate the extraction of economic profit from the body. Disciplinary diagrams of biopower articulate a flexible folding of forces, or a doubling of domination – 'the domination of others must be doubled by the domination of oneself' (Deleuze 1992: 101). In this context, the subject, the psyche, the very idea of interiority, is the product of this internal folding of external domination, or the product of a 'subjectivation' (Deleuze 1992: 101). The moulding of the child's interiority in Mettray is the intensification of a strategy, the affecting of a diagram of biopower, which can also be read as the articulation of Enlightenment pedagogy. As Kant says, 'one cultivates the child so that he eventually becomes free'.[1] Or rather, the disciplinary domination of the subject (the installation and cultivation of interiority) is made in the name of the subject's liberation. Gradually the capillaries of this normative power converge at the site of the body that transmits this political tactic as though it were a personal choice – we desire our oppression because we have come to believe that the practice of self-control is also the achievement of an emancipated autonomy. The freedom imagined by the Enlightenment dream of reason – the multiple liberations from ignorance, disease, tyranny, the *pathological* – is continually territorialised by strategies of economic domination. While disciplinary reforms are celebrated as the progressive humanisation of society, such reforms are also the strategic intensification of cost-effective systems of biopower applied by an expert class who set about installing normative regimens of self-discipline in the body in general. The carceral network of power-knowledge installed by a proliferating economy of expert judges of normality (psychiatrist, teacher, doctor) creates subjects who practise self-control, who are continually self-diagnosing, made docile by a fear of being and becoming pathological, Oedipalised by a fear of lack.

In what follows I experiment with Deleuze's productively opaque claim that we are entering a post-disciplinary (or hyper-Oedipal) era of control (Deleuze 1992), in order to open up the possibility that over the last few decades another radical shift in the tactics of biopower has occurred, one which, like at Mettray, flows through the bodies of children. If Deleuze locates 'extraordinary pharmaceutical productions' as part of the installation of the 'societies of control that are in the process of replacing disciplinary societies' (Deleuze 1992: 3–4), how might the installation of the psychopharmaceutical control of children illuminate the general method of a new system of post-human domination? What might we mean by a post-Mettray chemical economy of control? Moreover, is it now possible to speak of a *chemical politics*, in which new forms of *chemical citizenship* are produced by the installation of psychopharmacological power/knowledges?[2] For example, when the 'schizoaffective disordered' Phillipa King writes that 'the antipsychotic, antidepressant, antianxiety, and mood-stabilising medications I take hold my days together' (King 2007: 30), is she also announcing herself as a chemical citizen, one whose affects have been opened up to a prosthetic modification, moulded by the new folding of a chemical politics? Today, we can argue that the mentally ill form the macro-assemblage of a chemical population, or a psychopharmaceutical demographic, a Big Pharma target market. How might the overcoding of children by Attention Deficit Disorder-Ritalin™ machines mark the installation of a dispersed psychopharmaceutical overcoding?

Conditions of Release

In posing these somewhat unruly questions I am opening up the possibility that the coterminous abolition of corporal punishment in the school and the psychiatric invention of Attention Deficit Disorder during the post-Second World War era describe the strategic refinement of new chemical economies of Oedipal biopower. Today the disordered child is no longer caned, he is medicated. The child's body is released from external governmental regimes of disciplinary abuse into the dispersed space of an intimate chemical incarceration. In brief, the abolition of corporal punishment was made in the name of a progressive, child-centred, reform of disciplinary power. Corporal punishment is diagnosed as a form of child abuse. The psy-complex emerges as the benefactor of the child's body that is newly liberated from the tyrannies of abusive discipline. The *conditions of release* from abusive disciplinary power, however, require a new Oedipal folding of the subject, for the liberation from corporal punishment is at the same time a pathologisation of the relationship between disciplinary power and the child's body. Or rather, the child's body is released from disciplinary abuse on condition that it submit to the care of a new master in the form of the school counsellor or the child psychiatrist, who is also an expert in child abuse. And if this newly liberated body is rapidly territorialised by the medical-industrial complex that installs a new economy of therapeutic chemical control within the school, then, above all, this has nothing to do with a punishment of the unruly body, but is merely the modification of a very specific chemical imbalance – the careful, almost loving, enhancement of an individual's ability to learn.

While scholars such as Franz Kost (1985) and Ludwig Pongratz (2006, 2007) have argued that the shift from 'drill pedagogy' to 'reform pedagogy' creates new, softer systems of control – usefully pointing out how the dissolution of rituals of personalised corporal punishment enables the expansion of an impersonal 'network of circulating controls' – very little attention has been given to the relationship between reform pedagogy and the pedagogic application of drugs such as Ritalin™ and other Big Pharma drugs (Pongratz 2007: 5). For example, although Lawrence Grossberg's brief discussion of the medication of children under the rubric 'better discipline through chemistry', in his timely *Caught in the Crossfire: Kids, Politics and America's Future* (2005), is important, his focus is on the wider neo-liberal war against kids, and not merely that war's chemical component. The shift from the cane to the pill, from hitting to drugging, also describes the neo-liberal corporate exploitation of disorder. The economic inefficiency of the cane is replaced by the lucrative multiplicity of continually updated Big Pharma drugs. In this context, the disordered body is opened up to a direct economic harvest that is also a continual remoulding of the biopolitics of disorder. This new political anatomy of chemical control transmits a new normative language that animates the detailed machinery of pathologisation, which speaks of shifting chemical imbalances in the brain, intensifying the micropolitics of diagnosis, ensnaring the body in ever tightening chemical coils of control. For example, recent developments in pharmacogenomics have created third-generation antidepressants that 'claim to be fabricated at a molecular level to target the precise neuronal mechanisms that underlie depressive symptoms' (Rabinow and Rose 2003: 32). As a post-human disciplinary tool, the pill passes through the surface of the body in order to modify it at the molecular level.

As Pongratz observes, 'pedagogic punishment is modern society's "writing on the wall"' (Pongratz 2007: 8). The shift from the corporal punishment of school children to the biochemical control of the disordered child can be read as paradigmatic of other, wider changes in the transmission of power through the body which milk disorder through dispersed economies of chemical control. How might contemporary shifts around the pedagogic management of school children crystallise the installation of the societies of control and herald the becoming of a new political tactic that arises from the milking of disordered children by Big Pharma?

Such a tactic emerges around 1937 when, after conducting a series of chemical experiments on mentally handicapped and disturbed children in an asylum, the child psychiatrist Charles Bradley was able to claim that '[t]he psychological reaction of 30 behaviour problem children who received Benzedrine sulfate for one week was observed. There was a spectacular improvement in school performance' (Bradley 1937: 580). Seventy years later parents can purchase Ritalin™ online without consulting a doctor – 'Do you need a doctor to tell you your child is hyperactive and has a short attention span?' Big Pharma positions the doctor as a middleman: 'it can be even more expensive if your child hasn't been diagnosed with ADHD yet . . . Wouldn't it be easier if you could just buy your child's ADHD medicines on the Internet?'[3] Territorialised by what Deleuze calls 'the new medicine "without doctor or patient" that singles out potential sick people and subjects at risk, which in no way attests to individuation – as they say – but substitutes for the individual or numerical body the code of a "dividual" material to be controlled' (Deleuze 1992: 5), the child becomes the 'dividual' 'at risk' material to be controlled.

In *Foucault*, Deleuze makes the point that the disciplinary war against disorder is made in the name of the 'survival of the population' against those other populations that become 'a toxic or infectious agent, a sort of "biological danger"' (Deleuze 1988: 92). As a preemptive chemical strike against the biological danger of the 'at risk' dividual, preventive drugging is justified by the strategic creation of a pathological consumer demographic, a dangerous class or population, a target market. A genealogy of the pill as a normalising instrument of chemical control would require writing a history of the strategic composition of this 'biological danger' that today would encompass populations coded as 'at risk' from mental illness. But the history of chemical control cannot simply be collapsed with the history of psychiatry, for as Foucault and Deleuze and Guattari have shown us, psychiatry has always been more than a discrete discipline, it is also a way of life, a way of desiring and being Oedipus. There is a psychiatrisation of feminism, just as there is a psychiatrisation of children's rights. The liberation of the child's body from corporal punishment was partly achieved by feminist and children's rights movements.

Chemical.Revolutions

Between Charles Bradley's discovery of 1937 and today, a series of ideological, corporate and legislative shifts occurred in relation to the child's body which can be read as points of intensity that would mark the future composition of a genealogy of the pill, an 'ignoble archive' of chemical power which can only be gestured towards here (Foucault 1991: 203). For example: the American Academy of Child Psychiatry was founded in the same year – 1952 – that the American Psychiatric Association's *Diagnostic and Statistical Manual of Mental Disorders 1* (DSM) was published. In 1958 the National Defense Education Act installed the school-guidance counsellor.[4] In *Coming of Age in America* (1965), the sociologist Edgar Z. Friedenberg reported that students in an American high school voted against corporal punishment on the grounds that beating a child would make him more unmanageable, and suggested that the unruly child should be sent to the school psychiatrist instead (Friedenberg 1965: 76; Lasch 1977: 185). During the 1970s feminists, psychologists and advocates for children's rights established child abuse and neglect as a national problem and advocated the widespread reform of society.[5] In 1974 the American Psychological Association resolved to ban corporal punishment within schools and set up the Task Force on Children's Rights. In 1977 the International Society for the Prevention and Treatment of Child Abuse and Neglect was founded. During the same year, children subjected to corporal punishment in schools were diagnosed with the anti-social condition Educationally Induced Post-Traumatic Stress Disorder (EIPSD).[6] In 1980 the American Psychiatric Association established the new diagnostic category of Attention Deficit Disorder. By 1987 the National Coalition to Abolish Corporal Punishment in Schools combined the forces of education, law, medicine, feminism and the children's rights movement. By the late 1980s the medication of American school children with methylphemidate became a 'dominant child mental health intervention' (McCrossin 1995: 2). In 1994 UNICEF's *Progress of Nations* stated that all countries which had ratified the Convention on the Rights of the Child must abolish 'all forms of physical or mental violence' against children (Ludbrook 1996: 107). During the following decade the medication of preschoolers, school children and adolescents increased dramatically (Grossberg 2005: 35; Zito et al. 2000, 2002, 2007). The fourth edition of the *Diagnostic and Statistical Manual of Mental Disorders* states that the ADHD child '[o]ften fails to give close attention to details or makes careless mistakes in schoolwork. Often fidgets with hands or feet or squirms in seat. Often blurts out answers before questions have been completed' (Grossberg 2005: 33). In the most recent years, mental health promotion and prevention policies in the US (2002) and EU (2005) have favoured the widespread screening/treatment of all school children for mental illness.[7]

In order to think this dispersed shift from the cane to the pill it is worth contrasting two imaginary scenes of violence – not disconnected from historical realities, and separated from each other by around fifty years – which can be read as marking the edges of a transition from disciplinary power to new forms of chemical control.

Several decades ago a child wrote a swear word on a blackboard and was sent to the Master's office to be punished. He was given 'six of the best' by the Master who, depending on his disposition, canes his open palms lightly or with great force. Perhaps blood is drawn, and the child cannot write for a while. Or perhaps the child is told to bend over a chair, remove his clothes and submit to being whipped. 'Corporal punishment refers to intentional application of physical pain as a method of changing behaviour' (Greydanus et al. 2003: 285). Children were caned, slapped, spanked with belts, wooden paddles, whips, sticks, rulers; they were prevented from going to the toilet, shaken, kicked, punched, and made to stand still in corners for hours. They were humiliated, terrorised, subjected to a continuous regimen of punishment that installed the child within a 'punishing universality' (Foucault 1991: 194). The simple goal of corporal punishment was the breaking and remoulding of the child's will. Occasionally, although it was never official policy, the children were raped into submission.

In 2001 an eight-year-old boy writes a swear word on a whiteboard in a suburban West Australian primary school. He is taken to the school psychologist. If authority touches him, it is with the light caress of concern. His parents are called in, further experts are consulted, his general conduct is examined, and he is diagnosed with ADHD. The school offers the parents a choice, either the boy takes his medication or he will be expelled. It is an 'egalitarian' correction because the ADHD affects not only the child but the proper functioning of the schoolroom. Today the boy takes his 'meds' before school, many of which are often ™ or ® stimulants such as Ritalin™, Dexedrine and Cylert™, Concerta®, Adderall®, Daytrana™, Focalin®, Matadate™, Straterra®, Vyvana™ in combination with antidepressants such as Prozac™, Tegretal™ carbamazepine, Lithium and Melloril (thioridazine) clonidine, or perhaps an antipsychotic such as Risperdal™.[8] There have been side-effects and he has become thin, withdrawn, docile, chemically dependent, and finds it difficult to sleep. Unknown to him his growth is also being inhibited and he is at risk from irreparable cerebral dysfunction (Breggin 1999). But new improved 'meds' are currently being released. His doctor has recently been sent an advertisement by Novartis Pharmaceutical Corporation about Ritalin LA™ which announces:

> The improvement in attention and behaviour remained significant for the entire school day period for Ritalin LA 20mg . . . Ritalin LA may be swallowed as whole capsules, or, for children who have difficulty swallowing, it may be administered by sprinkling the beaded contents on apple sauce.[9]

Published in 1993 by Child Management Inc., and written by an expert in child discipline, *All About Attention Deficit Disorder: Symptoms, Diagnosis, and Treatment: Children and Adults*, by Thomas W. Phelan, is an unexceptional text within its genre, an almost cheerful celebration of the chemical solution to the newly installed category of the ADD subject. Phelan candidly describes ADD children as handicapped: '[t]he problem with ADD is the handicap is of the "hidden" variety. The child looks normal, so why can't he behave normally?' (Phelan 1993: 140). Such children are mentally handicapped precisely because they are undisciplined: 'ADD children have a hard time following rules and there are usually significant discipline problems. . . . ADD children don't clean their rooms, forget to feed the dog and don't do their homework' (19–20). As Peter Briggin and others have observed, ADD/ADHD is a psychiatric category of disorder that corresponds to 'a list of behaviours that annoy adults' (Grossberg 2005: 33). Untreated ADD children are 'obnoxious' and do not deserve to be engaged by their parents: 'Question 7: What if they say I don't love them and never did, or if they say that I never talk to them? (Martyrdom) Answer: Shut up' (Phelan 1993: 108). The diagnosis begins with school children and spreads backwards to infants and onwards to adults. The mental handicap of ADD manifests during infancy: Phelan writes that often baby ADDs 'sometimes make strange, repetitive vocalizations' (29), while 'we can detect 60–70% of ADD children by age two to three' (41), and 60% of ADD babies and children go on to become ADD adults who also need to be continually medicated with a changing cocktail of stimulants and antidepressants if they are to avoid problems at work (167, 168). The drugs improve grades, produce 'more compliant' subjects who are 'less disruptive in class' (123, 188), and enhance the chances of living a 'normal' life. The classroom is transformed into a laboratory of control, the teacher into a drug expert: '*the only reliable observer of positive and negative drug effects who is around while the drugs are active is the teacher*', amplifies Phelan (145). If this is the new Mettray, it is a space that is saturated by a chemical control that is more infinite and intimate than former disciplinary regimes.

Infinite Violence

Corporal punishment is a finite body-to-body violence done within the disciplinary enclosure of the school, while chemical control is an infinite and anonymous corporate-to-body modification which is dispersed across the social strata. At one point in time there is the disciplinary enclosure of the school, the child, the master, and his implements of punishment, and at another point there is the entire social strata, the child and his pills. The density of the disciplinary apparatus is radically compressed into a ™ 20mg pill. The limited violence of the teacher is dissolved along with the visible marks of abusive power. Now it is the child who must swallow his own condemnation indefinitely in the name of prevention and the management of symptoms. The surface of the body is no longer stained by a finite burst of violence within the disciplinary enclosure of the school, but undergoes an infinite internal chemical staining, experiencing side-effects that are corrected by more drugs, installing the body into a cycle of chemical control which requires regular examinations, blood tests, dosage corrections, the purchasing of new drugs. In the societies of control, writes Deleuze (1992: 5), we are never finished with anything. The wounds of chemical control are invisible – there are only the accidental side-effects of a drug that is enhancing, modifying and correcting a chemical imbalance in the child's brain. No longer is the punishment of unruly school children administered by the school, it is decentralised and outsourced to a pharmaceutical corporation that works through the school psychologist and other judges of normality. The pedagogic spectacle of corporal punishment, the tearing immediacy of pain, the marking of the skin with bruises and cuts, the tears and cries of punishment, the amplification of fear, shame and rage – all of these negative emotions, these inappropriate abuses of children, have given way to the quietly mundane process of swallowing a pill. The liberated body is calm, efficient and polite – Adult-friendly.

'We preferred the blows, but the cell suits us better', said the children of Mettray when praising the 'new punitive policies of the body' (Foucault 1991: 234). Today, children cannot say 'we preferred corporal punishment, but Ritalin suits us better', because the chemical reform of pedagogic control has never been an official policy. In other words, a particular silence about the normative pedagogic function of pharmaceutical corporations limits the conditions of speaking the transition between corporal and chemical punishment.

Oedipus as the Child Abuse Secret

If the shift from the cane to the pill, from beating unruly children to sprinkling drugs on their apple sauce, crystallises the micropolitics of the new societies of control Deleuze identifies as having emerged from the ruins of the disciplinary society, what are the conditions which have enabled this shift? Towards the end of 'Postscript on the Societies of Control', Deleuze writes:

The socio-technological study of mechanisms of control, grasped at their inception, would have to be categorical and to describe what is already in the process of substitution for the disciplinary sites of enclosure, whose crises is everywhere proclaimed. It may be that older methods, borrowed from the former societies of sovereignty, will return to the fore, but with the necessary modifications. What counts is that we are at the beginning of something. (Deleuze 1992: 7)

A socio-technological study of these emerging mechanisms of control requires thinking through the genealogy of post-Mettray pedagogy and the history of present pedagogic applications of chemical control.

Broadly speaking, we can identify at least three interconnected macro-assemblages that have contributed to the shift from the cane to the pill. These assemblages can also be read as features of the societies of control and part of a general dispersal of chemical correction, as the folding of a psychopharmaceutical domination.

1. After the Second World War there is an intensification of psy-complex regimes of normative control that are marketed as the democratic reform of previous systems of authoritarian discipline. This is known as the 'therapeutic turn'. A crisis in the disciplinary authority of the institution becomes a 'crises of reason' that produces an affective psy-politics and installs systems of therapeutic governmentality. Preventative psychiatry overcodes social problems as mental health issues. A rapid increase in the economic power of the medical-industrial complex results in the corporatisation of health and well-being. The diagnosis of new forms of mental illness requires the application of new pharmaceutical drugs.

2. During the 1970s an assemblage of child abuse and neglect emerges in the West from a coalition between second-wave feminism, psy-complex experts and the children's rights movement, which attaches expanding concepts of child abuse and neglect to a proliferating range of social problems and demands the widespread reform of every strata of the social. Within this context, corporal punishment is diagnosed as child abuse, and as a symptom of pathogenic disciplinary power. The child abuse and neglect assemblage constructs new forms of personhood such as the child abuse 'survivor', the 'wounded inner child', and 'multiple personality disorder' (Hacking 1995; Jenkins 2004; Showalter 1998).

3. The 'survivor population' emerges as a distinct category of deviance, and as the most pathogenic and criminogenic 'dangerous class' or a 'biological danger' that must be detoxified by therapeutic rehabilitation technologies. Adult perpetrators of child abuse

and neglect are diagnosed as victims of abuse who have not sought treatment, while children who are abused or neglected are diagnosed/stained as potential deviants. All those who transgress increasingly restricted definitions of normality are diagnosed as members of the 'survivor population'.[10] The pathological is increasingly linked to child abuse. The economic cost of this dangerous population is invoked to justify the intensification of mental health promotion strategies that seek to screen/diagnosis/treat children in general and the 'at risk' population.

These interconnected macro-assemblages can be read as hyper-Oedipal machines that have rechannelled what Luciana Parisi and Tiziana Terranova (2000) might call the 'turbulence' of child abuse and neglect into lucrative flows. The revelation that Freud's Oedipal complex was built on the suppression of child sexual abuse, this very liberation of the secret which Oedipus conceals, rather than opening up the becoming-child of an anti-Oedipal line of flight, releases Oedipus into wider circulation as *child abuse*.[11] As Deleuze and Guattari (1987: 290) suggest, Oedipus passes through the secret. The secret of child abuse becomes the new Oedipus, the new figure of lack, a new overcoding machine. In *Anti-Oedipus* Deleuze and Guattari write that 'the Women's Liberation movements are correct in saying: We are not castrated so you get fucked' (Deleuze and Guattari 1983: 61), while the 'paranoid social machine' of a psychiatrised feminism now says 'we lack because we were abused as children'. The Oedipal pathologisation of childhood and children, indeed a whole diagram of biopower, now flows through the very spaces that opened up Oedipus to the secret of child abuse (Foucault 1988: 271–85). As Deleuze and Guattari write towards the end of *Anti-Oedipus*:

> We have seen, following Foucault, how nineteenth-century psychiatry had conceived of the family as both cause and judge of the illness, and the closed asylum as an artificial family charged with internalizing guilt and with instituting responsibility, enveloping madness no less than its cure in a father-child relationship everywhere present. In this respect, far from breaking with psychiatry, psychoanalysis transported its requirements outside the asylum walls, and first imposed a certain 'free', intensive, phantasmal use of the family that seemed particularly suited to what was isolated as the neurosis. . . . After the family has been internalised in Oedipus, Oedipus is externalised in the symbolic order, in the institutional order, in the community order, in the sectorial order, etc. This progression contains a constant of all modern attempts at reform. (Deleuze and Guattari 1983: 359)

The Therapeutic Reform of Disciplinary Power

Creating a new biopower of lack, child abuse becomes a central component of the paranoid social machines that accelerated the emergence of
therapeutic control in the post-Second World War era. Progressive
liberal thought pushed for the substitution of punitive control of social
problems with therapeutic intervention: disciplinary power is gradually
reterritorialised as abuse by the increasingly powerful psy-complex. As
Ellen Herman writes:

> Psychology's rise to power during the postwar decades changed ordinary
> Americans' expectations of their lives by publicizing the pertinence of
> emotion, the virtues of insight, and the unavoidability of subjectivity in the
> conduct of private and public affairs. These feats earned experts high status
> and permanently transformed the way war, racial conflict, gender equality,
> and the responsibilities and possibilities of democratic self-government
> were understood. (Herman 1995: 305)

In effect, authoritarian disciplinary systems are converted into forms of
therapeutic control that stress mutuality and empathy over conflict and
punishment, while the conversion is marketed as liberal progress and
humanitarian reform. As a number of scholars have argued, contemporary modes of social control are therapeutic (Lasch 1977). Normative
technologies of therapeutic jurisprudence erase former regimens of punishment; as Bergan wrote in 1949: '[t]he concept of "treatment" has
replaced the concept of "punishment"' (Bergan in Kittrie 1971: 30–1).

Within this context, the emergence of 'mass preventive psychiatry'
shifts the focus from mental illness to mental health, overcoding a range
of social problems as mental health issues and offering proliferating
methods of treatment. Increasing in economic and social status after the
war, psychiatry announces a project of 'complete physical, mental and
social well-being' within 'the home, the church, the school, the prison,
industrial firms' (Lasch 1977: 98–9) and calls for the 'world-wide mobilisation of psychiatry' (Sullivan quoted in Lasch 1977: 97). Anxieties
about social disorder become crises in mental health and opportunities
for psychiatry-styled social reforms that medicalise the political agenda
and expand the political boundaries of the psy-complex. For a growing
body of sociological and cultural theorists the emergence of affective
politics has brought about a tightening of normative regimens: in the
name of mental health, happiness and well-being, contemporary forms
of therapeutic governmentality have intensified the micropolitics of
control. Frank Furedi, for example, observes that state-sponsored happiness programmes that aim to enhance well-being represent a 'new

politics of behaviour' which infantilises the subject as a discontented child (Furedi 2006). Just as society is imagined 'as a patient' (Frank 1948), or as 'diseased', citizens are treated as dysfunctional (Hazleden 2004) wounded children who require re-parenting by the psy-complex.

On the other hand, 'third way' sociologist Anthony Giddens reads the mass circulation of therapeutic or emotional literacy as an important contribution to a democratic 'reconciliation' of the sexes (Giddens 1992: 156). Indeed, Linda Nicholson has celebrated 'the therapeutic turn' as the democratisation of affects insofar as the personal sufferings of minority groups were translated as political problems during the 1960s. In making the personal political, the psyche also becomes political: 'early consciousness raising groups represented a new union of the therapeutic and the political' (Nicholson 1999: 160). Following from this union, a psychoanalytic philosophy of sexual-difference feminism has tended to diagnose phallocentric rationality as the dominant symptom of a global pathological repression of the affective alterity of the feminine. Liberating the body from the abusive disciplinary regimens of phallocentric rationality entails a return to the affective grounds of embodied thought. In this context, the crises of the rational subject are predominantly read in psychoanalytic or therapeutic terms as a breakdown of systems of patriarchal discipline and the liberating breakthrough of affective, empathic, other-sensitive, fluid feminine thought. While such positions often rest on crypto-normative psychoanalytic claims about healthy forms of embodiment, the 'psyche is political' paradigm continues to dominate the high end of feminist and cultural theory.

In thinking through the therapeutic turn as the installation of the new society of psychopharmaceutical or chemical control, it is important to recognise with Deleuze and Guattari that pathologising regimens of authoritarian discipline function to intensify a micro-Oedipal economy of affects. In this context, mobilising a discourse of child abuse against disciplinary power is a strategy that has been used by systems of therapeutic governmentality in order to mask the installation of new forms of social control. Here we can understand 'the therapeutic turn' as the pathologisation of the affective realm and the emergence of a therapeutic micropolitics of desire. Guattari asks: '[j]ust what is this deterritorialisation which rebounds to give rise to an upsurge of a new micro-fascism?' (1984: 228); one answer might be that this deterritorialisation occurs through the pathologisation of the macro-assemblages of the disciplinary society. The danger, then, is not merely out there, it is within the very theorisation of disciplinary power as a pathogenic abuse of the body. In this context, the strategic importance of Deleuze and Guattari's thinking lies in their analysis of the psy-complex as a machine that installs a micropolitics of therapeutic control through the diagnosis of *power as abuse*. Installed as the therapeutic solution to abusive power, psy-complex assemblages create the abused subject who is also the subject who must be 'healed', 'empowered' and, increasingly, rehabilitated with pharmaceutical drugs.

Oedipus on Drugs

One of the more significant historical outcomes of the therapeutic turn is the psychiatric moulding of the child abuse survivor through an individualising 'anatamo-politics' and a broader 'biopolitics of the population' (McNay 1994: 99): the child abuse survivor is both an individual subject, a 'survivor', and a member of a larger population of child abuse survivors, or a 'survivor population' a 'dividual'. Today the 'child abuse movement' can be recognised as a macro-assemblage that is rapidly territorialising a range of personal and social problems (Hacking 1995: 57; Jenkins 2004: 232). The movement to ban corporal punishment can be situated within a broad attempt at reform that encompassed not only the school, but the disciplinary enclosures of the family, the hospital and the courts, creating a new medico-politico-penal relationship to the child's body, which in turn transformed the articulation of the child's body as an object of control. Indeed a number of experts, such as the child psychiatrist Jack L. Westman, claim a direct correlation between the decline of American life and child abuse (Westman 1994: 199), while other experts locate the *untreated* child as the origin of a massive range of social problems (Polansky et al. 1981). In this context, preventative psychiatry lays claim to the child in the name of saving society from an emerging evil. The classification of children as a 'dangerous class' (Danzelot 1979) is shifted into the mapping of children as the biological danger that threatens the future order of society.

Under the regimes of therapeutic governmentality that mobilise a rhetoric of child abuse prevention, the child's body is opened up to a new folding of preventative psychiatry. In 2006, University of Chicago researchers announced findings which suggested that 'low levels of neurotransmitter serotonin may perpetuate child abuse across generations . . . The research suggests that treatments with drugs that increase brain serotinin early in an abused child's life could reduce the likelihood that the child will grow up to be abusive' (Maestripieri et al. 2006). Cleansing the subject of the pathogenic stains of abuse becomes the benevolent project of the new technologies of therapeutic chemical control that increasingly link an exposure to abusive power to chemical imbalances in the brain – post-traumatic stress disorder – while preventative medication is used to calm the stirring of anti-social/abusive power within the body – antipsychotic/depressant/anxiety pills.

This massive psychopharmaceutical mapping of the child's body is the control society's 'writing on the wall'. If the statement '[c]hildhood is madness' (Foucault 1993: 252) and the mad a type of child, functioned to organise the familial parody of the care of the insane Foucault identifies with the birth of the asylum at the turn of the eighteenth century – informing a whole pedagogy of self-restraint and installing the clinical gaze of parental reason within the subject – the last few decades have witnessed deepening revelations about the truth of madness *as* child abuse. The history of ideas about the childish barbarity of madness is now installed, not merely in the *idea* of immaturity, or through *narratives* of reason as the progressive overcoming of childhood's essential madness, but within the child's body itself. The discourse of madness now comes to rest within the body of the child, inciting confessions from his or her genetic and chemical composition. While Foucault writes in *Power/Knowledge* that 'the family-child complex' is 'the first and most important instance for the medicalisation of individuals' (Foucault 1991: 281), within control societies the family-child complex emerges as the first and most important instance of the *medication* of individuals. While Foucault writes that 'we are entering the age of the infinite examination and of compulsory objectification' (200), within control societies, we now enter the age of the infinite diagnosis and compulsory medication.

Side-Effects and Lines of Flight

Echoing Zygmunt Bauman's (2004, 2005) analysis of the waste economy of liquid modernity, Parisi and Terranova (2000) write that within the control societies 'nothing is wasted, everything is recycled'. In this context, the negative side-effects of chemical control, the accidental symptoms of an inefficient dose, are recycled in order to produce improved drugs: the chemical side-effect is recycled in order to refine the future control of affects. Every economy of chemical control produces a multiplicity of unexpected and unpredictable side-effects which are territorialised as resources for new forms of chemical control. But there are other side-effects, other kinds of chemical turbulence, which are not so easily recycled as profit. Contemporary protests over the medication of teenagers under the US government's TeenScreen programmes can be read as among the dispersed micropolitical side-effects which threaten the chemical flow of capital through the child by blocking the saturation of the school by Big Pharma.[12] Such minoritarian movements can be read as part of a larger anti-psychiatry rhizome attempting to deterritorialise the mapping of the body by Big Pharma, circulating an oppositional chemical politics and creating new understandings of chemical citizenship which read side-effects as productions that are not justified by diagnosis and the interpretation of lack. This politicisation of side-effects is anti-Oedipal in the sense that it is 'against overcoding' or against the diagnosis of the underlying meaning of the child's lack, and focuses instead on decoding 'the singular forces that produce systems and regularities' (Colebrook 2002: 121), or the death-bound forces of chemical control which aim to regulate difference and rechannel the turbulence of childhood. The anti-TeenScreen slogans, such as Educate Don't Medicate and I Am Not A Lab Rat, signal an emerging awareness of the chemical politics of control. We can imagine these forces as the untreatable side-effects of new biotechnologies of mass dosing, as the spitting out of Oedipus, as an anti-Oedipal depathologisation of childhood.

While I have argued that the post-Mettray child is installed within an economy of chemical control that is in the process of being decoded by anti-psy critiques of the political side-effects of Big Pharma, there are other ways of thinking about the children of Mettray. That we do not, after all, know what a child's body can do is evident when Foucault's description of the triumph of normative power over the bodies of children in Mettray undergoes an uncanny erotic decoding in the work of Jean Genet – Mettray's most glorious pathogen – whose *Miracle of the Rose* (1971), originally published in 1951, explores the libidinal rhizomes, the blossoming of a schizoanalysis, which connect the children in the colony. If Foucault's Mettray is a space in which normative power installs the docile individual, Genet's recalls a multiplicity of interconnected collectivities: 'Mettray swarmed with children, children with charming faces, and bodies and souls' (Genet 1971: 54). Genet's Mettray is a child-swarm which reterritorialises the language of discipline: 'The children had an extraordinary power of creating words as well. Not extravagant words, but in order to designate things, words which children repeat to each other, thus inventing an entire language' (Genet 1971: 55). An underground chemical economy also flows through the children in Mettray that enables Genet to take up a mutated sovereignty when he emerges from the disciplinary cell:

From the disciplinary cell, where I spent two weeks, I arranged with an infirmary assistant to split me some Phenobarbital in exchange for a few butts. This century is certainly the century of poison, an age in which Hitler is a Renaissance princess, in which he is, for us, a mute profound Catherine de Medici, and my fondness for poisons, the appeal they have for us, sometimes makes me merge with one or the other of these personages. Then the Phenobarbital led me to the infirmary in lordly state, pale and deathly-looking. (Genet 1971: 105–6)

The underground chemical economy in Mettray is part of the flow of 'the century of poison', a post-Renaissance age in which the creation of the complete human being culminates in the terrible sovereignty of fascist power. Taking Phenobarbital allows Genet to become the lordly sovereignty of Hitler as the Renaissance princess of poisons, a chemical becoming which is also a decoding of the intimate links between poison and power.

It is not insignificant that Deleuze writes: '"Control" is the name Burroughs proposes as a term for the new monster' (Deleuze 1992: 3). Intimate with the occluded economy of addiction and control, William Burroughs imagines a world in which the pharmaceutical industrial complex abjectifies the body as a chemical laboratory, hooking it into a chemical economy of domination which modifies and deforms in the name of well-being and freedom. The more addicted the 'soft machine' of the body, argues Burroughs, the easier it is to control. Burroughs' control-addiction machines operate according to the logic of an 'algebra of need' in which junk is not only a drug, but the desire to fill the installed organ of lack. In this sense *Oedipus is junk*, and the control-addiction machine another name for the Oedipal subject. Burroughs' control-addiction machines are part of a minoritarian literature of intoxication in which the macro-politics of chemical control are disorganised and recreated by multiple lines of flight which pass through the chemical experiments of De Quincey, Coleridge, Arthur Rimbaud, Charles Baudelaire, Antonin Artaud, Jean Cocteau, Aldous Huxley, Carlos Castenda, Timothy Leary, Irvine Welsh, Elizabeth Wurtzel and others. Such writing can be approached as the formation of a micropolitics of chemical citizenship, a counter-history of chemical control. However, as Deleuze and Guattari caution in *A Thousand Plateaus*, 'the line of flight of drugs is constantly being segmentarised under the most rigid of forms, that of dependency, the hit and the dose, the dealer' (Deleuze and Guattari 1987: 284). It is unwise to romanticise the addict as an anti-hero, to make opiates the religion of the subversive, or confuse underground chemical economies with freedom. But if Deleuze has found Burroughs' diagrams of control-addiction useful in thinking the present, and if a chemical economy of control is passing through children, it might be wise to think through the multiple ways in which the relationships between dependency, the hit, the dose and the dealer, describe connections which are trapping the always immature alterity, the playful affects and impolite dissent of the becoming of children and life.

References

Armstrong, L. (1981), 'The Cradle of Sexual Politics', *Frontiers: A Journal of Women's Studies*, 6 (1): 19–25.

Australian Principles Associations Professional Development Council (2007), *Kids Matter: Australian Primary Schools Mental Health Initiative*; http://www.apapdc.edu.au/kidsmatter

Bauman, Z. (2004), *Wasted Lives: Modernity and its Outcasts*, London: Polity.

Bauman, Z. (2005), *Liquid Life*, London: Polity.

Bradley, C. (1937), 'The Behaviour of Children Receiving Benzedrine', *American Journal of Psychiatry*, 94: 577–85.

Breggin, P. R. (1999), 'Psychostimulants in the Treatment of Children Diagnosed with ADHA: Risks and Mechanism of Action', *International Journal of Risk and Safety in Medicine*, 12: 3–35.

Colebrook, C. (2002), *Understanding Deleuze*, Sydney: Allen and Unwin.

Danzelot, J. (1979), *The Policing of Families*, New York: Pantheon.

Deleuze, G. (1988), *Foucault*, trans. S. Hand, Minneapolis: University of Minnesota Press.

Deleuze, G. (1992), 'Postscript on the Society of Control', *October*, 59: 3–7.

Deleuze, G. and Guattari, F. (1983), *Anti-Oedipus: Capitalism and Schizophrenia*, trans. R. Hurley, M. Seem and H. Lane, Minneapolis: University of Minnesota Press.

Deleuze, G. and F. Guattari (1987), *A Thousand Plateaus: Capitalism and Schizophrenia*, trans. B. Massumi, Minneapolis: University of Minnesota Press.

Foucault, M. (1979), *Discipline and Punish: The Birth of the Prison*, trans. A. Sheridan, Harmondsworth: Penguin Books.

Foucault, M. (1988), 'Sexual Morality and the Law', in L. D. Kritzman (ed.), *Michel Foucault: Politics, Philosophy, Culture. Interviews and Other Writings 1977–1984*, trans. A. Sheridan, London: Routledge.

Foucault, M. (1991), *Discipline and Punish*, trans. A. Sheridan, London: Penguin.

Foucault, M. (1993), *Madness and Civilization: A History of Insanity in the Age of Reason*, trans. A Sheridan, New York: Routledge.

Frank, K. (1948), *Society as the Patient: Essays on Culture and Personality*, Brunswick: Rutgers University Press.

Friedenberg, E. Z. (1965), *Coming of Age in America*, New York: Random House.

Furedi, F. (2006), 'Why the Politics of Happiness Makes me Mad', http://www.frankfuredi.com/articles/happiness-spiked-20060532.shtml

Genet, J. (1971), *Miracle of the Rose*, trans. B. Frechtman, London: Penguin.

Giddens, A. (1992), *The Transformation of Intimacy: Sexuality, Love and Eroticism in Modern Society*, Cambridge: Polity.

Greydanus, D. E., H. D. Pratt, R. C. Spates, A. E. Blake-Dreher, M. A. Greydanus-Gearhart and D. R. Patel (2003), 'Corporal Punishment in Schools: Position Paper of the Society for Adolescent Medicine', *Journal of Adolescent Health*, 32: 385–93.

Grossberg, L. (2005), *Caught in the Crossfire: Kids, Politics and America's Future*, London: Paradigm Publishers.

Guattari, F. (1984), *Molecular Revolution: Psychiatry and Politics*, trans. R. Sheed, London: Penguin.

Hacking, I. (1995), *Rewriting the Soul: Multiple Personality Disorder and the Science of Memory*, Princeton: Princeton University Press.

Herman, E. (1995), *The Romance of American Psychology: Political Culture in the Age of Experts*, Berkeley: University of California Press.

Herman, J. (2000), *Father–Daughter Incest*, Cambridge, MA: Harvard University Press.

Hazleden, R. (2003), 'Love Yourself: The Relationship of the Self with Itself in Popular Self-Help Texts', *Journal of Sociology*, 39 (4): 413–28.

Hyman, I., A. E. McDowell and B. Rains (1977), 'Corporal Punishment and Alternatives in Schools: An Overview of Theoretical and Practical Issues', in *National Institute of Education Proceedings: Conference on Corporal Punishment Schools: A National Debate*, February 18–20, US Government Printing Office 729 222/565.

Hyman, I., W. Zelikoff and J. Clark (1988), 'Psychological and Physical Abuse in the Schools: A Paradigm for Understanding Post-Traumatic Stress Disorder in Children and Youth', *Journal of Traumatic Stress*, 1 (2): 243–66.

Irigaray, L. (1985), *Speculum of the Other Woman*, trans. G. C. Gill, Ithaca: Cornell University Press.

Jane-Llopis, E. and P. Anderson (2005), *Mental Health Promotion and Mental Disorder Prevention: A Policy for Europe*, Nijmegen: Radford University Nijmegen.

Jenkins, P. (2004), *Moral Panic: Changing Concepts of the Child Molester in Modern America*, New Haven: Yale University Press.

Kant, I. (1960), *On Education*, trans. A. Churton, Michigan: University of Michigan Press.

King, P. (2007), 'A Mountain in My Mind', *The Times*, August 7: 30–1.

Kittrie, N. N. (1971), *The Right To Be Different: Deviance and Enforced Therapy*, Baltimore and London: Johns Hopkins University Press.

Kost, F. (1985), *Volksschule und Disziplin*, Zurich: Limmat.

Lasch, C. (1977), *Haven in a Heartless World: The Family Besieged*, New York: Norton.

Ludbrook, R. (1996), 'Children's Rights in School Education', in K. Funder (ed.), *Citizen Child: Australian Law and Children's Rights*, Melbourne: Australian Institute of Family Studies.

Maestripieri, D., J. D. Higley, S. G. Lindell, T. K. Newman, K. M. McCormack and M. M. Sanchez (2006), 'Early Maternal Rejection Affects the Development of Monoaminergic Systems and Adult Abusive Parenting in Rhesus Macques (*macaca mulatta*)', *Behavioural Neuroscience*, 120 (5): 1017–24.

McCrossin, S. (1995), *Ritalin and Attention Deficit Disorder: History of its Use, Effects and Side-Effects*, Boulder: Learning Enhancement Center.

McElroy, M. (2004), 'Mandatory mental health screening threatens privacy parental rights', September 15; http://www.ifeminists.net/introduction/editorials/2004/0915.html.

McNay, L. (1994), *Foucault: A Critical Introduction*, Cambridge: Polity Press.

Masson, J. (2003), *The Assault on Truth: Freud's Suppression of the Seduction Theory*, New York: Ballantine Books.

Miller, T. and M. C. Leger (2002), 'A Very Childish Moral Panic: Ritalin', *Journal of the Medical Humanities*, 24 (1–2): 9–33.

Moelis, C. S. (1988), 'Banning Corporal Punishment: A Crucial Step Toward Preventing Child Abuse', *Child Legal Rights*, 1: 2–5.

Nicholson, L. (1999), *The Play of Reason: From the Modern to the Postmodern*, Ithaca: Cornell University Press.

Parisi, L. and T. Terranova (2000), 'Heat-Death: Emergence and Control in Genetic Engineering and Artificial Life', *CTheory*, A084; http://www.ctheory.net/text_file. asp?pick=127

Phelan, T. W. (1993), *All About Attention Deficit Disorder: Symptoms, Diagnosis, and Treatment: Children and Adults*, Illinois: Child Management Inc.

Polansky, N. A., M. A. Chalmers, E. Buttenwieser and D. P. Williams (1981), *Damaged Parents: An Anatomy of Child Neglect*, Chicago: The University of Chicago Press.

Pongratz, L. (2006), 'Voluntary Self-Control: Education Reform as a Governmental Strategy', *Philosophy and Theory of Education*, 38 (4): 471–82.

Pongratz, L. (2007), 'Freedom and Discipline: Transformations in Pedagogic Punishment', in M. A. Peters and T. Besley (eds), *Why Foucault?: New Directions in Educational Research*, New York: Peter Lang Books.

Postman, N. (1982), *The Disappearance of Childhood*, New York: Delacorte Press.

Pride, Mary. (1986), *The Child Abuse Industry*, Wheaton: Crossway Books.

Rabinow, P. and N. Rose (2003), 'Thoughts on the Concept of Biopower Today'; https://www.lse.ac.uk/collections/sociology/pdf/RabinowandRose-BiopowerToday03.pdf

Rose, N. (2003a), 'Neurochemical Selves', *Society*, Nov/Dec: 46–59.

Rose, N. (2003b), 'The Neurochemical Self and Its Anomalies', in R. Ericson (ed.), *Risk and Morality*, Toronto: University of Toronto Press.

Rose, N. (2006), 'Disorders Without Borders? The Expanding Scope of Psychiatric Practice', *Bioscience*, 1: 465–84.

Rose, N. (2007), 'Molecular Biopolitics, Somatic Ethics and the Spirit of Biocapital', *Social Theory and Health*, 5: 3–29.

Rush, F. (1981), *The Best Kept Secret: Sexual Abuse of Children*, New York: McGraw-Hill.

Showalter, E. (1998), *Hystories: Hysterical Epidemics and Modern Culture*, London: Picador.

Westman, J. C. (1994), *Licensing Parents: Can We Prevent Child Abuse and Neglect?*, New York: Plenum Books.

Zito, J. M., D. J. Safer, S. dosReis, J. F. Gardner, K. Soeken, M. Boles and F. Lynch (2000), 'Trends in the Prescribing of Psychotropic Medication to Preschoolers', *American Medical Association*, 283: 1025–30.

Zito, J. M., D. J. Safer, S. dosReis, J. F. Gardner, K. Soeken, M. Boles and F. Lynch (2002), 'Rising Prevalence of Antidepressants Among US Youth', *Pediatrics*, 109 (5): 721–7.

Zito, J. M., D. J. Safer, D. Satish, J. Valluri, F. Garnder, J. J. Korditz and D. Mattison (2007), 'Psychotherapeutic Medication Prevalence in Medicaid-Insured Preschoolers', *Journal of Child and Adolescent Psychopharmacology*, 17 (2): 195–203.

Notes

1. The better part of this is from Kant's lecture 'On Pedagogy: How do I cultivate freedom alongside discipline?' His answer in relation to children is that 'one imposes discipline on him in order to lead him to the use of his own freedom' (1960: 711).

2. Here I am drawing on Rabinow and Rose who discuss 'emerging forms of genetic or *biological citizenship*' (Rabinow and Rose 2003: 4, my emphasis). They argue that 'the concept of biopower designates a plane of actuality' (3) which must

include an analysis of these emerging forms of biological citizenship. They read this as a product of a post-Second World War '*bioethical complex*' that 'has seen the rise of new kinds of patients' groups and individuals, who increasingly define their citizenship in terms of their rights (and obligations) to life, health and cure. And of course, new circuits of *bioeconomics* have taken shape, a large scale *capitalisation of bioscience* and *mobilisation* of its elements into new exchange relations: the new molecular knowledges of life and health are being mapped out, developed and exploited by a range of commercial enterprises' (13). Rose is interested in the third generation of antidepressants as a molecular knowledge of life which is being commercialised. I have not been able to engage with Rose as much as I should here. His 'Neurochemical Selves' offers an account of the rapid saturation of the body by Big Pharma. Here he writes that: 'If we are experiencing a "neurochemical reshaping of personhood", the social and ethical implications for the twenty-first century will be profound. For these drugs are becoming central to the ways in which our conduct is determined to be problematic and governed, by others, and by ourselves – to the continuous work of modulation of our capacities that is the life's work of the contemporary biological citizen' (Rose 2003a: 59). See also, Rose (2003b, 2006, 2007).

3. See http://pediatrics.about.com/cs/adhd/l/bl-buy-ritalin.htm. Which begins: 'Buy Ritalin Online Without a Prescription. Does your child have AHDA?' See also: http://www.vyvanseshine.com/early/Registrationasp. All about Vyvanse, coming soon for the treatment of ADHD, where you can join Shine today, and receive free trial medication. Shine is a pharmaceutical group that 'is here to provide you with consistent support' which 'offers a comprehensive treatment program for your child' and promises to enhance 'the challenging homework hours from 4 to 6pm'. 'Sign up for SHINE today!'

4. As Miller and Leger comment, '[a]lmost overnight, children were subjected to external testing and self-monitoring against norms of scholastic and occupational achievement derived from the psy-professions' (Miller and Leger 2002: 18).

5. See for example Ian Hacking (1995), Neil Postman (1982), Mary Pride (1986), Florence Rush (1981) and Elaine Showalter (1998). In brief, the argument in common here (and I hope I can be forgiven for collapsing differences) is that the 'discovery' of the extent of the sexual, physical and emotional abuse of children which mobilised an alliance between feminism, children's rights groups and therapists has enhanced the psychiatrisation of suffering.

6. The work of Hyman is pivotal here. See Hyman et al. (1977, 1988). Also C. S. Moelis (1988). Greydanus et al. state: 'If the goal of discipline is to facilitate moral internalisation, then corporal punishment fails to achieve this end' (Greydanus et al. 2003: 389). Corporal punishment fails because it creates mental and emotional disorder.

7. The New Freedom Commission on Mental Health in 2002 stated its mission as the promotion of 'successful community integration for adults with a serious mental illness and children with a serious emotional disturbance', which has led to the preventative strategy of TeenScreen and the 'screening' of 52 million students and 6 million adults who work at the schools. See McElroy (2004). E. Jane-Llopis and P. Anderson's *Mental Health Promotion and Mental Disorder Prevention: A Policy for Europe* states the following under the heading 'The need for action in Europe': 'A lack of positive mental health is a threat to the economy of public health, the quality of life and the economy of Europe' (Jane-Llopis and Anderson 2005: 4). Action includes 'define and identify high risk populations' (11); 'Screen and identify children and adolescents at risk of mental and behavioural disorders' (13); 'Identify groups at risk for mental disorders across the lifespan' (19), and so on. TeenScreen in the US has been running for several

years. See http://www/teenscreen.org about the 'growing momentum for mental health screening around the country'. The Australian Principals Associations Professional Development Council (APAPDC), in its *Kids Matter: Australian Primary Schools Mental Health Initiative,* warns that 'early signs of mental health problems can be detected in young children'; see http://www.apapdc.edu.au/kidsmatter

8. For a list of recent medications see http://www.vyvansehine.com. The site mentions in small print that 'amphetamines may lead to dependence' and that 'aggression, new abnormal thoughts/behaviours, mania, growth suppression, worsening of motion or verbal tics and Tourette's syndrome' are known side-effects.

9. See 'Data presented at APA meeting suggest Ritalin La (methylphenidate hydrochloride) extended-release capsules are an effective once-daily treatment for ADHD'; http://.pharma.us.novartis.com/newsroom/pressReleases.

10. See the telling website Advocates for Survivors of Child Abuse (http://www.asca.org.au/childabuse), which in the name of advocacy thoroughly pathologises and criminalises 'survivors'. See also texts such as Polansky et al. (1981), which pivots on the common-sense idea that abused children grow up to be abusive parents, and that this intergenerational cycle of abuse and neglect is responsible for the decline of society. They argue that 'protective service workers do seem to be trying to cope with an ever mounting human flood' (Polansky et al. 1981: 19) and suggest that the state performs 'parental prostheses'. In the forward to Westman (1994), Judge Charles D. Gill, of the Superior Court of the State of Connecticut, writes: '"where do all these monsters, predators, and punks come from?" . . . they were all reared by American adults. It is a rare predator who has had a successful childhood' (Westman 1994: viii).

11. Jeffrey Masson first published *The Assault on Truth: Freud and Child Sexual Abuse* (Masson 2003) in 1984. But before this event a number of feminists, including Luce Irigaray in her *Speculum of the Other Woman* (Irigaray 1985), had revealed Oedipus as the cover up of child sexual abuse. See also Judith Herman (2000), Louise Armstrong (1981), Florence Rush (1981).

12. See 'TeenScreen: A front group for the psycho-pharmaceutical industry'; http://www.psychsearch.net/teenscreen.html. Also 'TeenScreen: adolescent suicide and mental health screening program'; http://www.teenscreen.org. There is a rich and aggressive debate being conducted between activists and psychiatrists on this issue.

Chapter 6

Politics in the Age of Control

Saul Newman

In his 'Postscript on the Societies of Control', Gilles Deleuze diagnoses a new mode of control that pervades contemporary societies, surpassing the societies of enclosure and discipline so rigorously explored by Foucault. According to Deleuze, the old disciplinary paradigms are in the process of breaking down – or are at least undergoing a fundamental transformation. The control of individuals is no longer confined to the walls of the prison, school, factory or hospital, but rather spills out into other social spaces, functioning now as a free-floating, modulated form of surveillance made possible through the most sophisticated technologies. Little escapes its grasp, and yet this is a control which presupposes a certain freedom of movement and choice, thus immersing itself within the very fabric of 'liberal' societies.

My purpose here is to explore the political implications of this new technology of control. The emergence of the control society is, I would suggest, coextensive with the paradigm of biopolitics, as well as the global hegemony of neo-liberal capitalism. Moreover, techniques and practices of control have been intensified and given greater ideological consistency through the so-called 'war on terrorism' whose dark potentialities we have seen unfolding over recent years. However, we could equally say that such developments have themselves been made possible through diverse techniques, practices and technologies of control – technologies which have placed themselves in the service of both capitalism and the state. In any case, I will argue that societies of control mark a certain transformation in politics, coinciding with, as Jacques Rancière (1999) would say, the age of *post-politics*, where a dull, media-managed and technocratic consensus seems to have replaced the ideological conflicts of the past, and where the line between public and private domains becomes indiscernible. However, the reign of post-politics and the society of control does not mean the end of politics, only its reconfiguration. The central question, then, is what new forms of politics can take place in societies of control – and, in particular, what new forms of politics are needed to resist them. I will suggest here that a different 'micropolitics' is called for, one no longer organised around the themes of identity and difference, but rather around anonymity and 'disidentification'.

Technologies of Control

There can be little doubt that we are living today in a control society. The signs are all around us: ubiquitous CCTV cameras filming public spaces; the introduction of biometric scanning and facial recognition technology in major airports; the planned implementation of ID cards in the United Kingdom and elsewhere – cards which would contain biometric information;[1] widespread DNA testing for even minor offences, and the setting up of national DNA databases; the use of electronic monitoring bracelets for offenders or terrorist suspects placed under home detention; the use of 'smart cards' on public transport systems and for accessing health services, and so on. We are seeing the development – bit by bit – of an all-encompassing system of surveillance and regulation, the weaving of an intricate web of overlapping circuits of control, information gathering and identification. We live in a society that is more closely and minutely monitored, regulated and policed than ever before, where personal privacy is more or less non-existent, and where information about our whereabouts, personal details and spending habits is ceaselessly collected by both governments and corporations (the two entities are now all but indistinguishable). De Tocqueville, in his exploration of American democracy in the nineteenth century spoke of a new despotism there, 'an immense and protective power' that stands above the race of men and keeps them in perpetual childhood (de Tocqueville 1966: 667). Today we can find this protective power operating in societies of control – where surveillance technologies and government paternalism combine to hold us in a state of perpetual thraldom and dependency. From the TV monitoring of large crowds of people in public places, to the technological intrusion into individual bodies, desires and pathologies through DNA testing and the mapping of the human genome, we are subjected to a new technology of power which seeks to make everything visible in a way that even Foucault could not have dreamt of – the old panoptic techniques employed in the prison, school and workshop now seem almost laughable by comparison.[2]

Already Foucault had analysed the growth of disciplinary technologies during the eighteenth and nineteenth centuries, tracing their permeation of an ever wider array of social practices – medical care, punishment, military training, pedagogy, psychiatry. Such disciplinary practices, which – reversing the old medieval paradigm – imprisoned the body within the 'soul', were to be found functioning in enclosed institutions that we had hitherto seen as politically innocent: the school, the family, the hospital. Disciplinary power, moreover, coincided with a certain transformation of the law: increasingly, the law was being used to enforce the norm, creating certain standards of behaviour and rationality according to which the 'abnormal' was constituted as an object of perverse fascination (Foucault 2002: 1–89). As Foucault showed:

> There also appeared the idea of a penalty that was not meant to be a response to an infraction but had the function of correcting individuals at the level of their behaviour, their attitudes, their dispositions, the danger they represented – at the level of their supposed potentialities. (Foucault 2002: 67)

Today, this deployment of the law for the purposes of normalisation has become the most banal and uncontroversial feature of the societies of control: in the name of controlling what governments like to call 'anti-social' behaviour, we see the proliferation of an endless series of petty, ridiculous and excessive laws which regulate, at the most minute level, personal behaviours and actions. Ideological wars are now waged against 'noisy neighbours', 'rogue cyclists', 'inconsiderate motorists', 'skinny models', 'irresponsible parents', 'parents who smack their children', 'obese children', 'problem children', 'welfare cheats', smokers, paedophiles – and a series of fines, sanctions, punishments are enforced for the most trivial of infractions.[3] Any aberrant or deviant behaviour is immediately pathologised, medicalised, criminalised; it comes under the authority of social workers, teachers, doctors, police, judges, prison officials, psychiatrists – a whole diffuse and localised network that polices and monitors individuals. Here the most sophisticated of control technologies – DNA screening, electronic tagging, forced medication – work in tandem with the most rigid and draconian laws and policies of 'zero-tolerance' in order to reproduce the tyranny of the norm: the law becomes normalisation and normalisation becomes the law.

Such techniques of control have the effect of positioning individuals as continual subjects of risk and suspicion (Campbell 2004: 78–92): every young person is potentially a thug or a criminal, every Muslim potentially a terrorist. Control techniques are used not so much to identify a particular individual, but rather to identify a future risk and to attach this risk to certain types of individuals. Governments today, for instance, talk about identifying children 'at risk' of delinquency or of posing a potential threat to society – in some cases before they are even born! New surveillance technology is even being developed which claims to be able to predict crimes and terrorist attacks on public transport systems before they occur – CCTV recordings of members of people on buses and trains are matched against computer files of 'suspicious' behaviour, triggering an alarm when they correspond. We see here the automatic functioning of control technology – where computers rather than judges, police and psychiatrists become the arbiters of the norm. Perhaps we could say that whereas disciplinary societies constituted the subject as a fixed identity – defining him according to rigid categories such as normal/abnormal, sane/mad – societies of control seek to define the individual through a series of different, modulated and overlapping states of risk, with indeterminate and shifting borders: being 'at risk' of delinquency, terrorism (we see that the metaphor of the virus is now used to describe the risk of terrorism spreading through Muslim communities, fuelled by those demonic 'radical preachers'), sickness, mental illness, Attention Deficit Disorder, drug abuse, and so on. We are now all positioned as subjects of permanent risk, capable of certain unpredictable and criminal behaviours at any time.

Biopolitics and Global Capitalism

In this paradigm, moreover, the body itself becomes the site of permanent crisis and, thus, the target of control technologies. The body is policed, monitored, controlled – and yet is seen as constantly threatened by obesity, smoking, binge-drinking. Health standards such as the BMI (Body Mass Index) are enforced with all the ferocity of Victorian moral codes. Our bodies – particularly our genes – have become the source of all our pathologies, moral failings and deviant behaviours: it is no longer our sexuality, as Foucault maintained, but our DNA that is seen as the secret of our being. This obsession with the body would be characteristic of what Foucault himself termed 'biopower' – a new kind of power that functioned at the level of biological life, seeking to control its flows and functions and to harness its vital forces. The emergence of this new political technology coincided with developments, during the seventeenth and eighteenth centuries, in the biological, human and social sciences, and governmental discourses – bodies of knowledge and political rationalities which took the population and economic life as their proper domain. As Foucault says:

> For the first time in history, no doubt, biological existence was reflected in political existence; the fact of living was no longer an inaccessible substrate

that only emerged from time to time, amid the randomness of death and its fatality; part of it passed into knowledge's field of control and power's sphere of intervention. (Foucault 1979: 142)

It is within this paradigm of biopower that governments busy themselves with health matters, with 'obesity epidemics', for instance; that they take an interest in the health of individuals and the general population; that they centralise medical information in large national databases. Biopower, and the practice of *biopolitics*, in this sense, can be seen as providing a general strategy of coordination for the diffuse technologies of control. To put it simply, the general aim of power today is the control of life itself. As Foucault showed, politics no longer generally subscribes to the sovereign function of the power to kill, the power to end life – although as we shall see, this sovereign function has uncannily reappeared today at the heart of modern power regimes; rather, power now functions to preserve and sustain life. Yet, as benign as this might sound, it means that power now reaches deep into life itself, controlling, monitoring and regulating its palpitations. Moreover, the destruction of life in the name of preserving it functions as biopower's permanent and lethal underside.[4]

Deleuze's notion of control as superseding discipline can only be understood against the background of biopower/biopolitics. Already Foucault himself had charted a general shift from disciplinary power to biopower: while disciplinary power was focused on the individual, his body and his pathologies, biopower focuses on the population at large, monitoring its movements, migrations and epidemics; measuring its birth, mortality and longevity rates; assessing its economic output. It produces a sort of globalising effect. Secondly, where disciplinary power sought to enclose the individual within a physical or discursive space, biopower presupposes a certain freedom of movement and choice – therefore requiring a free-floating and modulated form of regulation and control (Foucault 2003). The superseding of disciplinary power by biopower – a process accompanied by a frequent overlapping between the two paradigms – seems to directly prefigure Deleuze's description of the emergence of the control society. Control societies seek an all-encompassing control over life – both at the global level of populations, and at the infinitesimal level of our biological substratum.

Moreover, the logic of biopolitical control coincides with and sustains the spread of global capitalism and the unchallenged hegemony of the neo-liberal economic model. Economic liberalism, as Foucault showed, was not a withdrawal of the state from economic life – as traditional laissez-faire notions would have it – but rather a much more complex interaction whereby the market is discursively constructed as an entity to be shaped and guided through certain governmental rationalities and strategies (Foucault 2004; Gordon 1991). Moreover, within this paradigm, individuals are seen as subjects to be regulated and policed through the market. In modern control societies, this occurs through the construction of the subject as a consumer who has a certain number of 'choices' defined by the market; and who is subjected to constant advertising. The individual is thus policed through the market. As Deleuze points out, control today takes place through marketing, and the individual is no longer the individual but the 'dividual' who is inserted into an endless series of samples, data and markets: 'marketing is now the instrument of social control and produces an arrogant breed who are our new masters' (Deleuze 1995: 181).

This new breed of masters is none other than the corporation: an entity which now has a global reach and achieves a planetary colonisation, turning the world into a giant market. The corporation is the 'soul', as Deleuze would say, of modern control societies. However, what we see is not simply the corporation taking over from the government and displacing its traditional role of service provider, but rather the corporation and the government melding together and becoming indistinguishable. Public/private sector 'partnerships' increasingly manage what were traditionally public services and infrastructure; governments and government institutions today are run like corporations, introducing private sector management techniques and free market mechanisms, and subjecting employees to continual performance reviews

Moreover, the economic and social dislocations wrought by neo-liberal economic policies require a more sophisticated form of social control: the workforce must be disciplined, and industrial and political militancy must be discouraged – the only acceptable form of freedom in modern neo-liberal societies is the narrow consumerist freedom of the market. The destruction of traditional working-class identities and communities due to retrenchment, downsizing and outsourcing must be patched over with a new ideological conservatism – one that stresses the dangers posed to community and family life from crime, drugs, anti-social behaviour and the breakdown of discipline. The communitarian discourse of New Labour in the UK – with its almost hysterical focus on 'law-and-order' issues – would be an example of this, functioning as nothing more than a flimsy disguise for its ruthless pursuit of Thatcherite economic policies. The spectre of crime or terrorism serves as an ideological scapegoat here: society needs its enemies, as Foucault would say, and the enemies of the control society – those who endanger our 'safety' and 'security' – are constituted as the 'other' in opposition to which society achieves an uncertain cohesion.

In our current paradigm of neo-liberal global capitalism, then, the technology of control is required to harness the productive energies of the population, while at the same time imposing on it a new form of social disciplining and surveillance. In what Michael Hardt and Antonio Negri (2000) refer to as a new capitalist Empire, social and biopolitical control and surveillance circulates through a diffuse hybrid network of localised points – thus producing a new form of global sovereignty, one without a defined centre of power. With the breakdown of the traditional model of the nation-state, where the state no longer exercises sovereignty over economic life within its borders, new forms of control are required which flow across borders, mimicking the very fluidity of capitalist flows themselves. As Hardt and Negri write: 'Empire thus appears as a very high tech machine: it is virtual, built to control the marginal event, and organised to dominate and when necessary intervene in the breakdowns of the system (in line with the most advanced technologies of robotic production)' (Hardt and Negri 2000: 39).

Deleuze and Guattari themselves see capitalism as a process of deterritorialisation – in which identities and institutions are destabilised and integrated into global circuits of flux and becoming. And yet, as they point out, for every deterritorialisation there is also a reterritorialisation: while capitalism releases flows of desire, and economic and social flows, it simultaneously imposes a 'code' on them, seeking to regulate and control them (Deleuze and Parnet 1987: 129). Control technology is the means by which this is achieved.

Controlling Terrorism

The reterritorialising effects of global capitalism also have a paradoxical effect on the state itself. The modern state is undergoing a kind of convulsion, whereby on the one hand its sovereignty is undermined – at least with respect to its control over economic life – and yet on the other hand we have also seen an aggressive reassertion of state sovereignty and power with the so-called 'war on terrorism'. In the wake of September 11, and with the emergence of this permanent global state of war, we have seen hitherto unthinkable control and surveillance measures being implemented in the dubious name of 'security'. Liberal democracies have been taking on the characteristics of totalitarian police states. While governments assure us that they are trying to 'strike the right balance between liberty and security', they have been introducing legislation that undermines even the most basic civil liberties such as the right to due process. The usual techniques and practices of control have been intensified and given new impetus and consistency in the 'war on terrorism'. The sophistication of technologies of control and surveillance find their strange counterpart in a rediscovery of torture and the practice of permanent detention;[5] the *mise-en-scène* of the control society is now to be found in the torture chambers of Abu Ghraib and Guantanamo.

Is it still reasonable, then, to talk about the control society – have we not gone back to a disciplinary or even a *pre*-disciplinary sovereign power; do the barbed wire of the prison camp, and the electric shocks delivered by the military torturer (now privately contracted of course), now not serve as the dominant symbols of power in the twenty-first century? Has not the 'softness' of control been replaced with the hardness and brutality of a now unlimited sovereign power? I would argue instead that the two modalities of power have intersected, and that the off-shore prison camps and extra-legal spaces of detention that have now become emblematic of the 'war on terrorism' are actually a kind of obscene excrescence of the society of control, symbolising – in an extreme form – the constraints and controls that are already characteristic of contemporary society.[6] And if Guantanamo Bay is closing down, this is only because the techniques of detention, discipline and control employed in such spaces are already infused – in more subtle ways – throughout the rest of society.[7] Control and sovereign exceptionalism become indistinguishable in the 'war on terrorism'.

How are we to understand the political nexus that allows this intersection to take place? First, the discourse of 'security' itself must be rigorously analysed. 'Security' is the word on everyone's lips today, from media outlets and politicians across the political spectrum. The ability to provide security from terrorism is now the single stamp of legitimacy for any government, and is considered the overriding responsibility of the modern state. However, as Agamben shows – referring to Foucault's work on eighteenth-century governmental discourses – 'security' consists not in the prevention of crises and catastrophes, but rather in their continual production, regulation and management. Therefore, by making security central to modern governance, there is the danger of producing a situation of clandestine complicity between terrorism and counterterrorism, locked in a deathly embrace of mutual incitement (Agamben 2002).

It is here also that the logic of the exception must be considered. For Agamben, as well as for other theorists of sovereignty like Hobbes and Carl Schmitt, sovereignty is conditioned by the exception – that is, the ability of the sovereign to stand inside and outside the law at the same time. In other words, in order to guarantee the law, the sovereign is not bound by the law but stands outside it, having the power to suspend it through a unilateral decision. In the words of Schmitt, the sovereign is 'he who decides on the state of exception' (Carl Schmitt, cited in Agamben 2005: 1). The hidden secret of sovereignty, then, is this radical indistinction between law and lawlessness, between politics and violence. However, what was once the secret of political philosophy has now become explicit. *The state of the exception has become the rule.* That is to say, the intensification of control and surveillance techniques, coupled with practices of extra-judicial detention and governments thumbing their nose at constitutional checks and human rights norms, suggests a normalisation of the state of exception. Governments in so-called liberal democracies are operating in an increasingly extra-judicial way; the state of exception is becoming the dominant paradigm of politics today (Agamben 2005: 1–31). However, we should be clear here that it is not simply that governments are acting illegally or outside the law as such: rather sovereignty and law enter into a 'zone of indistinction' in which their limits become unclear – a kind of grey zone in which sovereignty appears as law and law appears as sovereignty. For instance, the practice of extra-judicial detention is still authorised through legislation – but here the law appears in the form of its withdrawal. At the same time, we see the excessive production of petty laws and restrictions that characterises the societies of control, with governments working frenetically on their 'legislative agendas'. Both instances signify a kind of crisis of the law – marked simultaneously by its absence and its overabundance: the law, in other words, can no longer protect us from sovereign power and operates today simply as a vector for it.

The 'war on terrorism', then, has the effect of intensifying social control measures, as well as revealing the sovereign state of exception through which they are authorised. The 'war on terrorism' has to be seen as a kind of total and permanent war: a war whose real purpose is not the defeat of some shadowy terrorist enemy – the figure of the terrorist is itself constituted through this war – but rather the global control and regulation of populations.[8] Capitalist globalisation demands control, and this control is now articulated and intensified through a permanent state of war. Here the promised freedom and deregulation of the global free market find its ultimate answer in increased restrictions and surveillance. As Jean Baudrillard says:

> To the point that the idea of freedom, a new and recent idea, is already fading from minds and mores, and liberal globalisation is coming about in

precisely the opposite form – a police state globalisation, a total control, a terror based on 'law-and-order' measures. Deregulation ends up in a maximum of constraints and restrictions, akin to a fundamentalist society. (Baudrillard 2002: 32)

Therefore our understanding of the society of control should include not simply the subtle technologies that Deleuze speaks of, but also the whole panoply of control measures we see today: everything from the permanent detention of terrorist suspects, to the heightened policing of national borders, forms a new paradigm of power and a new logic of politics that must be critically analysed.

Post-Politics

These developments in the control society signify, I would suggest, a more fundamental transformation in contemporary politics. What passes for democracy in developed capitalist countries today is nothing but a gaudy mediatised spectacle of spin-doctoring and endless opinion polls – a banal reality show which masks the almost total ideological convergence between the major parties and the lack of genuine political alternatives. Modern politics is characterised by a kind of stifling ideological consensus: the dominant political discourse today is that which announces the eclipse of ideological conflicts between left and right, claiming to be 'post-ideological' and to be about solving society's problems in a rational, 'common-sense' way without the constraints of ideology. The idea of the social-democratic 'Third Way', which claims to seek a 'middle road' between socialism and capitalism, and which purports to represent the 'radical centre' of political opinion, would be paradigmatic of the 'post-ideological' consensus. Of course we should recognise that this so-called era of 'post-ideological' consensus simply means that the ideology of the neo-liberal market has become so entrenched, so sedimented, so accepted as economic orthodoxy on both sides, that we no longer recognise it as ideology as such. The 'post-ideological' consensus is simply a neo-liberal ideological consensus, and the so called 'Third Way' was never really a third way at all, but simply a way of disguising the formal Left's capitulation to neo-liberalism by providing it with some flimsy social democratic window dressing (Mouffe 2000: 93).

So far from this new consensus style of politics being a sign of the maturity of modern democratic politics, it is a sign of its degradation and imminent collapse. We are dealing here with a new mutation of politics, in which the triumph of 'democratic consensus' coincides with, and is symptomatic of, the complete eclipse of real politics. Indeed, Rancière has suggested that the very term 'consensus democracy' is a contradiction – one can either have consensus or democracy – and has proposed instead to call it *postdemocracy* (Rancière 1999: 95). According to Rancière, the global triumph of democracy during the 1990s, which came with the collapse of the Communist regimes, coincided with a kind of shrinking of the political space: democracy has not only given up on the people – on the idea of popular sovereignty – but this has also led, paradoxically, to an erosion of the power of even the formal parliamentary mechanisms of representation. Power in modern postdemocracies increasingly rests with unelected and unaccountable experts, technocrats and committees.

The dominance of this technocratic consensus model is concomitant with a remapping of the social terrain – specifically, a kind of folding of the public and private spheres. The public sphere has become increasingly privatised, with the private ownership and management of what were once public institutions and services. And on the other hand, the private sphere has become subjected to a kind of continual public surveillance – the spaces for personal privacy and autonomy become fewer and fewer, with most transactions and communications coming under various forms of electronic surveillance, with people encouraged to keep an eye on their neighbours, to 'report suspicious activity', and with the most mind-numbing reality TV shows now making a mockery of the right to privacy, throwing people's most personal and lurid secrets into the garish public light. Hardt speaks here of a 'post-civil' condition in relation to Deleuze's notion of the society of control: one in which the conceptual division between the state and civil society is no longer relevant, and in which the deployments of new surveillance techniques and technologies, instead of disciplining the citizen as a fixed social identity, seek to 'control the citizen as a whatever identity, or rather an infinitely flexible placeholder for identity' (Hardt 1998: 36). In other words, the folding of the public and private sphere produces a new social space in which one is no longer a citizen with rights and liberties – this liberal paradigm applied only when there was an autonomous civil society – but rather a citizen whose movements must be continually controlled and monitored, and whose identity must be continuously verified.[9]

More fundamentally, as I have argued, the post-civil condition is also a post-political condition: paradoxically, while governments today talk about e-government, and expanding democratic participation through electronic voting technologies, there has been an erosion of a genuine public space for politics – democracy is no longer a collective activity engaged in by the people, but rather a media-driven process determined by endless surveys, opinion polls and 'specialists', from which the category of 'the people' is entirely absent. The people or the democratic subject is not some sociological category to be prodded and poked by public opinion experts and pollsters, but rather, as Rancière argues, a kind of fractured or partial space of subjectification; it refers not to 'mainstream opinion' but, on the contrary, to an excluded part, the part that is 'miscounted', that demands to be included by claiming to be whole. In the paradigm of post-politics, however, this democratic subject is made invisible. The politics of dispute and disagreement – upon which any notion of democracy rests – is replaced by consensus, by a 'reasonable' politics of negotiation. In this model, decisions are made on the most efficient way of distributing social goods. Thus, the democratic subject is transformed into a consumer of government services, and also a consumer on the democratic 'marketplace' who selects the party that most closely corresponds with his 'preferences'. Disputes that arise are immediately translated into problems to be solved by experts and technicians: look at the way, for instance, that the riots in Paris in November 2005 were immediately interpreted by a whole army of sociologists, experts and TV panellists into a series of 'issues' like high youth unemployment and social marginalisation, issues which might be solved by 'well-targeted' government programmes. This is an aseptic universe where nothing can happen, where genuine disputes and conflicts are translated into 'policy challenges', and where we – in our radical comfort, as Baudrillard puts it – must be protected against any foreseeable security risk (Baudrillard 2002: 15).

Politics in Search of a People

When discussing the new society of control, Deleuze tells us that there is no need to fear or to hope for the best, simply to look for new weapons (Deleuze 1995: 178). Yet he does not tell us what these weapons might be. Confronting control technology must be a political question, but what kind of politics is required here?

The reign of post-politics or 'postdemocracy' does not mean the end of politics; it does suggest, however, that the traditional models of politics are no longer valid, and that new models are called for. In particular, there is a need to rethink radical political subjectivity – there is a need for a new conception of 'the people' after the exhaustion of the Marxist category of class and class struggle. As Deleuze says in his conversation with Negri on the question of radical politics today: 'We need both creativity *and* a people' (Deleuze 1995: 176). If this subject is invisible in contemporary post-political control societies, the challenge of politics today is to make the people *appear* – but in what form?

Some caution is needed here. To what extent can we assume 'the people' would be opposed to the technologies of control? In fact, do many people today not clamour for even *more* control, for more stringent 'law and order' measures, more surveillance and greater police powers? In dealing with this problem, we can gain some clues from Deleuze's notion of becoming-minor, and his distinction between majorities and minorities. For Deleuze, this distinction is not a question of size – for instance, women are a minority even though they are more numerous than men. Rather, the difference between majority and minority refers to a certain mode of subjectivity – a certain way of relating to one's identity:

> What defines the majority is a model you have to conform to: the average European adult male city-dweller, for example . . . A minority, on the other hand, has no model, it's a becoming, a process. One might say the majority is nobody. Everybody's caught, one way or another, in a minority becoming that would lead them to unknown paths if they opted to follow it through. When a minority creates models for itself, it's because it wants to become a majority, and probably has to, to survive or prosper (to have a state, be recognised, establish its rights, for example). But its power comes from what it's managed to create, which to some extent goes into that model, but doesn't depend on it. A people is always a creative minority, and remains one even when it acquires a majority: it can be both at once because the two things aren't lived out on the same plane. (Deleuze 1995: 173–4)

We can take from this that 'the people' is not simply a coherent or consistent identity, but rather one that is highly fractured – one that contains within it different modes of subjectification, different potential ways of being, and different possibilities for political engagement. It is impossible to speak of 'the people' as a unified entity, or circumscribe it within the contours of a national identity or a particular class or social group – this would only be considering the people as a majority or a macropolitical unity. As Deleuze shows, we have to explore the *micro*political potential of the people, its processes of becoming and its 'lines of flight'. The same people who complain about crime in their 'communities' and call for more CCTV cameras might also, in other circumstances, demonstrate against the WTO or G8 summits, or against their government's involvement in the war in Iraq. These examples are a case in point: one of the interesting things about the anti-war protests in 2003, as well as large anti-globalisation demonstrations, is that they are not identifiable in terms of the traditional models of politics. They are not necessarily working-class or Marxist movements, for instance, but rather are made up of people from all 'walks of life': white-collar office workers, church groups, anarchists, trade unionists, ecologists, old people, people of different ideological persuasions, and so on. This is perhaps what Deleuze means by 'becoming-minor': people disengage themselves from their established identities and social roles, and form, in a completely contingent and unexpected way, a new political entity. Yet this is a political identity that is at the same time beyond representation – becoming something completely new. Minor politics is always an *event*, and 'the people' is always an unpredictable subjectivity whose potential we can never really know.

A number of contemporary thinkers have explored new ways of looking at radical political subjectivity. Rancière, whom we have already discussed, sees 'the people' as a place of political subjectification which emerges through a fundamental disagreement or dispute (*la mesentente*) between an excluded part of society – illegal immigrants or the unemployed, for instance – and the dominant socio-political order which they claim to be part of, thus representing their struggle as universal, as embodying the interests of the 'whole of the community'. Ernesto Laclau sees 'the people' in terms of populist struggles, and as emerging in a contingent way through the hegemonic formulation of what he calls 'chains of equivalence' (Laclau 2005). Alain Badiou, in a different way, has tried to see the political subject as emerging through the 'event' of politics – a singular, unpredictable moment of rupture which destabilises existing conditions and identities and gives rise to a new, militant conception of truth (Badiou 2003). I do not have time to go into their arguments in any great detail here, but these different ways of seeing politics centre around a number of common themes. First, politics is always an *event* which emerges in a contingent way, and which cannot be wholly accounted for or determined by pre-existing conditions. Second, politics involves a kind of radical subjectification – a disengagement or, as Badiou puts it, a 'subtraction' from ordinary everyday social roles, identities and situations. For Rancière, politics is a process of 'disidentification' which does not rely on pre-existing identities and interests, but, rather, ruptures and destabilises them and produces something new: 'any subjectification is a disidentification, removal from the naturalness of place' (Rancière 1999: 36). Third, radical politics constructs a certain universality – it is something that goes beyond the logic of difference and particularity. However, this universality is understood in a contingent way, and does not rely on essentialist concepts such as the universal class (as in the Marxist notion of the proletariat) or a universal rational consensus (as in liberal discourse).

These themes of the event, disidentification and universality can help us to construct a conception of politics relevant to the society of control. It is clear, for instance, that a radical politics able adequately to resist the new globalised forms of social control must itself embody some sort of universal or global dimension. Yet this can be understood in a number of senses. First, radical politics can no longer be confined to specific identities or embody the logic of pure particularity. The model of identity politics prominent in the 1980s has reached its conceptual and strategic limits: difference – and the assertion of a differential identity – is no longer subversive in itself, as Foucault showed, and now seems to play into the hands of a fully multicultural and hybridised global capitalism.[10] Rather than a politics that claims to represent a particular identity, Foucault advocated a localised form of politics, organised around concrete struggles against particular sites of domination. Rather than a political vanguard speaking for the masses, moreover, the politics of resistance was something to be engaged in directly by those implicated in a specific situation of oppression – prisoners, homosexuals, students. Deleuze, in a conversation with Foucault, said to him: 'You were the first . . . to teach us something absolutely fundamental: the indignity of speaking for others' (Foucault and Deleuze 1977: 209). However, perhaps this model also needs to be transcended – perhaps localised struggles need to situate themselves on a global horizon, where links with other struggles can form in a 'rhizomatic' fashion (Deleuze and Guattari 1988: 9). Indeed, if the disciplinary model of power required a localised contestation of specific power relationships, then the society of control – which implies a more globalised and free-floating form of power – requires a different and more globalised mode of resistance. Moreover, radical political struggles can no longer be confined to national spaces – they can no longer take place solely within the representative institutions of the nation-state: rather, they must appear (and, indeed, *are* appearing) on a global terrain – not only spatially, in the sense of transcending national borders, but also conceptually, in the sense of taking globalisation itself as the central political issue and the central site of contestation. The anti-globalisation movement presents us with an initial model of this new form of politics.[11] This is a form of politics which transcends both the traditional Marxist model of class struggle, as well as the narrow politics of identity; it brings together a variety of different identities and struggles – which would otherwise have little in common – around the common terrain of contesting capitalist globalisation. Moreover, this is a movement of 'transversal' struggles which are not confined to national borders – activists not only travel to other countries to take part in demonstrations, but also attempt to highlight, through various forms of direct action, particular situations of oppression and exploitation that might be going on in other parts of the world.[12]

The other theme that I wanted to emphasise here is the one of disidentification: the idea that radical politics today involves not so much the assertion of a particular identity – sexuality, gender, ethnicity – as a subtraction or disentangling from one's established social identity. Is it possible to have a politics without identity, and, if so, how does this challenge the society of control? Agamben speaks of the 'coming politics', a politics and a community that no longer seeks to represent itself, no longer claims for itself a particular identity, and therefore cannot be incorporated within the representative structures of the state. The example he uses is the uprising in Tiananmen Square in 1989: this was a political gathering that did not articulate concrete demands – apart from vague references to 'democracy' – or otherwise try to represent itself as a specific identity. Its sheer incommunicability was perceived as an intolerable threat by the Communist regime: indeed, what the state cannot tolerate, according to Agamben, is that singularities 'form a community without affirming an identity, that humans co-belong without any representable condition of belonging' (Agamben 1993: 86). The radical nature of this political gathering lay in the fact that it was a community of 'whatever' singularities – people who no longer identified themselves in any particular or specific way, but simply came together, not on the basis of any pre-existing commonality, but rather as belonging to a community 'purely anonymously' (Wall 1999: 121). Perhaps a more politically trivial version of this might be found in the contemporary phenomenon of 'flash mobbing', where masses of complete strangers, upon receiving a mobile phone text message, gather together in a public place, make some unintelligible gesture or sound, and then depart.

In a control society based not so much around identity but *identification* – where individuals have to be constantly identified and monitored – perhaps the most radical gesture is that of anonymity and the refusal to be identified. And perhaps a politics of resistance can be constructed along the lines of a 'whatever community' – a new form of relationship in which people can come together anonymously, and where they can create new ways of communicating, new ways of being together that are not based on the need to identify oneself. Perhaps such a politics of the indiscernible and anonymous is what Deleuze and Guattari mean when they talk about becoming-minor.[13] Maybe in the society of control, the only way for the people to become visible – to affirm its place at the centre of politics – is to become *invisible*, to form a singularity that no longer seeks to represent itself.

Conclusion

Resisting the technologies of control is not simply a matter of destroying its machinery, although this might be an important aspect of it. Nor is it a matter of enthusiastically embracing technology and using it for subversive purposes – although once again, we should not discount the radical implications of things like 'hactivism', 'Internet activism', independent media, blogging and so on. Rather, resistance is a matter of understanding the logic of control, and creating new forms of politics – new ways of being together – which transcend it. As Deleuze says: 'But the machines don't explain anything, you have to analyse the collective apparatuses of which the machines are just one component' (Deleuze 1995: 175). Perhaps, then, to overcome the society of control, we need to construct a new collective apparatus – a new collective politics based on the people and its radical potential.

References

Agamben, G. (1993), *The Coming Community: Notes on Politics*, trans. M. Hardt, Minneapolis: University of Minnesota Press.

Agamben, G. (2002), 'Security and Terror', *Theory & Event*, 5 (4); http://muse.jhu.edu/journals/theory_and_event

Agamben, G. (2005), *State of Exception*, trans. K. Attell, Chicago: University of Chicago Press.

Badiou, A. (2003), *Saint Paul: The Foundation of Universalism*, trans. R. Brassier, Stanford: Stanford University Press.

Baudrillard, J. (2002), *The Spirit of Terrorism*, trans. C. Turner, London: Verso.

Butler, J. (2004), *Precarious Life: The Powers of Mourning and Violence*, London: Verso.

Campbell, N. D. (2004), 'Technologies of Suspicion: Coercion and Compassion in Post-disciplinary Surveillance Regimes', *Surveillance & Society* 2 (1): 78–92.

Day, R. J. F. (2005), *Gramsci is Dead: Anarchist Currents in the Newest Social Movements*, London: Pluto Press.

Deleuze, G. (1995), *Negotiations*, trans. M. Joughin, New York: Columbia University Press.

Deleuze, G. and F. Guattari (1986), *Kafka: Towards a Minor Literature*, trans. D. Polan, Minneapolis: University of Minnesota Press.

Deleuze, G. and F. Guattari (1988), *A Thousand Plateaus: Capitalism and Schizophrenia*, trans. B. Massumi, London: Athlone Press.

Deleuze, G. and C. Parnet (1987), *Dialogues*, trans. H. Tomlinson, New York: Columbia University Press.

Foucault, M. (1979), *History of Sexuality, Vol. 1: An Introduction*, trans. R. Hurley, London: Allen Lane.

Foucault, M. (2002), 'Truth and Juridical Forms', in *Michel Foucault: Essential Works 1954–1984, Volume Three: Power,* London: Penguin.

Foucault, M. (2003), *Society Must Be Defended: Lectures at the Collège De France 1975–76*, trans. D. Macey, London: Allen Lane.

Foucault, M. (2004), *Naissance de la biopolitique: Cours au College de France, 1978–1979*, Paris: Seuil/Gallimard.

Foucault, M. and G. Deleuze (1977), 'Intellectuals and Power', in *Language, Counter-Memory, Practice: Selected Essays and Interviews*, trans. D. F. Bouchard and S. Simon, Ithaca: Cornell University Press.

Gordon, C. (1991), 'Governmental Rationality: An Introduction', in G. Burchell, C. Gordon and P. Miller (eds), *The Foucault Effect: Studies in Governmentality*, Chicago: University of Chicago Press.

Hardt, M. (1998), 'The Withering of Civil Society', in E. Kaufman and K. J. Heller (eds), *Deleuze and Guattari: New Mappings in Politics, Philosophy and Culture*, Minneapolis: University of Minnesota Press.

Hardt, M. and A. Negri (2000), *Empire*, Cambridge, MA: Harvard University Press.

Laclau, E. (2005), *On Populist Reason*, London: Verso.

May, T. (2005), *Gilles Deleuze: An Introduction*, Cambridge: Cambridge University Press.

Mouffe, C. (2000), *The Democratic Paradox*, London: Verso.

Neal, A. (2004), 'Cutting off the King's Head: Foucault's *Society Must Be Defended* and the Problem of Sovereignty', *Alternatives*, 29 (4): 373–98.

Rancière, J. (1999), *Disagreement: Politics and Philosophy*, trans. J. Rose, Minneapolis: University of Minnesota Press.

de Tocqueville, A. (1966), *Democracy in America*, trans. George Lawrence, New York: Harper & Row.

Wall, T. C. (1999), *Radical Passivity: Levinas, Blanchot and Agamben*, Albany: SUNY Press.

Virilio, Paul (2000), *The Information Bomb*, London: Verso.

Žižek, S. (2000), *The Ticklish Subject: the Absent Centre of Political Ontology*, London: Verso.

Notes

1. It is interesting to examine the recent ID card 'debate' in the UK: after the government's argument that ID cards would be an essential weapon in the 'war on terrorism' was found to be unconvincing, it now claims that ID cards are really being introduced to crack down on illegal immigration and identity theft.

2. Perhaps we are seeing the installation of a global surveillance system – a 'globalitarianism' as Virilio (2000) calls it – where, through electronic satellite communication and real-time monitoring, the entire planet becomes subjected to a permanent and overexposed visibility; where everything is revealed and yet nothing is intelligible.

3. In the UK, the infamous ASBOs or 'Anti-Social Behaviour Orders' dreamt up by the New Labour government are now being used against people who play loud music, ride their bicycles on the footpath or even those who wear 'hoods' in an intimidating manner.

4. Foucault (2003) suggests, for instance, that the Holocaust could be seen as an instance of biopolitics: the attempt to eliminate the European Jewry was seen by the Nazis, perversely, as a way of preserving the biological health and integrity of the German population.

5. On a number of occasions the US Attorney General has sought to legalise and normalise the practice of torture, redefining it to include only practices which result in 'significant organ failure or death' – thus potentially allowing an almost medieval range of torture techniques.

6. On this see especially Andrew Neal (2004), and also Judith Butler (2004).

7. In response to the Supreme Court ruling that struck down military tribunals (Hamdan v Rumsfeld) the Bush Administration introduced legislation into

Congress that would essentially rewrite the Geneva Convention on questions of torture and the treatment of detainees.

8. Anti-terrorist legislation is increasingly being used against dissidents and protesters – for instance anti-globalisation and animal liberation activists.

9. One thinks here of the multiplicity of passwords and codes one has to remember in order to perform the most mundane daily activities – accessing one's bank account or paying utility bills.

10. For a good discussion of the limitations of multicultural identity politics, see Žižek (2000: 215–21).

11. Todd May (2005) also uses the anti-globalisation movement as a possible example of a Deleuzian politics.

12. We should also note that many direct action strategies directly contest aspects of the control society. Richard Day (2005) documents a number of direct action techniques that draw attention to the prevalence of surveillance technology: for instance, the Surveillance Camera Players (SCP) perform live plays in front of surveillance cameras – such as scenes from Big Brother. Also, the 'No Border' network – a loose coalition of affinity groups and grassroots organisations in Europe opposed to state border controls and restrictions on human migration – have campaigned against the Schengen Information System which is a government database used for information gathering and surveillance on 'illegal' immigrants (see http://www.noborder.org).

13. As Deleuze and Guattari state: 'There is nothing major or revolutionary except the minor' (1986: 26).

BECOMING

Chapter 7

Smash the Strata! A Programme for Techno-Political ®evolution

Tauel Harper

> Some people invoke the high technology of the world system of enslave-
> ment; but even, and especially, this machinic enslavement abounds in unde-
> cideable propositions and movements that, far from being a domain of
> knowledge reserved for sworn specialists, provides so many weapons for
> the becoming of everybody/everything, becoming-radio, becoming-
> electronic, becoming-molecular . . . Every struggle is a function of all of
> these undecideable propositions and constructs *revolutionary connections*
> in opposition to the *conjugation of the axiomatic*. (Deleuze and Guattari
> 2004b: 522)

Technology is latent with the possibility of developing a new mode of
techno-politics capable of redressing the instrumental abuses of modern
politics. No doubt such a possibility must contend with images of IBM
punch cards 'processing' humanity for murder during the Holocaust, as
well as deal with the one-dimensionality of the ubiquitous screens of the
spectacle. Nevertheless, in the work of Deleuze and Guattari there are
suggestions that we need not fear the role of technology in the struggle
against political oppression. Against a tradition of repression and discipline, they propose a programme of flight and flow. What I suggest here
is that Deleuze and Guattari present technological development as
fundamentally conducive to the emancipation of flows of desire.

Amongst theorists of techno-politics there is some trepidation when it
comes to reconciling the state and technology. Many of the state's services seem to require an authoritative 'General' which carries the legitimacy and control necessary for the provision of community services
such as education, security and common law over a geographical territory. Technology, on the other hand, seems to challenge the sources of
authority and reconfigure our sense of territory. In such a fluid world
where the desire for *ressentiment* urges individuals to cling on to what
security they can, against the security and discipline of a benevolent

Urstaat Deleuze and Guattari offer a vision of embracing anarchy. The role of the state therefore presents a confrontational element of Deleuzian thought: while Deleuze offers a plausible understanding of the transformation of the state under capital, this understanding seems to challenge the legitimacy of state organisation. For Deleuze and Guattari the state acts as an assemblage of capture that preserves the order of capitalism in the face of otherwise decoded flows. They suggest that even as flows of capital perpetuate the withering of the state as we know it, our Oedipal tendency is to feel this as lack and imagine a new General; the state is dead, long live the Urstaat.

The argument presented here is that new forms of technology such as the Internet and virtual reality might facilitate a rhizomatic reterritorialisation of the incumbent Urstaat. Whilst Deleuze and Guattari's perception of the irreconcilable antagonism between the Urstaat and the capitalist axiomatic appears to problematise Marxist readings of their work, the same capitalist axiomatic is a paean for Marxist understandings of the egalitarian distribution of technology (Poster 1997). With the constant sense of decoding and recoding provided by the axiomatic of capital, the deterritorialisation of existing technological assemblages may present a dynamic element of Deleuzian development that provides a fruitful outlet for desiring-production. More simply put, the fact that technology is continually developed by capital suggests that technology inherently deterritorialises and resists the ossification that otherwise poses a problem for political systems. Deleuze and Guattari's understanding of the importance of machines in determining the flows of desire makes them ideal theorists for exploring the political possibilities of technological development.

Initially I shall outline how different assemblages can be understood to encourage particular technological developments. The basic Deleuzian principle to be explored here is the idea that 'smooth' assemblages give rise to technologies of flight, whilst striated assemblages construct technologies of capture. I intend to use the example of the political assemblages of state and community to examine these technologies not only because of Deleuze and Guattari's avowed declaration that 'politics precedes being' (Deleuze and Guattari 2004b: 225) but because these particular assemblages serve as an illustrative example of the differing forms of capture and flight that are associated with politics. Following this I shall explore the suggestion that the deterritorialisation of the capitalist axiomatic presents a 'smooth space' which produces lines of flight. This exploration serves to identify how the current antagonism between the Urstaat and capital has created the conditions from which an emancipatory techno-political programme might emerge. The idea here is not to present a new axiom of development but rather to illustrate ways in which technological development, in all its nihilist entropy, opens up possibilities for a Deleuzian vision of micropolitics.

The Deleuzian Process of Technological Development

According to Deleuze and Guattari the starting point for technological development can be understood as deterritorialisation (2004b: 559–62). It is deterritorialisation which releases flows of desire which may either be reterritorialised, or give rise to lines of flight; and both of these moments have creative potential. According to Deleuze and Guattari, each assemblage is drawn towards stabilising and destabilising poles. As well as the cutting forces of the assemblage, there are always the stabilising forces, which seek to capture the flows that may otherwise lead to deterritorialisation (Deleuze and Guattari 2004b: 160). These stabilising forces are of archaeological interest to this techno-political program – they are the technologies of discipline and modulation that bind assemblages ever closer to the existing strata (Deleuze 1992). Of more interest to designers of technology are the movements of deterritorialisation. As an abstract machine brings the cutting forces of the assemblage together and concentrates them towards a deterritorialisation, it changes the composition of the assemblage from which it emerges. Technology is the tangible evidence of a deterritorialising assemblage.

It is important to understand that it is not the process of stratification that Deleuze and Guattari see as necessarily progressive. While the process of stratification seems to resemble the dialectical progress of historical materialism, in truth Deleuze and Guattari offer a far less determinist view of technological development, suggesting 'universal history is the history of contingencies and not the history of necessity' (Deleuze and Guattari 2004a: 154). The binding and slow change of stratification signals development but not necessarily evolution. Rather, it is the deterritorialisation of the assemblage which leads to the development of a line of flight that offers new connections to other assemblages and other machines. Technology is always already an assemblage with the potential of emancipation *and* capture. It is forever cutting towards a body without organs at the same time as it territorialises upon existing strata. What Deleuze and Guattari's theories gain in terms of avoiding dialectics is openness in regard to encouraging influences and connections – a willingness to experiment with creative subjects, even if they violate the imagined glory of a sacred whole.

Striated and Smooth Spaces: States and Communities

The determining feature of a line of flight that will evade capture and extend itself into a creative phase – a becoming – is that the line evolves from an assemblage constituted through its smooth space.[1] Conceptually, the constitution of a smooth space is determined by its level of rhizomatic connections. A smooth space can be understood to be a 'plane of intensity' that presents multiple rhizomatic connections. Opposed to this plane of intensity is the striated space of the assemblage of capture, of which the state serves as a paradigmatic model. As techno-politics is at issue here, I will briefly describe the operation of politics in these terms in order to further explicate the difference between the technologies developed by smooth and striated space.

The state is an illustrative example of a striated assemblage. The state is sedentary, remaining largely immobile despite the rapid amount of wild flow that surrounds it. Indeed as Deleuze and Guattari argue, the state acts to territorialise as many flows as possible. Even as the axiomatic of capitalism continues to break down all codes, the state manages to reterritorialise flows in such a way as to preserve its own being (Deleuze and Guattari 2004b: 560). It does this by creating striations in the state assemblage – assembling arborescent expert structures and extending the connections between the state and the existing strata.

The striated space of the state assemblage is most readily interpreted in the arborescent system of government which it legitimates. The whole process of representative democracy operates as a series of lines and junctions. The individual, which according to Deleuze and Guattari contains prior striations, interacts through its representative via a line of voting, or by registering one's intention to vote. These representatives then reconcile this political vector with existing striations in the assemblage. The social striations of majority voting were suggested 200 years ago by the ideologues of modern democracy, who acknowledged that this line drawing can never be truly representative. Voting and representation draw lines across both the state and the individual.[2] The technology of voting captures the flow of political expression and the abstract machine of representation channels it into the state assemblage. If the extent to which this forms a moment of capture is concerning, the effect of assemblage striations and nomads upon the direction of the captured line can be sickening. For instance, thanks to increasing lobbying expenditure, economic wealth has become a prerequisite for political influence, suggesting that if one wishes to be politically expressive, one must first be economically hyperproductive (Stratmann 2002). In such cases we can see that even if an abstract machine cuts away at the assemblage, nomadic forces may usurp the weak striation of the initial line of flight and contort it to yet another striation in the assemblage.

In conditions where technology is captured by the state, the technological assemblage under the piloting role of the state is directed towards enhancing the striations of the existing strata. The striations of borders which distinguish one state from another spring to mind, and in this context the 'war on terror' is an attempt to capture a line of flight caused by the deterritorialising impact of the flows of the international economy. In order to legitimise itself the state is keen to overcode and reterritorialise this surplus of flow – the state produces a ministry for homeland security, excuses intrusive security measures, or endorses the need for a £65 billion nuclear weapons upgrade. The state assemblage develops striations, emphasises them and then uses these divisions to justify a technological extension of the military-industrial assemblage under the auspices of the state. In such ways the state recaptures the flows of deterritorialised money and allegiance and in the process undermines the striation's capacity to develop into a line of flight. So we find that in the representative state it is arborescence that reigns supreme. Striations limit the possibility of lines of flight developing and escaping the captive assemblages.

Where the technological assemblage presents a chance of a new becoming is in the smooth spaces which orient it and in the deterritorialisations that occur upon it to develop lines of flight. These smooth spaces are rhizomatic, they don't feature the striation of arborescent assemblages and thus their acts of deterritorialisation suggest numerous opportunities for rhizomatic connections and numerous lines of flight. In opposition to the state, the smooth, nomadic space of the political assemblage can be conceived as community. Compared to the state, a community is a rhizome. Rather than depending upon an authoritative middle and distribution based upon lines (of paternal responsibility, of systemic imperatives), the assemblage of the community appears at all points to pertain to molecular analysis, as molar analysis of communities will always resort to a striated state-like space. So long as it remains molecular, rhizomatic, it remains smooth; in a sense it remains smooth entirely because community membership is itinerant rather than arbitrary. The multiplicity of possible connections, networks and interfaces is precisely what makes such models of organisation emancipatory.

Given this smooth space as a starting point, political expression can be understood to be an element of the war machine.[3] Seeing such creative potential within communities is complicit with Hannah Arendt's understanding that an emancipatory democracy must be entirely community based and itinerant. She argues that each time emancipatory political organisations have appeared 'they sprang up as spontaneous organs of the people, not only outside of all revolutionary parties but entirely unexpected by them and their leaders' (Arendt 1990: 249). Her point here is that, historically, communities which engage the spontaneity of expression with the normative weight of communicative legitimacy become revolutionary. The Deleuzian parallel is that the connective synthesis which gives rise to desiring-production is more likely to develop a line of flight if the assemblage itself is able to transform and transubstantiate so as to reduce the amount of disjunctive synthesis and avoid an anti-productive conjunctive synthesis.[4] In such conditions, the assemblage resembles an abstract machine of emancipation (Deleuze and Guattari 2004b: 564). Simply put, the more the assemblage can present a 'smooth', 'rhizomatic' territory, the more chances will exist for lines of flight to develop.

What this model reveals is the continuous and non-generalisable 'detachment' that Deleuzian theory offers us. Theorists such as Arendt are profoundly pessimistic about the role of technology in the political sphere, suggesting that it can only distort the ideal sense of self and reality.[5] However, Deleuze and Guattari insist against insinuating that there has ever been such an immutable and glorious ideal – to do so is to reincarnate the phallic myth which must always be experienced in terms of lack and in turn provides much of the Oedipal strength of the state (Deleuze and Guattari 2004a: 68, 114). Thus, Deleuzian theory encourages us to escape the idea of technological determinism and reinsert the influence of desiring-production into history. This aspect of Deleuzian theory is witnessed in the formula $n-1$, which describes the ever present possibility of becoming-other within a rhizome. It suggests that anything but totality is acceptable, but totality itself is unacceptable. As with Deleuze and Guattari's analogy of the orchid and the wasp as a rhizome, each territory exists in independent strata but the conjugation of the two strata produces a singularity, which can then be seen as constituent of the rhizome (Deleuze and Guattari 2004b: 11). It is the singularity, constituent of a zone of intensity, that is at the same time other and multiple, which provides the opportunity for exchange – for becoming-orchid or becoming-wasp – and generates the value of the rhizome. The General, the divine-right, the paternal state are all manifestations of Oedipus that essentially justify the capture of desiring-production by the capitalist axiomatic. Meanwhile, the rhizome, never representing a totality, nevertheless presents the interaction of many and multiple constituents. As such, the rhizome presents a fecund, collaborative basis for development that avoids the dangers of arborescence. According to Deleuze, it is in this way that technology evolves; through ignoring the possibility of tracings and urging the celebration of development and appreciation of rhizomatic relationships (Deleuze and Guattari 2004b: 13).

As designers we can also make the rather obtuse observation that at the basis of emancipatory technology lies a 'smooth space' of assemblage, and at the basis of captive technology lies a 'striated space' of assemblage. Behind the former is an acknowledgement of difference, multiplicity and partial objects; behind the latter is gravitation towards the objective that mandates a particular form of becoming. As theorists of techno-politics we can follow Deleuze and Guattari's notion that the role of philosophy is to identify the smooth spaces that can establish the becoming of 'new earths and new peoples' (Deleuze and Guattari 1994: 108). The venerable aspect of smooth spaces is that they don't channel desire into arborescent striations and they don't follow axioms like capital. Rather, they present a multitude of vectors as possible lines of flight. Smooth spaces, rhizomes, present moments of becoming; communities can become rhizomatic and smooth, or arborescent and striated.

With this in mind, I would like to suggest that open-source computer programming presents an embodiment of the process of rhizomatic becoming, where multitudes can conspire to produce a program which is never total and never complete. If we remember the rhizomatic formula $n-1$, never forming a totality and always being open to exchange, the Deleuzian framework offers an amazing promise of opportunities for collaboration in both technological and political development.

Techno-Politics as a Line of Flight

Having established that technology may be either captive or emancipatory depending on the striated or rhizomatic nature of the assemblage that gives rise to it, what I intend to do here is suggest how we might understand the capitalist axiomatic to be producing the conditions for a techno-political revolution. While it is true that the state has highly developed forms of capture, capital continues to decode flows and push towards its limits. Even a relative deterritorialisation on behalf of the state may produce its own lines of flight. I suggest that it is these lines of flight that are encouraging technology to develop towards communities.

Deleuze and Guattari insist that we are witnessing a deterritorialisation of the state, a process triggered by the decoding flows of capital (Deleuze and Guattari 2004a: 282). My argument is that the spaces of community, linked with rhizomatic technologies, present opportunities to redistribute political power in a way that maximises the emancipative force of desiring-production. This situation arises because capitalism has reached a limit – the limit of the legitimacy of the state as an overcoding assemblage (Buchanan and Parr 2007). Bearing in mind that capital only reaches limits when its limits can be reproduced on a wider scale (Deleuze and Guattari 2004a: 281), I shall explore the market as a new manifestation of the Urstaat, which undermines many of the striations of the typical state system. I shall explore ways in which the market opens up smooth spaces in an effort to re-establish the legitimacy of its overcoding and I suggest that by doing so, the market has created the conditions for a techno-political revolution.

The most contentious point here is that the capitalist state is pushing against a limit which it cannot expand upon using the state assemblage. Deleuze and Guattari warn that such a situation is always imminent – as capitalism wears down the legitimacy of states 'they recode with all their might, with world-wide dictatorship, local dictators, and an all powerful police, while decoding – or allowing the decoding of – the fluent qualities of their capital and their populations' (Deleuze and Guattari 2004a: 282). For instance, the forces of capital have deterritorialised the state to the point where the pressure of private industry upon the state to limit taxes has led to the privatisation of the majority of state services. The same capitalist axiomatic has eroded the possibility of meaningful attempts to limit the flow of capital across state borders.[6] The state thus finds itself witnessing an increase of flow along with reduced traditional legitimacy. With the loss of rational power, the Urstaat seeks to compensate through increasing the power of its Oedipal appeal. As Deleuze and Guattari imply in the passage just quoted, the state has used 'terror' as a universal fear to bolster the state's appeal to the increasingly dividual motives of voters. Despite the apparent success of these reterritorialisations a 'war on terror' is the last recourse of a state that is having difficulty territorialising, precisely because it cannot striate the international assemblage in a way that would make this extension of power legitimate.

The state constructs the legitimacy of the 'war on terror' through increasingly spectacular assemblages of capture. This construction, in turn, exacerbates the legitimacy of the state as a political assemblage. Thus technology is both reterritorialising and deterritorialising in the same instance. For instance, consider the role of the recently designed F-22 Raptor, which, at $121 million a unit, serves as a 'stealth fighter' for the US Air Force (Tirpak 2003: 25). In one sense the Raptor is able to capture desiring-production through implicating an Oedipal lack, its spectacular cost inducing one's consciousness to make the leap: 'One hundred and twenty one million? We really must need protection.' As a conjunctive synthesis such a thought reterritorialises sovereignty and the need for the state to protect us from insidious 'others'. However, as a spectacle the Raptor imbues a connective synthesis about the possibilities and power of the technical assemblage that in essence constitutes those it stands to 'shock and awe' within a smooth space that expands beyond state boundaries. Meanwhile, its cost presents a real limit for the state. Here we see that the state's demand for desiring-production is no longer sustained by that which is generated through the connection to the *state* assemblage; rather the state requires the desiring-production generated through connection to the technical assemblage. In terms of political expression, as the role of state technology becomes more spectacular, state institutions become less and less gratifying.

So what has happened to the line of flight created by deterritorialised political expression? Some suggest that this form of desiring-production is increasingly captured by ethnic groupings who seek to replace the Urstaat with a 'smoother' assemblage which comes replete with Oedipal striations (Brown 1998).[7] Others suggest that in a number of ways our political expressiveness is now channelled into the market assemblage in a way that is in fact axiomatic (Klein 2000). What makes the market particularly interesting as a new assemblage for desiring-production is that the market presents itself as a theoretically smooth space and seeks to court the legitimacy forfeited by the state.

It is perfectly understandable that within this milieu the market is the latest expansion of the Urstaat, the new 'state' that provides the overcoding of desire. The previously described move from state economy to market economies can be understood as the initial act of state deterritorialisation. Subsequently our desiring-production is reterritorialised as a false choice between private companies. Branding codes our political expressiveness in the material assemblage oriented towards conspicuous consumption. In terms of media, reality television programmes such as *Big Brother* and *Pop Idol* reterritorialise choice and judgement within the assemblage of entertainment. Communication technology has reterritorialised political expression through facilitating homepages, blogs and discussion boards. All of these acts are reterritorialisations through which the market has been able to capture the line of flight of creative political expression and contain it within the assemblage of existing epistrata. However, Deleuze and Guattari suggest that we need not fear this subsidence of the state, instead we should imagine the possibilities of harnessing the opportunities presented by these moments of deterritorialisation. In doing so, we are encouraged to

> Mimic the strata . . . Lodge yourself on a stratum, experiment with the
> opportunities it offers, find potential movements of deterritorialisation,
> possible lines of flight, experience them, produce flow conjunctions here
> and there . . . it is through meticulous relation with the strata that one suc-
> ceeds in freeing lines of flight. (Deleuze and Guattari 2004b: 178)

The market not only frees flows from capture in codes, it also develops
networks of exchange and reciprocity that are relatively free of
arborescent interference (Holland 2006: 203; Bay 2006: 100). The
development of the market has allowed us to see ways of reorganising
around itinerant communities rather than nation-states, localities or
ethnic groupings. Capital shows us the way to challenge the axiomatic
of state's monopoly on political power. Indeed the market is built upon
the promise of a 'smooth space' of transaction, a level playing field that
undermines the striations of race, class and borders.

Hence, the primary function of capital in undermining state-political
power is the development of communities as assemblages. The affectation of community is a part of the reterritorialisation contained within
the act of branding, where community membership and distinction are
promised as a benefit of consumption. It is true that these communities
are designed to imply a lack and their dominant striation remains
membership-through-consumption. Nevertheless, the striation of consumption is a blemish on the otherwise smooth and expansive surface
that capital tries to create. The more a brand tries to manipulate the
community's abstract machine of creative expression, the more pro-
nounced the striation of consumption becomes and the more cutting
edges of deterritorialisation take hold. Thus, the process of branding has
emphasised the connective synthesis that generates desiring-production
and yet it frustrates desiring-production to a point where it seeks to
escape the existing assemblage.

In an attempt to capture this desiring-production, market technologies have sought to become more responsive to consumer needs and
maintain their composition of communal consumption. Attempts to
register consumer opinions have extended the technological assemblage
necessary to establish communicative communities. As with extensions
of assemblages such as railways and electricity grids, capital has
developed the technologies to make the exchange between markets and
communities as immediate and real as possible (DeLanda 2006: 260). In
the process of capturing and harnessing the line of expressive communication, this has decoded the claims to legitimacy of many communities.
The more a corporation insinuates that it cares for a community, the
more the corporation's legitimacy depends upon responding to that

community's expressive concerns. Following Habermas (1996), in asking organisations and institutions to redeem the claims to truth they make, we can see that there are cutting edges to these deterritorialisations that may assist in freeing expressive communication.[8]

Further, the communicative methods necessary for meaningful political organisation may well be developed by market research. The development of cyberanalytics and the extension of information processing now harnessed by marketing techniques may be used to record and measure political opinion. Such technologies have grown directly out of the existing striations within the market yet when applied to the market as a political community, or as a collection of communities, these roots appear to have radicles – the striations descend and dissipate amongst a rhizome of an active community (Deleuze and Guattari 2004b: 16). If we are bound to continue with a staged representative politics, mediated selection processes such as those witnessed on *Pop Idol* and *Big Brother* produce a more concise and responsive scrutiny of candidates than the equally mediated representation of political elites we are currently subjected to.[9] As Arendt noted with regard to public display, there is something about the public nature of the judgement and alliance that enlivens such spectacles (Arendt 1958: 198). As seen in the recent pseudo-public confrontations about racism and bullying on reality TV, even banal entertainment can become-political.

The dangers of these methods of capture are exacerbated by the Urstaat's current control of the technological assemblage, but there is no reason to feel we must acquiesce to societies of control. This is not an either/or discussion but a series of extensions through experimentation. There is no reason why branded communities, encouraged by brands themselves, might not meet in a virtual forum to identify their own personal, unbranded, desires. To extend this line, the immersive technology necessary for gratifying ideal speaking forums may well be developed by a teledildonics company. These possibilities multiply exponentially as long as technology works for communities. As long as the market attempts to resurrect the Urstaat the more will it employ technology to develop communities. This certainly provides opportunities for other becomings.

The culmination of the market spreading over the entire earth as though it were a smooth space has been the increasing prominence of information and communication technologies as the market's assemblage. If one perceives the market as inherently striated, the extension of the Internet is yet another form of control through modulation. Along with their damning indictment of binary and their refusal to countenance any form of technological miracle (Deleuze and Guattari 2004a: 253),

Deleuze and Guattari also proclaim that a language of decoded flows, such as binary, is the ultimate flow of capitalism (Deleuze and Guattari 2004a: 261). Yet binary could equally be regarded as the ultimate encoded flow, which for the most part ensures the expansion of proprietary software but carries with it the technological stipulation that communities may configure their interfaces to interpret the binary according to their own codes. Insofar as these technologies present themselves as serving smooth spaces, the rhizomatic assemblage of the Internet presents an assemblage that is full of cutting edges and lines of flight.

Certainly, the 'publics' created on the Internet are more reflective of the contemporary material political conditions within which dividuals find themselves. Rather than being constrained to striated territories defined by their physicality, Internet public spaces can encompass the smooth assemblages of communities engaged in discussion. Hence the Internet has been conducive to developing micropolitical spaces as well as macropolitical alliances on international issues such as labour and environmental standards. What is perhaps most revolutionary about this development is its indication that the habit of critique has the infrastructure to follow capital. Corporations and big business have developed globally to overcome the alleged incommensurability of state assemblages; the Internet allows communication and critique to achieve the same global spread. 'Technopolitics thus helps labour create global alliances in order to combat increasingly transnational corporations' (Kellner 2001: 20). By reflecting the molecular rather than necessarily molar subjectivities of dividuals, the Internet provides malleable and multiple communities that may respond elegantly and appropriately to contemporary political issues.

Finally, there is every reason to believe that the act of computer programming provides an ideal outlet for the desiring-production generated through the passive synthesis of connection. Or rather, the processes of deterritorialisation evidenced in open-source software creation are replete with opportunities to develop lines of flight and acts of becoming. Computer programming is always a process of deterritorialisation – it never accepts a totality, it proceeds through alpha, beta and gamma models in a continual process of deterritorialisation and reterritorialisation which obeys no General and is based upon a point of intersection of multiple assemblages. Open-source and collective experimental methods make such collaboration a living programme of n–1. Taking from Holland's illuminating work, truly creative and emancipatory becomings are 'immanent to the activity itself, not imposed by a transcendent instance from above; where itinerant following and group creation prevail over the issuing and obeying of commands' (Holland 2006: 195).

The continual reflexivity of open-source software enables communities to constitute themselves as acts of desiring-production.

The other great benefit of computer programming as an outlet for desiring-production is its virtuality. Virtual is 'real without being actual, ideal without being abstract' (Deleuze 1988: 96–7). Political expression within virtual communities has the opportunity to be decentred, without need for a General, and completely gratifying. Perhaps most importantly, virtual communities provide an opportunity to be productive without being material. The lack of materiality means that open-source-designed communicative communities can proliferate to reflect every community that has a political will – be they virtual or real. This proliferation can satisfy and employ desiring-production in a fluid way that generates a communal dividend with minimal environmental impact.[10] Virtual worlds can be built and squandered, yet through interaction with the political assemblage such worlds may always relate to and define the real.

From here it is understandable that we therefore seek to create Internet forums that will provide an outlet for the expressive tendencies of new communities. I suggest that the conditions for a techno-political revolution spring from rhizomatic communication technologies providing universal access to coding practices.[11] Hannah Arendt saw this condition as being something close to a political utopia:

> A council-state of this sort, to which the principle of sovereignty would be wholly alien, would be admirably suited to federations of the most various kinds, especially because in it power would be constituted horizontally and not vertically. But if you ask me now what prospect it has of being realized, then I must say to you: Very slight, if at all. And yet perhaps, after all – in the wake of the next revolution. (Arendt 1972: 233)

The assemblage of rhizomatic communication allows us to organise communication to reflect communicative communities in such a way as to bypass the physical limitations of territory and usurp the development of communities by the market. What I have in mind here is beyond the communicative broadening and strengthening of NGOs. What I have in mind is an open-source movement of reterritorialisation, where the technical language is constantly becoming-open, where its body without organs remains the open functioning of the space, and where a community is possible which makes the most of the desiring-production generated through the synthesis of connection. Such a virtual community possesses the potential of unlimited and ideal creativity. Production collectives, consumer organisations, environmental agencies, they can each construct their desiring machines in order to become-rhizomatic, become-political.[12]

The Dangers

Before concluding that what remains before us is the inevitable development of an emancipatory techno-political programme, we would do well
to remind ourselves of the four dangers – fear, clarity, power and the
great disgust (Deleuze and Guattari 2004b: 250–5). These present real
threats to a techno-political programme of emancipation and should be
used to moderate any technological designs.

The first danger is fear. Fear is understood to be gravitation towards
the safety of the known, the tendency towards Nietzschean *ressentiment*: 'We are always afraid of losing. Our security, the great molar
organisation that sustains us, the arborescences that we cling to, the
binary machines that give us a well defined status, the resonances we
enter into, the system of overcoding that dominates us – we desire all
that' (Deleuze and Guattari 2004b: 250). Like any journey, the possibility of venturing away from a familiar assemblage can be frightening. It
is often only once the journey is begun that the sense and inevitability of
the departure becomes apparent. The greatest threat to techno-politics is
that the fear of the unknown will stop us making the journey at all and
bind us closer to the existing strata. However, as I have identified here,
there are many other forces encouraging us to leave, such as the market
and the repressed desiring-production of political expression. Deleuze
and Guattari leave us in no doubt: since the 'great' democratic revolutions *everything* has changed except democracy. The idea that the
current democratic assemblage is fulfilling political will has not been
tenable for the last fifty years.[13] It is fear that maintains this assemblage
and, by implication, its striations.

The second danger is clarity. The danger with clarity is that we see
things too well and in place of clinging to the known for fear of the
unknown, we cling to our own lines of flight with absolute faith and
thus come to dominate rhizomatic engagements. The error here is the
same as with the first danger, to assume a totality that defies n–1 and
presume that our flight is the only response. In the case of techno-politics
the danger is that a dissemination of politics to the level of community
will only result in more definitive striations between dividual aspects of
community. Amongst the viral effects of this danger is a technical plu-
tocracy, which spreads its influence throughout all the communities it
encounters by virtue of its paternal affectations.[14] It is important to keep
in mind that these are ideas for designs not designs for ideas. We are to
create spaces for desiring-production to become political, but only in the
hope that these spaces remain multiple and fulfilling, not determining.

The third danger is power. The danger of power is that it manipulates the line of flight and the original striation in an attempt to capture the line and increase power by inculcating other assemblages. A techno-elite is a very real danger within techno-politics, just as a media-elite threatens the 'proper' function of state politics. In both cases the powerful depend upon the assemblage to give them power, but extend their power through capturing lines of flight. In a sense, we need to be wary of the nomads who would be Generals. The transition from striated to smooth spaces is particularly dangerous in terms of allowing new striations to be imposed by other lines. The needs of techno-politics in response to the danger of power are to ensure that technological language remains open and that technology itself is a conduit to community rather than a determinant of community. Any over-reliance upon technology is liable to create striations within the community that supports that technology. We must avoid the temptation to network control and resurrect the Urstaat.

The fourth and final danger is the great disgust. The great disgust involves the fear that lines of flight, with their entropic nature, are continuously invoking a passion for abolition that may become an end in itself. In terms of technology I believe this suggests inbuilt obsolescence, fashion or taste as absolute deterritorialisation. It is an immersion in the virtual at the complete expense of the real, a retreat once again to the perfection of nothingness. A broader failure to consider the virtuous employment of desiring-production is manifest in the technology of 'standby' modes and the electric chair . . . the gas chambers and the human *de*-ssembly line of the Holocaust. Deleuze and Guattari are particularly scathing of such technological developments as an infusion of anti-production and stupidity necessary to maintain enough 'lack' to sustain capitalist acquisition (Deleuze and Guattari 2004a: 256). In order to avoid the great disgust we must remember that deterritorialisation is not an end in itself. The goal is not a victory of nihilism but to allow legitimacy and action to once again be constituted through an assemblage that is immanent to our own desiring-production.

These four dangers invoke a need for consideration and, mostly, a need to be rhizomatic in order to enable and facilitate becomings rather than determine them. While the latter three dangers of techno-politics have been enunciated strongly by contemporary theorists, these elaborations only serve to endorse the first danger of fear. This is an argument against fear. If we remain mindful of these dangers, we need not fear technology that harnesses the political will of communities. Such technology should, in fact, present new opportunities for becoming-political that harness desiring-production in a way that will benefit the development of both communities and technologies. What makes me optimistic that technology may give rise to smooth spaces of assemblage is the continual deterritorialisation which accompanies technological development. As long as this deterritorialisation takes place, systems will leak, reterritorialisations will be incomplete, and lines of flight will develop.

Finally, as strong as our desire to see the state resurrected may be, it is dangerous to entertain the possibility that we might, from this situation, create a benign paternal state. If the state manages to further capture technology, this will only serve to develop the repressive power of an already untenable state assemblage. Such an occurrence will only serve to further the possibility of the great disgust. Against statist versions of techno-political revisionism, Deleuze and Guattari present political (r) evolution as a process of flow. Although they recognise the cultural destruction wrought by capitalism, they do not seek to turn back the tide of history, but rather to harness the historical moment of the capitalist axiomatic. The decoding power of capitalism unleashes flows which give rise to new connections for desiring-production. I would like to suggest that if we are witnessing an absolute deterritorialisation of the state, then the smooth space of community presents an alternative positive space within which to develop the roles of the state. And if we are witnessing a relative deterritorialisation of the state, this process has given rise to lines of flight that are equally positive. To take up an outdated idiom, techno-politics will proceed through either evolution or revolution.

References

Arendt, H. (1958), *The Human Condition*, Chicago: University of Chicago Press.
Arendt, H. (1972), *Crises of the Republic*, San Diego: Harvest/Harcourt Brace Jovanovich.
Arendt, H. (1990), *On Revolution*, London: Penguin Books.
Bay, T. (2006), 'I Knew there were Kisses in the Air', in M. Fuglsang and B. M. Sorensen (eds), *Deleuze and the Social*, Edinburgh: Edinburgh University Press.
Brown, D. (1998), 'Why is the Nation-State so Vulnerable to Ethnic Nationalism?', *Nations and Nationalism*, 4 (1): 1–15.
Buchanan, I. (2008), *Reader's Guide to Anti-Oedipus*, London: Continuum.
Buchanan, I. and A. Parr (2006), 'Introduction', in I. Buchanan and A. Parr (eds), *Deleuze and the Contemporary World*, Edinburgh: Edinburgh University Press.
DeLanda, M. (2006), 'Deleuzian Social Ontology and Assemblage Theory', in M. Fuglsang and B. M. Sorensen (eds), *Deleuze and the Social*, Edinburgh: Edinburgh University Press.
Deleuze, G. (1988), *Bergsonism*, trans. H. Tomlinson and B. Habberjam, New York: Zone Books.
Deleuze, G. (1992), 'Postscript on Societies of Control', *October*, 59: 3–7.
Deleuze, G. and F. Guattari (1994), *What Is Philosophy?*, trans. G. Burchell and H. Tomlinson, New York: Columbia University Press.

Deleuze, G. and F. Guattari (2004a), *Anti-Oedipus: Capitalism and Schizophrenia*, trans. R. Hurley, M. Seem and H. Lang, London: Continuum.

Deleuze, G. and F. Guattari (2004b), *A Thousand Plateaus: Capitalism and Schizophrenia*, trans. B. Massumi, London: Continuum.

Dewey, J. (1927), *The Public and Its Problems*, Chicago: Swallow.

Ebo, B. (ed.), (2001), *Cyberimperialism? Global Relations in the New Electronic Frontier*, Connecticut: Praeger Publishers.

Froomkin, M. (2003), 'Habermas@Discourse.Net', *Harvard Law Review*, 116 (3): 749–873.

Habermas, J. (1996), *Between Facts and Norms: Contributions to a Discourse Theory of Law and Democracy*, trans. W. Rehg, Cambridge, MA: MIT Press.

Holland, E. (2006), 'Nomad Citizenship and Global Democracy', in M. Fuglsang and B. M. Sorensen (eds), *Deleuze and the Social*, Edinburgh: Edinburgh University Press.

Kellner, D. (2001), 'Globalisation, Technopolitics and Revolution', *Theoria*, 98: 14–36.

Klein, N. (2000), *No Logo*, New York: Picador.

Patton, P. (2000), *Deleuze and the Political*, London: Routledge.

Pitkin, H. (1998), *The Attack of the Blob: Hannah Arendt's Concept of the Social*, Chicago: University of Chicago Press.

Poster, M. (1997), 'Cyberdemocracy: Internet and the Public Sphere', in D. Holmes (ed.), *Virtual Politics: Identity and Community in Cyberspace*, Thousand Oaks: Sage.

Schumpeter, J. (1954), *Capitalism, Socialism and Democracy*, London: Allen & Unwin.

Stiglitz, J. (2002), *Globalisation and its Discontents*, London: Penguin Books.

Stratmann, T. (2002), 'Can Special Interests Buy Congressional Votes? Evidence from Financial Services Legislation', *Journal of Law and Economics*, 45: 345–73.

Tirpak, J. (2003), 'The F/A-22 Gets Back on Track', *Journal of the Air Force Association*, 86 (3): 22–8.

Williams, J. (2005), 'On the Popular Vote', *Political Science Quarterly*, 58 (4): 637–46.

Wolin, S. (1993), 'Democracy: Electoral and Athenian', *PS: Political Science and Politics*, 26: 475–8.

Notes

I would like to thank Ian Buchanan for his invaluable guidance and feedback on this project.

1. This dichotomy forms a central part of the schema of *A Thousand Plateaus* (Deleuze and Guattari 2004b: 388–551) and is explored thoroughly in Paul Patton's *Deleuze and the Political* (Patton 2000: 88–132). Possibly, the perception of 'smoothness' is forever determined by perspective and comparison, or by the instruments we use for analysis. One may consider marble smooth when viewed next to a rock. The same marble appears striated and irregular when viewed through an electron microscope (although here again, relatively smooth spaces may appear).

2. The political alienation that an individual experiences in modern democracy was notably anticipated by Jefferson and by de Toqueville and has been described by Hannah Arendt in her critique of utilitarian public space. This she sees as being dominated by lines of authority and instrumental formulae which, as Deleuze and Guattari expect, condition the experience of self in a machinic fashion (Arendt 1958).

3. As understood by Paul Patton to refer to those assemblages that develop in antagonism to the state (Patton 2000: 110–11).
4. The relationship between these syntheses and desiring-production is explored by Ian Buchanan (2008).
5. This point is most thoroughly explored by Arendt in *The Human Condition* (1958: 238, 289) and forms the centrepoint of Hannah Pitkin's critique in *The Attack of the Blob* (1998).
6. For evidence of the role of the World Bank and World Trade Organisation in enforcing this deterritorialisation as emblematic of the subsidence of the state under the forces of capital, see Stiglitz (2002).
7. Deleuze and Guattari discuss this phenomenon themselves (2004a: 114).
8. Given Habermas' insistence on exploring the contingent conditions of communicative legitimacy rather than universal truth (and thereby avoiding the Oedipalisation of a glorious whole) it seems antagonistic for Brian Massumi to regard Habermas' project as 'Prussian mind-meld' in his introduction to *A Thousand Plateaus* (Deleuze and Guattari 2004b: xii).
9. For an exploration of participation in reality TV 'elections' as a line of flight see Williams (2005)
10. For a thorough explanation of fluidity and contemporary technology see David Savat's chapter in this edition.
11. Some evidence that rhizomatic networks give rise to ideal communicative communities is assembled by Froomkin (2003).
12. This new form of citizenship has been explored by Eugene W. Holland in a previous volume in this series (Holland 2006: 202).
13. See Arendt (1958), Dewey (1927), Habermas (1996), Schumpeter (1954), Wolin (1993).
14. See Ebo (2001) for an analysis of this situation.

Chapter 8

Deleuze and the Internet

Ian Buchanan

> I've found myself more and more wary of Google out of some primal liz-
> ard-brain fear of giving too much control of my data to one source.
>
> John Battelle

There can be no doubt that the Internet has transformed practically
every aspect of contemporary life, especially the way we think about the
body and its relation to identity and to place, once the twin cornerstones
of social existence – in social life you are always someone from somewhere, the son or daughter of so-and-so from such-and-such town.
These details of our existence, which are essentially historical, although
they may sometimes take a form biologists think belongs to their domain
(gender, race, body shape), segment us in different ways, slicing and
dicing us this way and that so that we adhere to the conventions and
demands of the socius itself.

> We are segmented in a *binary* fashion, following the great major dualist
> oppositions: social classes, but also men–women, adults–children, and so
> on. We are segmented in a *circular* fashion, in ever larger circles, ever wider
> disks or coronas, like Joyce's 'letter': my affairs, my neighbourhood's
> affairs, my city's, my country's, the world's . . . We are segmented in a
> *linear* fashion, along a straight line or a number of straight lines, of which
> each segment represents an episode or 'proceeding': as soon as we finish
> one proceeding we begin another, forever proceduring or procedured, in
> the family, in the school, in the army, on the job. (Deleuze and Guattari
> 1987: 208–9)

These segmentations penetrate our being, they appear and even feel
bodily, especially the apparently natural attributes of gender and race,
but they are not for all that visceral. Deleuze and Guattari are very specific about this. They describe these socially orchestrated captures of the
body – gender, race, class, work, family, and so on – as 'incorporeal
transformations'. If today – as Deleuze foresaw with typical acuity in his

short essay on what he labelled 'the society of control' – our credit card and social security numbers are more significant identity and place markers than the colour of our skin or where we went to school, that isn't because the 'meat' of our bodies has lately been superseded in its cultural significance by our bloodless digital 'profile'. Rather what has happened is that one incorporeal 'apparatus of capture' has been succeeded by another – the segmentations of gender, race and class have been supplanted by the segmentations of debt and credit. 'A man is no longer a man confined but a man in debt' (Deleuze 1995: 181).

In effect, our body has been replaced as the principal site of power by our profile. But this does not mean that the age of the body has been succeeded by the age of the body without organs, as many of the Internet-inclined have argued, because the disciplined or segmented body was just as much a body without organs as is the ghostly profile that government agencies and banks now make of us and store in their databases for referral whenever we want a loan, a driver's licence, or to leave the country for a vacation. It will no doubt come as a surprise to many that the clearest confirmation of this point, that the disciplined body is already a body without organs, is to be found in Foucault's *Discipline and Punish*, which is often read as a history of the body.[1] Referring to Kantorowitz's influential thesis that the King effectively has two bodies, one that lives and dies and another that is immortal, Foucault writes:

> If the surplus power possessed by the king gives rise to the duplication of his body, has not the power exercised on the subjected body of the condemned man given rise to another type of duplication? That of a 'non-corporal', a 'soul', as Maby called it. This history of this 'micro-physics' of the punitive power would then be a genealogy or an element in a genealogy of the modern 'soul'. Rather than seeing this soul as the reactivated remnants of an ideology, one would see it as the present correlative of a certain technology of power over the body. It would be wrong to say that the soul is an illusion, or an ideological effect. On the contrary, it exists, it has a reality, it is produced permanently around, on, within the body by the functioning of a power that is exercised on those punished – and, in a more general way, on those one supervises, trains and corrects, over madmen, children at home and at school, the colonised, over those who are stuck at a machine and supervised for the rest of their lives. (Foucault 1979: 29)

The soul is the body without organs seen in its disciplined aspect, but it is not the whole of the body without organs. Foucault's vision of the duplication of the body is an impoverished one in comparison to Deleuze and Guattari's, and he pays the price for this conceptual diminishment by leaving himself with no plausible means of explaining how or why one might adhere to the conventions and demands of the socius itself except through coercion. The full body without organs is the soul animated by desire. Foucault's description of the modern soul is instructive nonetheless because it points up the degree to which the body without organs is a social rather than individual concept: we all have our own body without organs, but it is plugged into a larger entity that is the body without organs of all bodies without organs, or the plane of consistency. This larger entity that all our individual bodies without organs are plugged into is society's own body without organs and it is my contention that we can only properly understand this particular concept if we apprehend it at this level.

The Priority of Marx

As a first measure in standing this concept back on its feet, then, it has to be recognised that although Antonin Artaud is the source of the phrase 'body without organs' his work plays only a very small part in its theorisation as a concept. This is not to say that Artaud is unimportant to Deleuze and Guattari, but the truth is they tend to treat his work as pre-philosophical, as a source of symptoms or ideas rather than concepts. Moreover, focusing on Artaud reinforces the misperception that the body without organs is the exclusive preserve of individuals. Correcting this view requires that we look to the concept's more important conceptual sources: Lacan, Spinoza and Marx. This list may be in either ascending or descending order of importance depending on how you look at things: Deleuze and Guattari attribute the invention of the concept to Lacan, but this seems to be of significance only inasmuch as they can use it against Lacanians. They suggest that the architecture of the concept was foreshadowed by Spinoza, and they take from this source the notions of longitude and latitude which they use to map the body without organ's components. They reserve for Marx, however, the special distinction of showing us how this concept works in everyday life at the level of the mode of production. In light of this, I want to argue for the priority of Marx in any reading of the body without organs on the grounds that, to follow a Jamesonian logic, the Marxian position subsumes the other two (Jameson 1981: 10, 47).

On its first or Lacanian approximation, the body without organs is simply the constellation of partial objects constituting our desire in its transitive mode. It is described by Deleuze and Guattari as the 'real inorganisation' of desire such as one finds on the reverse side of the Big O:

'[There] desire is shifted into the order of production, related to its molecular elements, where it lacks nothing, because it is defined as the natural and sensuous objective being, at the same time as the Real is defined as the objective being of desire' (Deleuze and Guattari 1983: 311). Desire, on this understanding, constantly surpasses the neat triangle of mommy-daddy-me imposed by psychoanalysis.

On its second or Spinozist approximation, the body without organs is 'the immanent substance, in the most Spinozist sense of the word; the partial objects [that is, Lacan's *petit a*] are like its ultimate attributes, which belong to it precisely insofar as they are really distinct and cannot on this account exclude or oppose one another' (Deleuze and Guattari 1983: 327). But the significance of this insight can really only be seen when it is rewritten into a Marxian discourse, as Deleuze and Guattari do for us in the opening pages of *Anti-Oedipus*. If we want to have some idea of the forces exerted by the body without organs, then we must first establish a parallel between desiring-production and social production. To put it another way, we have to establish that desire functions on the same level as the real. However, Deleuze and Guattari then go on to say this parallel is to be treated as strictly heuristic, at least in the first instance.

> Its one purpose is to point out the fact that the forms of social production, like those of desiring-production, involve an unengendered nonproductive attitude, an element of antiproduction coupled with the process, a full body that functions as a socius. This socius may be the body of the earth, that of the tyrant, or capital. This is the body that Marx is referring to when he says that it is not the product of labour, but rather appears as its natural or divine presupposition. (Deleuze and Guattari 1983: 10)

This is the body without organs in its social aspect: 'It falls back on (*il se rabat sur*) all production constituting a surface over which the forces and agents of production are distributed, thereby appointing for itself all surplus production and arrogating to itself both the whole and the parts of the process, which now seem to emanate from it as a quasi cause' (Deleuze and Guattari 1983: 10).

In *A Thousand Plateaus* Deleuze and Guattari transform this insight into an analytic principle: the body without organs has two phases, an initial phase of construction and a subsequent phase of making things circulate (Deleuze and Guattari 1987: 162). Judith Butler (1990) has demonstrated that the concept of gender – not the actual experience of gender – follows precisely this course. What she effectively claims, without using this terminology, is that gender is an incorporeal transformation: the very labels 'man' or 'woman' seize and transform us. Gender is an attribute – an effect – that penetrates our bodies and functions there as 'quasi cause' of everything we do. We are not born into our gender, we assume it, but once it has taken hold we act in its name. This effect interacts with other effects, such as race and class. As Butler points out, even if one accepted that it was possible to choose one's gender, it is nevertheless impossible to choose not to have any gender at all. You thus desire on gender, it is part of your body without organs. Gender is a rigged game – you can choose to be man, woman, or transgendered, but you cannot choose to be non-gendered because the very notion of 'sex' as some neutral biological (that is, non-cultural) given is simply the other half of the equation.

Gender and sex work together in a manner Deleuze and Guattari describe as biunivocal. Each effect functions as the concrete proof of existence of the other – this is what it means to say they are quasi causes. We oscillate between the two, jumping from one circle of hell to the other. Gender, Deleuze and Guattari argue, is the mechanism power needs to exert itself. Part of the difficulty Butler has in explaining how gender and sex differ from one another (yet operate together) stems from the fact that these terms have the appearance of being, as it were, unengendered or naturally occurring. But, as she effectively wants to argue, but doesn't quite have the vocabulary to do so, they are very far from naturally occurring – they are engendered but in such a way that they seem to fall back on themselves and smother their origins from view so as to appear unengendered. This is how the body without organs operates. Its chief operation is to 'fall back on' itself and create a smooth plane for desire. This example points to what is perhaps the key feature of the body without organs: it functions as pure presupposition, that is, the thought or idea which thought cannot grasp. It is like our soul, always there, always in need of work, and always unreachable.

The body without organs is not a 'feedback loop', as Bard and Söderqvist suggest, because what occurs on the body without organs is not the same thing, and isn't constructed in the same way, as the body without organs itself (Bard and Söderqvist 2002: 113). What occurs on the body without organs doesn't feed back into it. To continue the example above – if I cross-dress I may be playing with (my) gender, but I'm not thereby altering it, whether on an experiential level or a theoretical level. By the same token, because the body without organs is a virtual entity, Katherine Hayles' complaint that it doesn't pay enough heed to physical constraints is without foundation (Hayles 2001: 154). More to the point, conceptually the body without organs should be understood as our way of coping with physical constraints. It is our means of fabricating a mental position from which to view the conditions of our everyday life as making sense.

The Internet's Body Without Organs

Presuppositions can sometimes be brought to light by asking: what ought to be? In the first years of the Internet – that is, the early 1990s, with the emergence of the World Wide Web – when it was still small enough to be contained on a single mainframe computer, the key permutation of this question was (according to Bill McKibben) whether it would be like TV, just another distraction, or whether it would really allow for the kind of connectedness it seemed to enable. McKibben thinks the answer 'is still not clear – more people use the Web to look at unclothed young women and lose money at poker than for any other purposes' (McKibben 2006: 4). Setting aside the moralising tone, the contrast with TV is instructive because in its early days television was subjected to considerable scrutiny and regulation by government – of a kind that varied quite widely from nation to nation. The Australian government, for instance, regarded it as a service and placed it in the same policy category as health and education. Interestingly, TV was thought too important and too dangerous (government grasped immediately the propaganda power of the new medium) to leave in private hands and policy was developed accordingly. The basic tenets of Australian policy were that TV should be free, available to all (the infrastructural cost of this is staggering when you consider the dispersed nature of the population), and informative (all stations were required to provide news services as well as educational programming for children). It did not opt, however, for complete state control as Britain did, but neither did it leave it all to the market as the US did, although even there the government placed severe restrictions on content. Australia aimed for a kind of middle ground that allowed for commercial applications, but kept a close eye on what those applications were. TV was essentially a national technology and the issue of what it could and should be was a matter of national debate.

   The Internet has never been a national technology in this sense so its development has not been overseen by a governmental body, except in the most ad hoc way via band-aid legislation which, in the case of child pornography say, can do no more than ban certain practices and create the judiciary conditions needed to punish the offenders, but cannot actually stop it. And that is how things should be according to the majority of Internet pundits, whether e-business billionaires or left-wing academics: Internet equals freedom.[2] This is the Internet's body without organs: the great and unquestioned presupposition that it is an agent of freedom. The 'material problem confronting schizoanalysis is knowing whether' the bodies without organs we have are any good or not, or more to the point, knowing whether we have the means of determining whether they are any good or not (Deleuze and Guattari 1987: 165). The body without organs is an evaluative concept which, as Guattari instructs in his last book *Chaosmosis*, should be used dialectically, which is to say with a view towards an understanding of how it is produced (Guattari 1995: 12). In other words we should ask two basic questions: how is a particular body without organs produced? and what circulates on it once it has been produced?

Just how enfeebled a concept of freedom the Internet rhetoric implies was exposed by the press reaction to the story of Google's entry into the Chinese market, which is said to be growing by 20 million users a year and was already worth an estimated $151 million per annum in 2004 (a figure that is literally tiny by US standards, but it doesn't take a genius to see that the potential for growth is huge, and with everyone predicting that China is going to be the next superpower one can understand why Google would want a foothold). To be allowed to set up servers on mainland China and create a Google.cn service, which will be faster and better suited to purpose than the regular US version Chinese people already have access to, Google had to agree to adhere to the Chinese government's regulation and control of Internet content. This means complying with its three Ts rule: Tibet, Taiwan and Tiananmen are all off limits, as are such search categories as 'human rights', 'Amnesty International', 'pornography', and of course 'Falun Gong'. It is believed that there are 30,000 online police officers monitoring chatrooms, blogs and news portals to ensure that these topics aren't discussed and these kinds of sites aren't accessed. Although this isn't the first time Google has agreed to cooperate with government and effectively censor its search results (in Germany it restricts references to sites that deny the Holocaust, while in France it restricts access to sites that incite racial violence), the scale of its compliance with the Chinese government's censorship requirements far exceeds anything it has done before.

That Google chose to make these compromises as the necessary price of doing business in the world's fastest growing economy was read by many as a betrayal of the values of freedom for which Google is supposedly an emblem. The fact that these jeremiads were largely confined to the business pages of liberal papers suggests that the notion of freedom they had in mind was largely of the freedom-to-do-business kind wrapped up in the rhetoric of freedom of speech. The obviously self-serving acquiescence to censorship is defended by the company on the grounds that 'providing no information (or a heavily degraded user experience that amounts to no information) is more inconsistent'.[3] What this case demonstrated is that Google isn't really concerned about our access to content at all. All the bluster about compromised values was really just a verbal smokescreen to cover up this one glaring truth: Google's priority is its access to new markets and it will not hesitate to compromise its putative ethic of 'do no evil' in order to achieve that goal. If we regard Google as a gigantic multinational corporation – which with a net worth in excess of $80 billion (making it bigger than Coke, General Motors or McDonald's) it in fact is – and not simply a search tool, then there should be little to surprise us in its about-face in China. It is only if we continue to buy into the fantasy that it, and somehow the Internet as a whole, is a bastion of freedom that we find these events dismaying. If the Internet was ever a 'commons', to use the word anti-corporate commentators like Naomi Klein have made fashionable, then there can be no doubt that it is rapidly being 'enclosed', the implication being that Amazon, Google and eBay are still only at the 'primitive accumulation' stage. Information is in effect a natural resource, like oil, that Google exploits without regard for the environment (as oil companies do when we aren't watching and sometimes even when we are).[4]

Nowhere is this more evident than in the Google-led hype surrounding the convergence of Internet and mobile phone technology. In an op-ed for the *Financial Times* Google CEO Eric Schmidt went on record saying that Internet-enabled mobile phones would effectively solve the problem of how to gain access to emerging markets in underdeveloped countries where the absence of landline infrastructure would otherwise have proved an impassable obstacle. He doesn't put it like that, of course. He's never so indelicate as to mention the dirty word 'market'. His rhetoric is liberatory and egalitarian. The Internet has democratised information, Schmidt claims (2006: 15), or at least it has for those who have access to it. And that he says is the problem: not everyone has access! In sub-Saharan Africa, Schmidt laments, less than 1 per cent of households have a landline. If that statistic wasn't bad enough for a business that presupposes the existence of such basic utilities as a functioning telephonic network, then there is the worse news that even if broadband was available to every household it wouldn't change things all that much because very few people in this part of the world can afford computers. Mobile phones will liberate this technologically dark region by overcoming these twin obstacles to online access. On the blessed day when everyone has Internet-enabled mobile phones, a 'schoolchild in Africa will be able . . . to find research papers from around the world or to see ancient manuscripts from a library in Oxford' (Schmidt 2006: 15). Until then, however, the 'digital divide' prevents this democratising magic from having its effect. According to Schmidt, thanks to the Internet we don't have to take what business, the media or politicians say 'at face value' and this is empowering. Schmidt's view is that what is actually said online isn't as important as the 'freedom' to say whatever one happens to want to say. Thus, he says, governments should stop focusing on how to control the Web and 'concentrate on how to give Internet access to more people in more countries' (Schmidt 2006: 15). Government should, in other words, help Google to expand its market.

By the same token, as Google's negative response to requests from US law enforcement agencies for assistance in tracking down users of child pornography illustrates, Google thinks the government shouldn't be allowed to impinge on its market. Although Yahoo, MSN and AOL have been willing to help out, Google has held fast, citing the right to privacy as its rationale. But Google patently speaks with a forked tongue on this subject. Co-founder of Google, Larry Page, defended the company's refusal to help identify child pornographers by saying, rather tellingly, that the company relies on the trust of its users and that giving out data on users would break that trust. His implication is obvious: if Google gave out data on its users it would effectively turn customers away and eventually lose its pre-eminent place as market leader. Protecting market share is how we should understand Page's call for legislation that stops government from being able to ask for such data in the first place.[5] But this doesn't mean Google actually respects the privacy of its users, if by that one means it doesn't keep them under surveillance: it is constantly gathering data on users, individually and collectively, and even publicises this fact (under the innocuous sounding rubric of Google Trends) by releasing 'maps' of most frequently searched topics broken down by region. Eschewing any pretence to being scientific, these search maps make for titillating reading as one ponders what it means in cultural-geographical terms that the most frequent Google searches in the city of St Albans in Hertfordshire were for gyms, weight loss and the Atkins diet. Does this make it the 'most self-absorbed city in Britain', as claimed by *The Sunday Times* (UK) in a half-page piece studded with such titbits of spurious psycho-social information gleaned from Google Trends?[6] Obviously more of a lifestyle puff than a hard news piece, although it was in the news section, what is particularly striking about this article is its complete lack of sensitivity to the fact that such maps are the product of electronic surveillance (that is, precisely the kind of thing *The Sunday Times* normally rails against). That a liberal paper like this doesn't see Google Trends as surveillance is evidence of just how little critical attention is paid to this dimension of the Internet in the public sphere.[7] I don't, however, want to give the impression that this is some kind of conspiracy because the fact is Google is very open about its snooping – one Google executive, Marissa Mayer, has even said we should expect it.[8]

The Rhizome

Is the Internet a rhizome? All the straws in the wind say 'yes' it is.

> Whereas mechanical machines are inserted into hierarchically organised social systems, obeying and enhancing this type of structure, the Internet is ruled by no one and is open to expansion or addition at anyone's whim as long as its communication protocols are followed. This contrast was anticipated theoretically by Gilles Deleuze and Félix Guattari especially in *A Thousand Plateaus* (1980), in which they distinguished between arboreal and rhizomic cultural forms. The former is stable, centred, hierarchical; the latter is nomadic, multiple, decentred – a fitting depiction of the difference between a hydroelectric plant and the Internet. (Poster 2001: 27)

There are of course excellent grounds for thinking that the Internet meets some if not all of the basic criteria of the rhizome, which Deleuze and Guattari (1987: 21) list as follows:

- The rhizome connects any point to any other point (connections do not have to be between same and same, or like and like).
- The rhizome cannot be reduced to either the One or the multiple because it is composed of dimensions (directions in motion) not units. Consequently no point in the rhizome can be altered without altering the whole.
- The rhizome operates by variation, expansion, conquest, capture and offshoots (not reproduction).
- The rhizome pertains to an infinitely modifiable map with multiple entrances and exits that must be produced.
- The rhizome is acentred, nonsignifying and acephalous.
- The rhizome isn't amenable to any structural or generative model.

So, how well does the Internet map against these six principles? At the 'bare machine' level it seems to agree with the first principle very closely. The ideal of the Internet is that any computer can be connected to any other computer. How well this works in practice is another matter altogether, as anyone who has experienced the frustration of trying to access 'big' sites using low bandwidth connections (such as dial-up) or has had to rely on servers clogged by high volumes of traffic can readily attest.

But the more interesting philosophical question here, which applies as much to Deleuze and Guattari as to the Internet, is the premium we place on intention: until the advent of search engines of the capability of Google, it was extremely difficult to implement one's intent in relation to the Internet. The phrase, 'surfing the Internet', reflects this: using the Internet used to be (and in some cases still is) like looking for a needle in a haystack, and basically what one did in order to find something was 'surf' from one site to another until one found it (hence the proliferation in the early 1990s of books listing 'useful' websites, which themselves tended to be indexes or directories enabling you to find other sites – by the same token, little attention was given to domain names at this time, with the result many of them looked like nightmarish calculus equations rather than the user-friendly mnemonics we're accustomed to now). You moved from one Web address to another as though from one fixed point in space to another, which interestingly is not at all what surfers do.[9]

This brings us to the second principle: here the match is a little less straightforward. For a start, the practical reality of the Internet is nothing at all like the multi-dimensional sensorium envisaged by William Gibson when he first used the term 'cyberspace' in his groundbreaking novel *Neuromancer*, but then again he famously didn't even own a computer at the time. However, Gibson's vision of cyberspace has had a lasting influence and many people do think of the Internet as the realisation of the Deleuzian ideal of multiplicity. But the incredible proliferation and constantly expanding number of websites does not by itself mean that the Internet can be classed as a multiplicity in Deleuze's sense. Are websites dimensions or units of the Web? There is a simple way to answer this question – what happens when we add or subtract a site? The answer is that it isn't clear that the addition or the subtraction of any one site actually affects the whole. If several million sites were to vanish then that would clearly make a difference, but the loss of a few hundred or even several thousand might not. If sites were dimensions then according to Deleuze and Guattari's definition of the rhizome their removal would alter the whole, so we have to conclude that individual websites are units of the Internet, not dimensions. Empirically we know that the number of websites is important; there is for example a vast difference between the Internet of today, which has hundreds of millions of specific sites, and trillions of pages to go with them, and the Internet of 1990, which had fewer than two hundred sites and could be contained in its totality on a single PC. But this doesn't mean we have to abandon the idea that the Internet is a multiplicity because there is another way we can come at this problem.

Thus we come to the third principle, that the rhizome operates by variation, expansion, conquest, capture and offshoots (not reproduction), which is essentially a matter of population, and which in contrast to the numbering number can be grasped in dimensional terms. Darwin's two great insights, according to Deleuze and Guattari, were that the population is more significant than the type in determining the genetic properties of a species, and that change occurs not through an increase in complexity, such as the proliferation of individual websites or multiplication of weblinks entails, but rather the opposite, through simplification. Internet usage certainly bears this point out, as recent trends confirm – the Internet is the standard source of product information, everything from details of the latest designs to replacement user manuals are lodged there; it is also becoming the preferred point of sale as more and more business is conducted online; and it is steadily taking over from its rivals TV and radio the role of content provision, as podcasts and downloads become more the rule than the exception. In the process the Internet is changing how we understand 'media' – on the one hand, it is steadily displacing the variety of media that used to exist (newspapers, magazines, TV, radio and cinema) onto itself, while on the other hand, it is absorbing new interactive functions, such as data searches and direct online sales, the other media can't offer. Paradoxically, then, from the perspective of the user the Internet is without doubt the most powerful homogenising and standardising machine invented since money. Firstly, all pre-existing forms of media have been compelled to adapt themselves to suit the Internet environment; second, having stripped the traditional media of its exclusive preserve to make and distribute news, movies or whatever, the Internet has 'enabled' a whole new kind of media production, from the so-called 'citizen journalists' we hear so much about today, to bloggers, to home-movie makers and amateur pornographers. Viewed from the perspective of the media as a whole (that is, from a population perspective), the Internet has simplified what media means and in the process set off a massive expansion of media operations into virtually every corner of existence. It is having the same effect on retail.

The fourth principle, that the rhizome pertains to an infinitely modifiable map with multiple entrances and exits that must be produced, is, I would hazard, the most important. But its implications are neither obvious nor fully explained by Deleuze and Guattari. In effect, however, what it means is this: the rhizome is not manifest in things, but rather a latent potential that has to be realised by experimentation. This can be linked to the sixth principle, namely that the rhizome isn't amenable to any structural or generative model because basically what Deleuze and Guattari are saying is that you can't either prescribe the rhizome into existence or expect to find it naturally occurring. It has to be invented. The rhizome is the subterranean pathway connecting all our actions, invisibly determining our decision to do this rather than that. Insofar as we remain unaware of its existence and indeed its operation we do not have full control over our lives. The rhizome is in this sense a therapeutic tool. 'For both statements and desires, the issue is never to reduce the unconscious or to interpret it or to make it signify according to a tree model. The issue is to *produce the unconscious*, and with it new statements, different desires: the rhizome is precisely this production of the unconscious' (Deleuze and Guattari 1987: 18). The rhizome of the Internet cannot simply be the pre-existing network of connected computers. Rather we have to conceive it in terms of the set of choices that have been made concerning its use and determine the degree to which the resulting grid is 'open' or 'closed'.

The fifth principle – that the rhizome is acentred, nonsignifying and acephalous – appears to be one that could be left unchallenged. Yet, if we were to grant that the Internet is acentred, nonsignifying and acephalous in appearance and indeed in its very construction, the reality of its day-to-day use still does not live up to this much-vaunted Deleuzian ideal. Here we have to remind ourselves that Deleuze and Guattari regard the rhizome as a tendency rather than a state of being. It must constantly compete with an equally strong tendency in the opposite direction, namely towards what they term the 'arboreal'. The Internet exhibits arboreal tendencies as well rhizomatic tendencies and any balanced assessment of it would have to take these into account too and weigh up their relative strength. To begin with, one still moves from point to point through the Internet – there is no liberated line of flight in cyberspace. Moreover, Google searches are very far from disinterested, as John Battelle's pathbreaking book *The Search* makes abundantly clear. Now that retailers can pay Google to link certain search items (what Google calls AdWords[10]) to their business name, so that a search for a book, for instance, will always lead to Amazon or Abebooks or whoever, the minimal conceptual distinction that used to separate Google from the Yellow Pages has basically vanished.[11] The operating premise of Google searches may not be that when whenever we are searching, no matter what we are searching for, we are actually looking for something to buy, but its results certainly appear to obey this code. Insofar as we rely on Google as our user's guide to the Internet, the Internet we actually see and use is thus 'stable, centred and hierarchical', that is, the very opposite of rhizomatic. Google searches are conducted on a 'stable' electronic snapshot of the Internet, not the living breathing thing itself, which it indexes very precisely; the search engine is patently a centring system, de facto and de jure, and what could be more hierarchical than PageRank? This is not to say that Google isn't an extremely useful tool, because plainly it is; but it is to insist not only that it has its limitations, some of which are quite serious, but that it isn't the only means of searching for information available.

A New Problematic?

If we were to follow Deleuze's watchword, that philosophy has the concepts it deserves according to how well it formulates its problems, then we would not start from the idea that the Internet might be a body without organs or that it looks like a rhizome or indeed from any other pre-existing point of view. Instead we would try to see how the Internet works and develop our concepts from there.

In its first flush, the Internet seemed to be about connectedness, but that idea has since been exposed as a perhaps necessary but nonetheless impossible ideal (like the Lacanian conception of sexual relations) that we are at once compelled to try to realise but destined never to succeed in doing so. Now, though, Battelle's work has made it clear that the Internet is much more about searching than connecting. Although connecting people – strangers with strangers, friends with friends – is a major feature of the Internet's cultural role, it is predominantly used to search for objects, that is, commodities, and in the case of pornography and celebrity gossip one may well say it is searching for people in their guise as commodities. A lot of quite utopian claims have been made on behalf of the Internet, the strongest being that it has so changed the way people interact that it has created a new mode of politics. But it now seems clear that it is just another 'model of realisation' – Deleuze and Guattari's term for the institutions capitalism relies on to extract surplus value from a given economy. That business couldn't immediately figure out how to make money out of the Internet, that is, turn it into a 'model of realisation', meant that in the early years of its existence the utopian image of it as an affirmative agent of cultural change was able to flourish, giving the Internet a powerful rhetorical legacy it continues to draw on even as it is moulded more and more firmly into a purely commercial enterprise.

Google is effectively the common-sense understanding of what using the Internet actually means, both practically and theoretically. It is at once our abstract ideal of searching and our cumulatively acquired empirical understanding of it. But more importantly, searching is what we think of as the proper practice associated with the Internet – one writes with a pen, makes calls with a phone, and searches the Internet. When our searches don't yield the results we're after we tell ourselves it is because we don't properly understand Google, that we don't have enough practical experience with it, or sufficient competence to use it fully, rather than dismiss the search engine itself as fundamentally flawed. It is in this precise sense that Google has become, in noological terms, the 'image of the search' (Deleuze and Guattari 1987: 374). Google's significance is clearly more cultural than technical because it determines our view of Internet technology itself, deciding for us – in advance and without discussion – what it is actually for. If the problem in the early days of the Internet was that no one could foresee the range of its applications – and seemed to stand around waiting for history to decide instead of putting in place the appropriate legislation and policy to guide its development some now think of as missing – the problem today is that everyone thinks they know what its application should be, namely, the facilitation of sales, and any sense that it might have a more progressive use has been consigned to the dustbin of fantasy. If there is something the matter with the Internet it is that its utopian beginnings block critical thoughts about its future, as though somehow its starting point was already the fabled end of history when the concrete and abstract become one.

John Battelle says he wrote *The Search* because it was his sense that Google and its rival search engine companies had somehow figured out how to 'jack into' our 'culture's nervous system' (Battelle 2005: 2). His account of the seemingly inexorable rise of the search engine giant, which is largely a standard corporate biography, is by turns alarmist and infatuated, he is in equal measure amazed by Google's power and disturbed by it. It is, however, Battelle's attempt to use Google's history to say something about contemporary culture that makes for the most fascinating reading, and whether we agree with his prognosis or not I think we have to take it seriously. There can be no doubt that the Internet is going to play an increasingly significant role in shaping cultural attitudes, behaviours and practices in the future. Battelle's decision not to write a book about Google per se but rather something like a Google-effect is undoubtedly wise. As much of a behemoth as Google is, there's no guarantee that it will be around forever. It may disappear, as AOL appears to be doing as its business model founders in the face of Google's, or it may be swallowed up by an even more aggressive predator such as Microsoft (presently three times the size of Google measured in terms of market capitalisation), which virtually wiped out its one-time competitor Netscape Navigator in the so-called 'browser wars' of the 1990s. By the same token, none of the other major corporations – not eBay nor Amazon nor even the venerable Microsoft – can be considered immune to such forces of change. Indeed Wall Street is worried that Microsoft won't be able to shake off the competition – it has no answer to Apple's iTunes and it is losing the battle to control the Web.[12] It has also lately been reported that Google and Yahoo, as well as Microsoft, are cooking up plans to encroach on eBay's turf, though so far the results are disappointing to investors. But the business sector at least sees it as both inevitable and desirable – commercial users of eBay apparently feel they have maxed out on that service and to reach new customers they need access to new providers.[13]

The Internet seems to engender a kind of restlessness in us to always want see what's just over the horizon, one click away. The success of Amazon, Google and eBay (amidst the blaze of spectacular dot.com failures of the past decade) is intimately related to the way their sites facilitate searching. Google's strength in this regard is obvious, but we shouldn't overlook just how good Amazon and eBay are in their own highly localised domains. What these companies have cottoned on to is something we might call 'search engine culture'. The Internet thrives not because it can be searched, but because the search engines we use to navigate it respond to and foster the desire to search by constantly rewarding us with the little satisfactions of the unexpected discovery. A potent search engine makes us feel that the world really is at our fingertips, that we are verily 'becoming-world'. One can find objective evidence of the intensifying influence of 'search engine culture' in the constant consumer demand for increased bandwidth and memory capacity to facilitate it. Most households in the West possess vastly more computing power than they could hope to use, except for such activities as searching the Web. It may be that online business is only just now starting to take off and show genuine profits because it has only lately developed an appreciation of the architecture of the desire called 'searching'. As John Lanchester puts it, Google 'has a direct line, if not quite to the unconscious dreaming mind of the world, at least to the part of it which voices its wishes' (Lanchester 2006: 5). I believe the same is true of Amazon and eBay and indeed a range of other Internet services such as online dating and grocery shopping that are yet to produce corporations of the gigantic proportions as these icons.[14] But I don't accept that Google is the global id, as Lanchester puts it, because to do so would be to accept that our deepest atavistic desire is to buy something and there could be no more dystopian outlook than that. Neither is it the global body without organs, though with a bit of work it could be, and who knows what changes that might ring?

References

Bard, A. and Söderqvist, J. (2002), *Netocracy: The New Power Elite and Life After Capitalism*, London: Pearson Education.

Battelle, J. (2005), *The Search: How Google and Its Rivals Rewrote the Rules of Business and Transformed Our Culture*, London: Nicholas Brealey Publishing.

Butler, J. (1990), *Gender Trouble: Feminism and the Subversion of Identity*, London: Routledge.

Deleuze, G. (1995), *Negotiations*, trans. M. Joughin, New York: Columbia University Press.

Deleuze, G. and F. Guattari (1983), *Anti-Oedipus: Capitalism and Schizophrenia*, trans. R. Hurley, M. Seem and H. Lane, Minneapolis: University of Minnesota Press.

Deleuze, G. and F. Guattari (1987), *A Thousand Plateaus*, trans. B. Massumi, Minneapolis: University of Minnesota Press.

Foucault, M. (1979), *Discipline and Punish: The Birth of the Prison*, trans. A. Sheridan, London: Penguin Books.

Guattari, F. (1995), *Chaosmosis: An Ethico-Aesthetic Paradigm*, trans. P. Bains and J. Pefanis, Sydney: Power Publications.

Hayles, N. K. (2001), 'Desiring Agency: Limiting Metaphors and Enabling Constraints in Dawkins and Deleuze/Guattari', *SubStance: A Review of Theory and Literary Criticism*, 30 (1–2): 144–59.

Hui, W. and K. Chun (2006), *Control and Freedom: Power and Paranoia in the Age of Fibre Optics*, Cambridge, MA: MIT Press.

Jameson, F. (1981), *The Political Unconscious: Narrative as a Socially Symbolic Act*, London: Routledge.

Jameson, F. (1991), *Postmodernism, or, the Cultural Logic of Late Capitalism*, London: Verso.

Lanchester, J. (2006), 'The Global Id', *London Review of Books*, 28 (2): 3–6.

McKibben, B. (2006), 'The Hope of the Web', *New York Review of Books*, LIII (7): 4–6.

Poster, M. (2001), *What's the Matter with the Internet*, Minneapolis: University of Minnesota Press.

Schmidt, E. (2006), 'Let More of the World Access the Web', *Financial Times*, May 22: 15.

Solove, D. (2004), *The Digital Person: Technology and Privacy in the Information Age*, New York: NYU Press.

Notes

1. Foucault's heartfelt acknowledgment of the importance of Deleuze and Guattari's work to his own thinking is obviously not unimportant in this respect.
2. It is perhaps worth observing that in this sense the Internet is fundamentally anti-socialist: it will not accept dirigisme of any description.
3. *Guardian*, January 25, 2006: 3.
4. Jameson's (1991: 35) claim that culture is the new nature is thus shown to be substantially true.

5. *Guardian*, January 25, 2006: 3
6. *The Sunday Times*, May 21, 2006: 13
7. This issue has not been ignored in academic discourse – see, for example, Solove (2004) and Hui and Chun (2006) – but the emphasis there is overwhelmingly on the activities of governments.
8. *Observer*, January 22, 2006: 24
9. As Deleuze himself recognised, surfing is one of those sports in which the 'key thing is how to get taken up in the motion of a big wave, a column of rising air, to "get into something" instead of being the origin of an effort' (Deleuze 1995: 121).
10. As clear an instance as one could find of language 'falling under the domain of private property' (Poster 2001: 39).
11. But in a sense, all Google is doing is making a commercial strength out of what has always been a weakness in its operating system: Google's famous PageRank algorithm is anything but immune to influence. Its basic premise that the more traffic a site receives the more significant it is has meant that it is prey to the influence of spammers who simply bombard a particular site until its rank changes. There are even companies promising that for a fee they can elevate a site's ranking, thus enhancing its market presence (popular wisdom has it that people rarely look beyond the first page of results – a ranking of 50 or worse is basically death for an Internet business relying on Google traffic). Google is alert to this and black-bans companies it thinks are guilty of such practices. But ultimately its best defence against this has been to abandon (albeit unofficially) the idea of 'organic' searches, that is, searches which aren't influenced by the 'invisible hand' of market forces.
12. *Guardian*, May 14, 2006, Business section: 3.
13. *The Sunday Times*, February 5, 2006, Business section: 39.
14. Having said this, it also needs to be pointed out that the online businesses other than the big three make up more than 80% of the business as a whole. As Battelle (2005: 154) informs us, Amazon's 2000 revenue was $2.76 billion at a time when Internet business was worth $25 billion annually.

Chapter 9

Swarming: Number versus Animal?

Eugene Thacker

'It seems that concepts have their own existence. They are alive, like invisible creatures. . .'

Deleuze, letter to Kuniichi Uno (July 25, 1984)

'Molecule!'; or, Deleuze and Biotechnology

Returning home one evening, I entered the elevator and, unknowingly, entered into 'the molecular'. I was not alone in the elevator; a small group of four or five other people were also inside. In the awkward silence that accompanies so many elevator rides – a silent stillness of ascending or descending movement – one of the others suddenly shouted 'molecule!' Before I was able to recall the children's game that had just been announced, everyone had made their bodies compact and had begun bouncing about, bouncing off each other, bouncing off the walls. I had no choice but to become a molecule myself, for even had I wished not to play, my veering away while trying to avoid the other bodies/molecules would have already implicated me in the game.

'Molecule' is a strange sort of children's game, one of those performative, physical exercises with no real educational value or, for that matter, goal. Some play in order to collide, others play in order to steer clear and swerve, and still others simply want to 'go with the flow'. Presumably 'molecule' is played until either complete boredom or complete exhaustion sets in. On one level, the molecule game is an absurdist re-enactment of mechanistic philosophy, in which the world is understood in terms of body, causality and motion (one imagines Descartes, Gassendi and Hobbes playing 'molecule'. . .). More likely, however, the game references modern physics, and is perhaps in some ways an outgrowth of suburban Cold War culture (luckily the game is not called 'particle accelerator'). But the playing of the molecule game, and the sort of ad hoc, experimental embodiment it requires, points not just to differing views of 'the body', but both to the continuum of 'multiplicity' in which bodies are intermeshed and to the fact that bodies are 'animated' because of this intermeshing.

We should pause here, however. Isn't this making too much of a simple children's game? Would we be going too far if we now cited Deleuze? ('The discovery in any domain of a plurality of coexisting oppositions is inseparable from a more profound discovery, that of difference, which denounces the negative and opposition itself as no more than appearances in relation to the problematic field of a positive multiplicity' [Deleuze 1994: 204].) What, indeed, do philosophical concepts such as 'multiplicity' describe? Do they point to things, objects, or to a 'content' that demonstrates the concept? It is because of questions such as these that any attempt to talk about 'Deleuze and X' (whatever 'X' may be – literature, film, politics, religion, media, biology) raises questions about the nature of the philosophical concept – or, more precisely, questions about the relation between 'concept' and 'life'. Take, for example, the many concepts found in the work of Deleuze ('alone' and with Guattari) that reference the life sciences: not only 'the molecular' but also the 'body without organs', 'becoming-animal', 'folding' and embryogenesis, 'nucleic acids of expression' and 'proteins of content', 'phylogenesis' and the 'machinic phylum', and so on.[1] Arguably the question of biology – of how to think 'life' – has been a long-standing concern for Deleuze. Already, as early as Deleuze's writings on Bergson, there is the engagement with evolution and vitalism, and *Difference and Repetition* contains extended sections on natural history, comparative anatomy, and the Cuvier–Geoffroy debate.[2]

Thus the tendency may be to accept Deleuze's 'biological' concepts as being themselves comments on biology and the life sciences, and to the extent that they 'take up' concepts from the life sciences, this would not be inaccurate. Taking note, for instance, of Deleuze's specific engagement with natural history, anatomy, biology, genetics, and so on, we could even 'upgrade' his arguments and 'apply' them to the contemporary fields of genomics, biotechnology and nanotechnology. But to do so would also be to limit the life of such concepts to being about their content; and indeed Deleuze never wrote a book about biology or the life sciences, even if a certain thinking about 'the living' runs through his writings (and in this way intersects with the philosophy of biology). The concept of 'the molecular' for instance, is not necessarily about 'molecules' per se; though there may be 'molecular molecules', not all molecules are 'molecular' (especially the 'master molecule' of DNA).[3]

In addressing this question of 'Deleuze and X' – and let's say that 'X' is the question of 'life' – we need to pay attention not only to 'content' but also to 'expression' and to the interplay between them. In doing so, it becomes apparent that Deleuze's interest in biology and the life sciences is really not about so much about 'life' as it is about 'multiplicity', or rather, about 'a life' that is specific to and indissociable from multiplicity. To pursue this thought, we will begin from a set of case studies that deal with the phenomenon of swarms (and its analogues such as flocks, packs, and so forth). We will then consider the more traditional approach of philosophical thinking about 'life' and the animal, before looking to Deleuze's intervention into this tradition (and Badiou's intervention into Deleuze's intervention).

Swarming: Three Case Studies

Consider three contemporary case studies, each of which we might describe as a 'swarm'. The first example of swarming comes from the sciences of complexity, especially as they have influenced fields such as myrmecology and the study of 'social insects'.[4] Swarming here has to do with the capacity of insects such as ants, bees and wasps to perform complex tasks without any overarching, centralised control. This view focuses on the random, local interactions (both insect–insect and insect–environment) that enable insects to forage for a food source, to cooperatively transport large objects, to build a nest, or to regulate the temperature of a hive. For example, in the army ant species *Eciton burchelli*, the search for food begins with multiple, random searches by groups of ants, which fan out from the bivouac (hosting the queen and brood) in a branching pattern to form a swarm front. As many as 200,000 ants may blanket an area over fifteen meters wide in search of a food source. The ants communicate to each other through pheromones, chemicals they lay on the ground like a trail as they continue their search. When any ant discovers a food source and brings it back to the bivouac, their trail is reinforced with pheromone, and the correlation of time (rate of return to bivouac) and intensity (rate at which pheromone is reinforced) in turn encourages other ants to follow one trail or another. Eventually, what begins as a widely dispersed swarm fan becomes a series of discrete, linear 'highways' to reliable food sources.[5]

The complexity view of swarming thus places a great deal of emphasis on the principle of 'local actions, global patterns'. In such 'self-organising' swarms, 'pattern formation occurs through interactions internal to the system, without intervention by external directing influences . . . Moreover, the rules specifying interactions among the system's components are executed using only local information, without reference to the global pattern' (Camazine et al. 2001: 8). This view – represented by complexity researchers Eric Bonabeau and Guy Théraulaz, and by myrmecologist Deborah Gordon – stands in contrast to a more traditional one, in which social insects are understood as highly regimented and governed by a set of fixed behaviours, which are themselves the result of genetic and evolutionary adaptation. This view is best represented by Edward O. Wilson's work on ant colonies, which made plentiful use of political and military metaphors to depict a hierarchical, deterministic and closed system of governance in which all individuality is sacrificed for the good of collective 'colonial existence' (a view which has also been criticised for its implied naturalisation of racism and sexism). As Wilson and co-author Hölldobler note, in an oft-quoted phrase, 'Marx just had the wrong species' (Wilson and Hölldobler 1995: 9).[6] What the complexity view brings to the traditional study of swarms is a set of more flexible, open-ended principles for understanding swarming behaviour as nondeterministic.[7] Swarms are dynamic in that they 'require continual interactions among lower-level components to produce and maintain structure' (Camazine et al. 2001: 29), they exhibit 'emergent' properties, they are affected as a whole by small changes ('parameter tuning'), and they may exist with some consistency across more than one 'metastable' state. The upshot of this view – which can also be found in studies of bird flocking, fish schooling, wolf packs and bats – is the necessity of a network-wide perspective on the complex organisation of such group animals: 'An emergent property cannot be understood simply by examining in isolation the properties of the system's components, but requires a consideration of the interactions among a system's components' (Camazine et al. 2001: 8).

This emphasis on complexity and networks leads us to the second case of swarming. We can take, as an example, the burgeoning field known as 'swarm intelligence', which combines findings in the study of social insects just described with computer science.[8] In a sense, swarm intelligence can simply be thought of as the instrumentalisation or the 'actionability' of insect swarms and their ability to solve complex problems:

> Recently a growing community of researchers has been devising new ways of applying swarm intelligence to diverse tasks. The foraging of ants has led to a novel method for rerouting network traffic in busy telecommunications systems. The cooperative interaction of ants working to transport a large food item may lead to more effective algorithms for robots. The way in which insects cluster their colony's dead and sort their larvae can aid in analyzing

banking data. And the division of labor among honeybees could help stream-line assembly lines in factories. (Bonebeau and Théraulaz 2000: 74)

In this way, the example of ant foraging is not just a survival mechanism for an insect species, since, from a communications perspective, it solves an optimisation problem centred on the most efficient way to deliver a message through a network.[9] In other words, the case of insect swarms becomes transmogrified into a network of nodes and edges, a mesh of interrelations between particles, a bidirectional graph. Swarm intelligence proposes a whole *technê* to insect swarming, one that is made accessible through this 'complex', network science view.

Perhaps the ramifications of this transition are best expressed in the computer animation of swarming, most often found in science fiction and horror films. Since the late 1990s, one of the most prevalent uses of computer animation in film has been in the imaging and animation of aggregate forms: soldiers on a battlefield (*The Lord of the Rings* trilogy), the attack of enemy insects (*Starship Troopers*), the flocking of bats (*Batman Begins*) or birds (*Night Watch*), the swarming of intelligent machines (*Matrix Revolutions*), and the chaos of a starship battle (*Star Wars Episode III*). Something interesting takes place in such examples: the study of insect swarms, which, along with studies of other group animals, informs such computer animations, is often used to depict insect or other animal swarms. Insects serve as the model for their own modelling in a virtual world. No doubt part of this trend is due to the fact that the study of flocking in birds and swarming in insects has been a popular resource for studying how such self-organisation takes place.[10] For instance, simulations of flocks often show that bird flocks follow a set of simple rules, carried out at the local level between individual birds: aggregation (moving towards the flock), steering (steering clear of other birds; avoiding collision), and rate variability (adjusting speed to match nearest neighbours). These loosely defined 'rules' are carried out not at the level of the flock as a whole, but at the level of individual birds and their awareness of their immediate neighbours (Reynolds 1987).

However, this chain of associations – swarms (of insects) into algo-rithms (of swarms) into swarms (of bots, of data packets, animated agents, and so on) – also says a great deal about the cultural and political meanings that are given to such phenomena, especially when humans are involved. The very idea of instrumentalising swarms – something that by definition has no central control – raises a set of political concerns, and this leads to our third case study. Recently, activists and political theorists have attempted to define a new model of civilian-based political protest based on swarming concepts. While traditional protest models were based on a centralised, mass gathering, unified by a single set of mottos or demands, this new type of 'distributed dissent' takes place through a multiplicity of smaller units that coordinate their movements with the aid of mobile and wireless technologies. In other instances, the actual protest itself may be more traditional (centralised massing), but the means of its organisation and coordination is emergent or bottom-up. The wide range of such events have been variously referred to as 'multitudes, 'netwars', 'smartmobs' (in their less political vein), or simply 'the movement'. They include, among the more well-known examples, the 1999 Battle for Seattle, the G8 Summit in Genoa, the 'People Power II' demonstrations in Manila, the 2003 F15 antiwar protests, and the long history of the Zapatista struggle in Mexico.[11]

For RAND researchers John Arquilla and David Ronfeldt, the network mode of organisation is key to understanding such movements: 'The term netwar refers to an emerging mode of conflict (and crime) at societal levels, short of traditional military warfare, in which the protagonists use network forms of organisation and related doctrines, strategies, and technologies attuned to the information age' (Arquilla and Ronfeldt 2001: 6). Michael Hardt and Antonio Negri (2004) – who reference Arquilla and Ronfeldt – argue that the political concept of *multitudo* ('multitude' as opposed to 'people') is something always being created, never totally arriving, the very possibility of counterpowers. In their historical analysis of proto-multitude insurgencies, which include guerilla warfare and the new social movements, Hardt and Negri place particular emphasis on the notion of 'the common' that stitches together any self-organised political event, and for this reason Negri has continually argued that the concepts of labour, production, cooperation and collectivity must be thought as simultaneously political and ontological (Hardt and Negri 2004: 69–91).

However such netwars and/or multitudes do not concern the military context; for this Arquilla and Ronfeldt develop a military-based theory of swarming they call 'Battleswarm'. For them, swarming is 'the systematic pulsing of force and/or fire by dispersed, internetted [*sic*] units, so as to strike the adversary from all directions simultaneously'(Arquilla and Ronfeldt 2000: 8). Swarming has, of course, been a military tactic for some time, and can arguably be traced back to the ancient world (Edwards 2000). In its militaristic sense, 'swarming forces must be capable of sustainable pulsing, coalescing rapidly and stealthily on a target, then redispersing and recombining for a new pulse' (Edwards 2000: xvi). While technological advantage is always temporary, technology appears to be a crucial – even a constituent – part of both military and civilian-based swarming. Both have relied to a great deal on emerging network communications technologies.[12]

Life in the Swarm, Life of the Swarm

We have, then, three types of swarming, all of which are concerned at some level with how complex, global organisation arises from simple, local interactions. Perhaps, if only for the sake of simplicity, we can dub the first case of insect swarms 'biological', the second case of swarm algorithms 'technological', and the last case of distributed protest movements 'political'. Each view provides some explanation for the swarming phenomenon, be it biology-genetics, technics-code or politics-ideology. But, just as we have set up this fairly neat division of biological, technological and political swarming, we can immediately see the fuzziness between them: biological studies of swarms are replete with political and cultural concepts ('colony', 'queen', 'worker'), swarming algorithms are used to represent swarms culturally in film and TV as terroristic threats, and distributed protest movements are often dismissed in conservative circles as a primitive, animalistic type of 'mob rule'.

Despite this, one feature common to each of these perspectives has to do with the unique type of 'organisation' that takes place in swarms. The lesson that these and other fields suggest is that there exists a complex whole that cannot be reduced to any of its parts. Broadly speaking, the theses proposed are: (1) that coordinated, local actions can produce complex, global patterns of activity; (2) that such phenomena are dependent upon a high degree of connectivity or communication among individual members; and (3) that individuals within the group do not simply play a single, uniform role. The result – a wholehearted 'network science' approach – emphasises the two essential characteristics of all networks: their flexibility (ability to adapt or to improvise) and their robustness (ability to maintain a goal while taking into account contingencies).

But even more important than the emphasis on organisation is the qualifier that such organisations are somehow 'living' in a way that is, arguably, different from the 'life' of any individual unit. On the one hand the anti-reductionism of complexity research argues that you will not find the key to the 'life' of the ant colony in any one of the individual organisms that compose it. On the other hand, this critical move has had the effect of placing the question of 'life' in a sort of no man's land of the ineffable, a non-site that can only be approached through the language of 'emergence', dynamism and spontaneity.

Perhaps we can address this difficulty by making a distinction between the life *in* the swarm and the life *of* the swarm. The former – life in the swarm – is the discrete life of the organism, itself individuated through the sciences of biology (an ant, a wasp, a locust). The latter – life of the swarm – is the more difficult, even 'vitalist' life that is posited of the swarm as a whole. Thus our question would not just be 'to what degree can the claim of "life" be made of a swarm?' but rather, 'are the criteria for the life in the swarm and the life of the swarm different?' We can take this questioning further and ask 'to what degree is the life of the swarm identical with the notion of "vitalism" as the ineffable, the unnamable and the unaccounted for?'

'Now, that man is more of a political animal than bees or any other gregarious animals is evident' (Aristotle 2001: 1129). For Aristotle, the human being was first a living being, with the additional capacity for political being. In this sense, biology becomes the presupposition for politics, just as the human being's animal being serves as the basis for its political being (this would be the case for Hobbesian 'natural right' as well). But not all animals are alike. Deleuze and Guattari distinguish three types of animals: domestic pets (the Freudian, anthropomorphised Wolf-Man), scientific animals (state animals, official taxonomic species), and packs (group-animals, 'multiplicities') (Deleuze and Guattari 1987: 240–1). For Deleuze and Guattari, this third type of animal – the pack, the swarm – presents a challenge to the first two, principally because it challenges the anthropocentrism through which human beings think not only the animal but the question of 'life' and the living: 'Schools, bands, herds, populations are not inferior social forms; they are affects and powers, involutions that grip every animal in a becoming just as powerful as that of the human being with the animal' (241). This third type of animality exists not via characteristics (species and qualities) but rather through 'contagion', 'propagation', a 'swarming', a 'peopling'.

Clearly it is this last type of animal – the pack, the swarm, the peopling – which provides the most direct counterpoint to the Aristotelian formulation, and which leads us to again reformulate our question: what is it that cuts across the biological, technical and political perspectives on swarms? What do we make of interdisciplinary studies in biocomplexity and swarm intelligence which suggest that there is no 'queen' but only a set of localised interactions which self-organise into a pattern we call a 'swarm'? Such studies seem to suggest that Aristotle based his formulation on the wrong kinds of animals. Of course, 'you can't be one wolf, you're always eight or nine, six or seven' (Deleuze and Guattari 1987: 29). This brings us to our central question: *is there a vitalism that is specific to multiplicity*? Does such a vital multiplicity, an animal multi-plicity, a living multiplicity, ever escape the persistent anthropomor-phism that defines the boundary between human and animal? What if, in an examination of swarms, the question of multiplicity is seen to be indissociable from the question of 'the living'? Would not the notion of animal life become *extrinsic* to itself, and would not the paradoxical task of thinking – and writing – this 'life' specific to multiplicity also have to become extrinsic to itself? Do plants swarm? Rocks? Ideas?

Philosophy and Animality

With the possible exception of Aristotle (that is, Aristotle the 'biolo-gist'), we are lacking the philosophical treatises on the animal that would compliment those on the human: Descartes never wrote a companion volume on the animal to the *Treatise on Man*, Hobbes never wrote the animal version of *De homine* (*On Man*), and Rousseau's organicism in *The Social Contract* never extended into a full-blown trea-tise on what Michel Serres calls the 'Natural Contract'. It will help at this point to consider briefly how philosophy has traditionally thought 'the living', and specifically how it thinks animal life. What we find is that philosophy not only compares the human with the animal (for example, defining humans as 'featherless bipeds'), but more specifically philosophy returns to the comparison between human and insect. How can an animal so 'alien' evoke so many continuities and congruencies?

Aristotle, who often takes for granted the givenness of the natural world, provides us with a comparison that has since become the stock material of science fiction: the comparison between humans and insects as the paradigm for the human–animal relationship (for human beings are 'more of a political animal than bees'). No doubt Hobbes had com-parisons like this in mind when, in *Leviathan*, he notes that 'certain living creatures, as Bees, and Ants, live sociably with one another (which are therefore by Aristotle numbred [*sic*] amongst Politicall [*sic*] crea-tures) and yet have no other direction, than their particular judgements and appetites' (Hobbes 2003: 119). Hobbes' intention – much against Aristotle – is specifically to define the body politic as an artificial entity established by the creation of an absolute sovereign, through the rea-soned agreements of individual members, with their own 'safety and security' in mind. Insects have a 'natural community' while humans have an 'artificial covenant'. The human ability to emerge from the warring 'state of nature' and to relinquish rights to a sovereign power is, for Hobbes, a hallmark of human – and not animal – politics.

But the human–insect comparison concerns not simply governance, for many of our contemporary associations with insects are with insect 'colonies' in which various types of work are performed. Insects seem to be workaholics. Marx was aware of this role of labour vis-à-vis nature. In the first volume of *Capital*, he acknowledges that insects do indeed perform complex types of labour. The spider builds a web, the bee builds a nest, and so forth. 'But what distinguishes the worst architect from the best of bees is that the architect builds the cell in his mind before he constructs it in wax. At the end of every labour process, a result emerges which had already been conceived by the worker at the beginning, hence already existed ideally' (Marx 1990: 284). This, we might add, is the unique character of the 'species-being' of the human. From this, labour-power would be not only a physical and material phenomenon, but a conceptual and 'ideal' one. It would seem that the human ability to perform this labour (and is this not a type of 'immaterial labour'?) is a constituent part of the physical, material aspect of labour-power. If 'nature builds no machines', then insects make no models.

It is, however, Bergson's sporadic comments on insects that finally shore up the discomforting aspect of the human–insect comparison, a discomfort rooted not in the mode of governance, nor in labour, but in the phenomenon of organisation itself. Bergson, drawing upon the then-current knowledge in the biological sciences, argues that Darwinian approaches to the temporal dynamics of the living are too restrictive, viewing selection as a negative, reductive process. Organisms may perfect themselves in more than one way, and according to criteria that have not yet been established. Humans (vertebrates) are highly developed in terms of what Bergson calls 'intelligence', while insects (arthropods) are highly developed in terms of what he calls 'instinct'. He not only posits the metastability of multiple evolutionary strands, he also emphasises the creative and generative aspects of evolution – the *poiesis* of 'the living'. In this regard, Bergson cannot help but point to the uncanny liveness of insects *as a whole*:

> When we see the bees of a hive forming a system so strictly organised that no individual can live apart from the others beyond a certain time, even though furnished with food and shelter, how can we help recognising that the hive is really, and not metaphorically, a single organism, of which each bee is a cell united to the others by invisible bonds? (Bergson 1998: 166)

Bergson has, unsurprisingly, been accused of that most unforgivable of ontological sins – 'vitalism' – but his sentiments had been echoed in nineteenth-century entomology and they are still a part of the contemporary scientific field of swarm intelligence.

Arguably, this is the element that renders the comments of Aristotle, Hobbes and Marx somewhat ambivalent. It is not simply that we humans have language or reason, that we volitionally form governments, or that we engineer our production processes, but rather that insects communicate, form 'societies', and perform complex tasks *as aggregate and differentiated forms*. This would seem to both bear a comparison to human groupings, and, in the context of neo-liberal individualism, to mitigate against any such comparison. 'Insect societies' appear so uncanny because they differ from us humans on so many of the *same* issues (sociability, sovereignty, labour, collective being. . .).

Vitalist Multiplicity

At the risk of homogenising the above thinkers, let us enumerate some of the guiding assumptions in philosophical thinking about humans and insect animals. To begin with, we note that the basic unit of comparison is the individuated being (subject, body, organism). At times this takes a more biological turn (as it does in Bergson), at times it becomes an ontological issue (as it is in Heidegger's ruminations on the 'tick'). But the shared premise is that the condition for the comparison between the human and the animal is the individuated being. Even in biological studies of 'group' animals, one always begins with individuation, which results in the individual. Individuals, after all, form groups. Or do they? Do groups form individuals? This then leads to a further point: not only do we begin from the individuated being, but embedded in this is the notion that individuals precede groups. This is not only a presumption about animals; it also informs much of Western political thought. Plato, in the second book of the *Republic*, begins by suggesting that the Idea of 'justice' in the 'little body' of the human being can only be understood via the 'big body' of the state (Plato 2003). What follows from this is that the state, as an aggregate of individuals, can only be understood by an *individuation of the group*. The group becomes an epiphenomenon of the individual, a secondary formation, a kind of meta-individual. Even today, the discourse of business management in the high-technology sector is inclined to speak of a 'hive mind' and 'group think'.

We can see a process in which the basis of any possible comparison between human and animal is conditioned by four principles: (1) that the basis of comparison is an individuated being, (2) that the individual precedes the group, (3) that the individual constitutes the group, and (4) most importantly, if the group has a 'life' of its own, it will be that of a super-individual. In a sense, groups can never be alive; or, the 'life' of a group is always proper to the individual that is the group. *Aggregates are only 'living' at the cost of being individuated.* Thus, one of the primary challenges in the paradoxical task of thinking animal being – of thinking vitalism inseparable from multiplicity – is to *begin* from the group, the many, the multiple. What then is 'animal being' without individual animals?

It would seem that Deleuze and Guattari's comments on the pack or the swarm offer a counter-example to such anthropomorphising and meta-individuating tendencies. The pack, for them, is nearly synonymous with multiplicities: 'becoming-animal always involves a pack, a band, a population, a peopling, in short, a multiplicity' (Deleuze and Guattari 1987: 239). The organisation of the pack must, for Deleuze and Guattari, be understood temporally. It does not proceed, as in natural history, by way of the series (A resembles B, B resembles C, and so on), since this posits a unilinear chain of causality, whereas packs, swarms, and so on, function through a network of local interactions. Neither does it proceed through structure (A is to B as C is to D), for what is at issue is not the similarities and differences between an ant and a wasp, a bird and a fish, but rather the 'abstract' relations that each swarm or pack engenders. Finally, if the pack or swarm does not proceed through series or structure, neither can it be deduced through a homology of internal relations (what A is to B, A′ is to B′), for the animality of the pack or swarm is not limited to the anthropological systems of totemism or sacrifice in which they obtain meaning for human beings.

What, then, is the pack or the swarm? Deleuze and Guattari give a deceptively straightforward answer: 'A becoming-animal involves a pack, a band, a peopling, in short, a multiplicity' (Deleuze and Guattari 1987: 239). The swarm or pack does not, then, exist statically as 'an' animal, as if in a vacuum; its 'being' is identical with its 'becoming', and its becoming inseparable from its 'unnatural participation' in a swarm or pack. In short, *time* – or better, the temporality specific to morphology – becomes the central element in the concept of the pack or swarm. The swarm or pack functions through becomings of all sorts, a 'becoming-animal traversing human beings and sweeping them away, affecting animal no less than human' (237). The pack is not an arbitrary or unorganised sort of becoming, but a becoming that exists through 'modes of expansion, propagation, occupation, contagion, peopling' (239). Animality – in this sense – is simply what spreads, what disperses, what one can 'catch'. In this sense, becoming-animal has little to do with animals per se, be they the domesticated, anthropomorphic pet or the scientific species. The becoming specific to the pack or swarm has to be understood within the context of the 'complex' whole that results – that is, in relation to the concept of *multiplicity*. We might say that the pack is a multiplicity expressed via a topological temporality, and it is its topology that is 'living'.

It may be helpful at this point to pause over this cluster of concepts – animal/'life', pack/swarm, becoming and multiplicity. We recall Deleuze and Guattari's three types of animals – pet, species, pack – and that their level of thinking operates at the level of this third type, an 'animality' that has nothing to do with 'animals'. We return to our initial questions: 'How does global organisation emerge from local actions?' 'How is the life of the swarm distinct from the life in the swarm?' These two questions are related. One is a question of the one and the many, a question of ontology, a question of topology. The other is a question concerning the living and nonliving, the organic and nonorganic, a question pertaining to the philosophy of biology. We can suggest that, for Deleuze, these two questions are intertwined. In fact, what Deleuze calls the 'mathematico-biological' domain is precisely this intersection between ontology and biology, the question of 'being' and the question of 'life'. The domain in which they intersect may be called 'multiplicity'.

We can delve into Deleuze's elaboration of the concept of 'multiplicity', and this in turn will help to explicate this intertwinement of ontology and biology. What is 'multiplicity'? In *Difference and Repetition*, Deleuze suggests that multiplicity opposes itself both to the 'One' and the 'many': 'multiplicity must not designate a combination of the many and the one, but rather an organisation belonging to the many as such, which has no need whatsoever of unity in order to form a system' (Deleuze 1994: 182). One, many, multiplicity. These are, to be sure, 'ancient' philosophical terms. Plato's notion of the Idea (*eidos*) contained a unity that was lost in its derivative manifestations; there exists an essential unity or oneness of the Idea of 'justice' that is lost once we deal with actual 'just acts', and even more so when we speak of the simulation of justice or the use of justice for ends other than itself. This 'image of thought' is based on the notion that the truth of the matter lies in the transcendent, the universal, the Idea as 'One'. If you want to truly understand the rock, the plant, the animal, you must always move higher up, along a verticality that leads from the blasphemy of simulacra, to the imperfections of the physical world, to the abstract knowledge systems that describe that world, up to the wisdom of the essence, the Idea itself. Plato never asks the question: is there an animal Idea? This is the image of thought that Deleuze both despises and seeks to invert ('an image of thought that has effectively stopped us from thinking').

Deleuze thus 'inverts Platonism' by stressing the immanent and not the transcendent, difference and the differential instead of the identical and the same, and a movement of thought that 'spreads out' rather than a thought that 'raises up'. However, if this was all that Deleuze did, his attack on Platonic thinking would amount to no more than a simple replacement of opposing terms. A close reading of *Difference and Repetition* actually reveals Deleuze 'un-packing' the Platonic *eidos* from within. Instead of either affirming a more traditional reading of Plato (the Idea as transcendent, as identical, as One) or positing its opposite (the anti-Idea as immanent, different, many), Deleuze re-reads Plato to extract from his works a notion of *multiplicity* and *univocity*, difference and repetition, the 'One-All': 'Being is said in a single and same sense of everything of which it is said, but that of which it is said differs: it is said of difference itself' (Deleuze 1994: 36). It is not that something called 'multiplicity' opposes itself to the Idea as the many opposing the One; instead what Deleuze calls 'multiplicity' is precisely that which courses through both the One and the many, which is different because it is always different; recurrently different, different again. This is, moreover, something at least implied in Plato's late dialogue, *Parmenides*, where Plato effectively deconstructs his own notion of the Idea-as-transcendent, the Idea-as-One.[13]

Let us turn to another, different definition given by Deleuze: 'An Idea . . . is neither one nor multiple, but a multiplicity constituted of differential elements, differential relations between those elements, and singularities corresponding to those relations' (Deleuze 1994: 278). Dense though this is, it will help if we unpack it a little. Deleuze provides us with three conditions for any multiplicity. First, there are *elements* ('differential elements'). Elements 'have neither sensible form nor conceptual signification, nor, therefore, any assignable function' (183). Elements are thus not objects or things, but the potential or the non-actual constraints which would define a multiplicity. They are related to what Deleuze calls 'dimensions', or 'the variables and co-ordinates upon which a given phenomenon depends' (182). Second, there are *relations* ('differential relations') which are relations between the elements (which themselves are not actual things or objects). Relations are continuous, they are reciprocally determined and allow for no independence.[14] Everything is connection, 'non-localisable ideal connections'. Relation is like the change of change. Thus, not only are the elements differentially changing, but the relations between these differentially changing elements are themselves changing. Finally, there are *singularities*, which, through elements and relations (both differential), actually incarnate terms, forms, qualities and species (things, objects, organisms, nodes).[15] But this is with the important addendum that the singularities do not change without the multiplicity itself changing.

The first thing to note here is that, for Deleuze, multiplicities are not simply discrete nodes that interact and form a network. Multiplicities are not networks. Again, Deleuze works against a notion that says first there are things, and then there are relations between those things. His three conditions for multiplicities – elements, relations, singularities – do not begin with things and then proceed to relations between them. If anything, Deleuze asks us to think relation *before* we think thing, object, node. In terms of swarms and packs, this means that the actual components of the swarms – the individual organisms, the ant, the bat, the rat – are not the 'cause' but rather the effect of both differential elements and differential relations between elements, which then combine to incarnate actual organisms or animals. Multiplicities not only have *conditions*, they also have *modalities* – real and possible, actual and virtual. For Deleuze, it is crucial to think modality in relation to the conditions of multiplicities. And modality is not simply the real–possible pair (for example the real as the statistical probability of a defined set of discrete outcomes), it is also the actual–virtual pair (the actual does not negate the virtual, for the virtual is coextensive with the actual, it is what 'makes a difference'). In the case of swarms, the elements, for instance, are not manifested in actuality, but exist 'virtually' as the very ability of matter and energy to be organised in such as a way as to 'swarm'. Together, the elements and the relations of multiplicities are not simply the arbitrary possibility of being anything, but the non-actual, generative, 'abstract' constraints that, in our example, swarm: they generate dispersals, trailing, branching, swerving, fanning, involuting, dilations, expansions. The implication is that, in thinking swarms and packs, we would have to do two things at once: think the 'abstract' pattern of swarming that cuts across any specific swarm, but, at the same time, think this in a non-transcendental, non-universal way, as completely immanent to the way the swarm is composed of differences-upon-differences.

What do these conditions and these modalities tell us about swarms and packs? For one, they stress that the organisation of the pack or swarm is directly correlated to its internal heterogeneity, its internal 'consistency'. Recall that, for Deleuze and Guattari, the pack is not simply an homogeneous, amorphous unit. The pack continually differentiates, and this internal differentiation can be understood to be the motor behind its creativity, variability and involution (a 'creative involution'). Each pack contains one or more 'exceptional individuals', those pack elements which serve as the threshold or membrane of the pack, those elements with which one makes a *pact* in order to become a *pack*.[16] The exceptional individual is not an individual at all, but the conditions of de-individuation that are the conditions of the pack. At the same time, every pack also has its 'anomalous', or those elements that diverge, swerve and abandon a given course.[17] If the exceptional individual is the condition of de-individuation for becoming a pack, then the anomalous is the condition of singularisation for sustaining a pack. The anomalous are those elements in the pack that define a different threshold, a 'phenomenon of bordering', a tensile dimension of the pack, its 'intension' rather than its spatialised 'extension'.[18] We might say that the zone between local actions and global patterns is occupied by the anomalous. The result of these forces – the exceptional individual, the anomalous being, the phenomenon of bordering – is a view of multiplicity as defined through a certain notion of time: 'a multiplicity is defined not by the elements that compose it in extension, not by the characteristics that compose it in comprehension, but by the lines and dimensions it encompasses in 'intension' (Deleuze and Guattari 1987: 245). In short, what Deleuze and Guattari discuss as the pack-multiplicity is a swarming, one that cuts across the domains of biology (ant foraging), technology (network protocols), or politics (smartmobs). We see again that the greatest challenge posed by multiplicity is its being thought as such.

Number versus Animal

But perhaps we can be a bit sceptical here: Is there not something contradictory in our very designation of 'a' pack or 'a' swarm, something beyond mere nominalism and having to do with the very ontological status of multiplicity, especially inasmuch as the swarm designates an animal being, a living being? This is the question raised by Alain Badiou in his treatment of Deleuze's concept of multiplicity (Badiou 2004). Two of Badiou's points are worth mentioning in the context of animals, swarms and multiplicity. First, while Deleuze proposes to have done with Hegelian becoming by offering the series one–many–multiplicity, Badiou wonders if such a project doesn't end up reinscribing multiplicity within a version of 'the One' (but a renewed 'One' that has been flattened, informed by Spinoza more than by Plato or Hegel). Deleuze's inversion of Platonism – his formulation of the 'univocity of being' – is thus haunted by the challenge of what Badiou calls a 'multiple-without-oneness', the challenge of considering the 'intrinsic resources of the multiple' in itself, without resorting to a notion of a chaotic, turbulent, univocal One (Badiou 2004: 68–9).

This leads to a second point Badiou makes, which has to do with Deleuze's approach to the many or the multiple (Badiou prefers the term 'multiple' for reasons associated with mathematics). In Badiou's reading, Deleuze bifurcates multiplicity, between a quantitative, 'closed' multiplicity that is reduced to number, and a qualitative, 'open' multiplicity that is innovated by the virtual: 'multiplicity appears as suspended between two forms of the One: on the one hand, the form that relates to counting, number, the set; on the other, the form that relates to life, creation, differentiation' (Badiou 2004: 71). Badiou's summary of Deleuzian pack-multiplicities is that, for Deleuze, there have only ever been two approaches to the multiplicity: number and animal. The result is that Deleuze's 'way out' is only in the passage from one multiplicity to the other, a false solution which, in Badiou's words, only reifies multiplicity as a 'vitalist terrorism', a 'natural mysticism'. Badiou summarises his 'critique' of Deleuze in this way:

> [T]he attempt to subvert the 'vertical' transcendence of the One through the play of the closed and the open, which deploys multiplicity in the mobile interval between a set (inertia) and an effective multiplicity (line of flight), produces a 'horizontal' or virtual transcendence which, instead of grasping singularity, ignores the intrinsic resource of the multiple, presupposes the chaotic power of the One, and analogises the modes of actualisation. When all is said and done, we are left with what could be defined as natural mysticism. In order to have done with transcendence, it is necessary to follow the thread of the multiple-without-oneness – impervious to any play of the closed and the open, canceling any abyss between the finite and the infinite, purely actual, haunted by the internal excess of its parts – whose univocal singularity is ontologically nameable only by a form of writing subtracted from the poetics of natural language. (Badiou 2004: 79–80)

As is well known, Badiou's response comes through his contentious proposition that 'ontology is mathematics', an assertion that leads him to an in-depth engagement with the philosophy of set theory in his *Being and Event*. But Badiou's particular engagement with Deleuze centres on this perceived dichotomy between the two types of multiplicity, between the set and vitalism, between 'number' and 'animal'.

For Badiou, Deleuze approaches the concept of multiplicity through 'a preliminary deconstruction of the concept of "set"' (Badiou 2004: 70). Whenever we speak of a 'set', we imply not only a collection of items, but, more importantly, criteria for ordering those items as included or excluded, as part of the set or not part of the set (the set of all things not part of this particular set), or subsets (sets within sets). In his reading of Deleuze's dichotomised concept of multiplicity, Badiou's argument is that for Deleuze *set* is always reducible to *number*. In other words, Badiou's claim is that Deleuze conflates the relation between 'set' and 'number'. Deleuze presumes that 'set' is always reducible to 'number' (for example that 'couples' are always reducible to the number '2'). Because, for Deleuze, set is reducible to number, set is always defined by the dialectic of the One and the many. The Deleuzian result, as we've seen, is that 'number' becomes split between two types of multiplicity: closed versus open, static versus dynamic, discrete versus continuous, difference-in-degree versus difference-in-kind, numerical versus vital. In Badiou's reading, Deleuze theorises multiplicity versus the One–many, which is itself another dichotomisation. As Badiou notes, this opposition is based on a temporalisation of 'set' of an 'intervallic' type (virtual–actual, possible–real, being–becoming). However, for Badiou all this does is reinscribe multiplicity within a transcendental domain, in its new guise of 'the virtual'. It leads, as Badiou jibes, to a 'Platonism of the virtual' (2000: 44.6).[19] Thus Deleuze's stated aim to 'invert Platonism' and the Platonic 'image of thought' actually ends up resurrecting the Idea as the virtual, as a paradoxical and transcendental time-beyond-time. Badiou's own argument is, *contra* Deleuze, that 'set' is not reducible to 'number' – and not every set is a number. Furthermore, number itself presupposes the 'prior availability of an ontology of sets'. Number is dependent on the concept of set, which itself poses ontological problems that pertain to existence, individuation, identity and the mathematical philosophy of the 'actual infinite'. Thus for Badiou the theory of sets demonstrates that multiplicity always exists in the actual, and has no need of a Platonic, transcendent 'virtual'. This is, for Badiou, a true multiplicity, a 'multiple-without-oneness'.

We return to our 'practical' question, on the ground, as it were. How does all this inflect our understanding of the conceptual chain animal–swarm–multiplicity? What of Badiou's characterisation of 'number' versus 'animal'? From one perspective, do not the technoscientific examples cited above – swarm intelligence, network science, multi-agent systems – appear to take up Deleuze and Guattari's notion of the pack, contagion and multiplicity, while eschewing the division between number and animal, the quantitative multiplicity and the qualitative multiplicity? As we've noted, contemporary variants of graph theory, group theory, differential calculus, even fuzzy logic, all inform the computerised simulation of packs, swarms, flocks, and so on. In a way, do not such examples seem to echo Badiou's proposal concerning set theory, that, 'far from the set being reducible to number, it is rather number . . . which presupposes the prior availability of the ontology of sets' (Badiou 2004: 71)? In this regard, the animal multiplicity of the pack or the swarm is not that which is irreducible to number; rather, number is, in Badiou's sense, the ontological principle that conditions the generativity, the contagion, the propagation of the multiple: 'This is why, in elaborating an ontology of the multiple, the *first* rule is follow the conceptual mathematical constructions – which we know can overflow in all directions, no matter what the empirical case' (74).

But we are still left with the perennial, exhaustive question of the animal, the 'bare life' of animality, the animality specific to multiplicity. Clearly, for Badiou 'number' is superior to 'animal' just as the ontology of sets is superior to what he perceives as Deleuze's careless, romantic 'vitalism'. A thought: perhaps what Deleuze means by 'animal' is what Badiou means by 'number'. *Deleuze's 'animal' = Badiou's 'number'?* If the pack is the animal, is the animal also number? If number informs the pack, is number also a pack? Is there a *vitalist matheme* that would encompass the dual question that runs through the concept of animal multiplicity: that of number and that of 'life'? Perhaps, then, the multiplicity specific to packs and swarms – the relation between multiplicity and animality – is to be found in this vitalist matheme, one that would produce not just animal swarms, or data swarms, or political swarms, but an affective swarming, a transversal that cuts across the fields of biology, technology and politics. Such an affective swarming would need to raise several topological issues: the relation between connectivity and collectivity (being-in-exchange and being-together), the relation between pattern and purpose (a problem of teleology), and the notion of edges-without-nodes (swarming as a network-in-time).[20] These and other topological issues point to the possibility of a renewed transversality, or, perhaps, a 'pathology' between number and animal, something at least hinted at by Badiou:[21] 'everywhere where mathematics is close to experience but follows its own movement, it discovers a "pathological" case that absolutely challenges the initial intuition. Mathematics then establishes that this pathology is the rule, and that what can be intuited is only an exception' (Badiou 2004: 74).

Formless, Faceless Enmity

By way of closing, consider how the concept of swarms effects the most basic political relation: that of enmity. The friend–enemy distinction is, as Carl Schmitt notes, the basis of political decision, but the political decision is also that which constitutes enmity (Schmitt 1996). Are you friend or foe? Everything depends on how one 'faces' the situation; it all depends on where you're standing. Enmity is always a face because enmity is always 'faced' or constituted by a confrontation. I stand alongside my friend; I stand opposite my foe. My friend and I only 'face' each other insofar as we stand opposite and 'face' our common foe. The Schmittian friend–foe distinction is not just politico-military, but politico-ethical too. The basis of the friend–foe distinction is intimately related to the relation between self and other. But this self-other relation need not be a rapid fire of glances, gazes and recognition (as we see in the Hegelian-Kojevian model). For Levinas, ethics is first constituted by the ambiguous calling of the 'face' of the other, for there is an affective dynamic at work between self and other that revolves and devolves around the 'face' (a verb more than noun) (Levinas 1989). Ethics is thus not how a pre-constituted self decides to behave towards others who are equally pre-constituted. Rather ethics is itself this challenge offered forth by an 'Other' that pre-exists the self and continually calls the self into question. Friends, foes, selves – there are faces everywhere. There are faces everywhere, except, of course, where there are no faces – or where there is only a *defacement* of enmity.[22] But how can enmity have no face? Recall our three case studies of swarms ('biological', 'technical', 'political'). Swarming attacks from all directions, and intermittently but consistently – it has no 'front', no battle line, no central point of vulnerability. It is dispersed, distributed and yet in constant communication. In short, it is a faceless foe, or a foe stripped of 'faciality' as such. So, a new problematic emerges. What is the shape of the ethical encounter when it 'faces' the swarm, defined by its being faceless? If there is no foe to face, how does one face a foe?

In addition to swarms and packs, the issue of faces, facing – or rather 'faciality' – is another of Deleuze and Guattari's concerns. But they also take 'facing' (facing the other, facing a foe) to be a kind of pattern-recognition, a certain ordering of holes, lines, curves: 'The head is included in the body, but the face is not. The face is a surface: facial traits, lines, wrinkles; long face, square face, triangular face; the face is a map, even when it is applied to and wraps a volume, even when it surrounds and borders cavities that are now no more than holes' (Deleuze and Guattari 1987: 170). Faciality is, in a more mundane sense, our recognition of other human faces, and thus our habit of facing, encountering, meeting others all the time. But for Deleuze and Guattari, the fundamental process of faciality also leads to a deterritorialisation of the familiar face, and to the proliferation of faces, in the snow, on the wall, in the clouds, places where faces shouldn't be. . .

Are there places where 'faces' shouldn't be? Is that, in fact, what 'swarming' is? In a sense, the swarm, *swarming-as-faciality*, is a reminder of the *defacement* proper not only to distributed insects, but to distributed humans; in fact, perhaps swarming is simply a reminder of the defacement that runs through all instances of 'facing' the other: 'The face is produced only when the head ceases to be part of the body' (Deleuze and Guattari 1987: 170). Perhaps the reason why swarms, packs and multiplicities elicit such fascination is that they pose a question about 'life', but a question more fundamental than that of the difference between human and animal life. A question about local actions and global patterns, about an ambivalent, tensile topology that asks us to consider *sovereignty* and *multiplicity*, or *control* and *emergence*, in the same breath.

References

Aristotle (2001), 'The Politics', in R. McKeon (ed.), *The Basic Works of Aristotle*, trans. B. Jowett, New York: Modern Library.

Arquilla, J. and D. Ronfeldt (2000), *Swarming and the Future of Conflict*, Santa Monica: RAND.

Arquilla, J. and D. Ronfeldt (eds) (2001), *Networks and Netwars: The Future of Terror, Crime, and Militancy*, Santa Monica: RAND.

Badiou, A. (2000), *Deleuze: The Clamour of Being*, trans. L. Burchell, Minneapolis: University of Minnesota Press.

Badiou, A. (2004), 'One, Multiple, Multiplicities', in *Theoretical Writings*, trans. R. Brassier and A. Toscano, London: Continuum.

Bonebeau, E. and G. Théraulaz (2000), 'Swarm Smarts', *Scientific American*, 282 (3): 72–9.

Bonabeau, E., M. Dorigo and G. Théraulaz (1999), *Swarm Intelligence: From Natural to Artificial Systems*, Oxford: Oxford University Press.

Camazine, S., J-L. Deneubourg, N. R. Franks, J. Sneyd, G. Théraulaz and E. Bonabeau (eds) (2001), *Self-Organization in Biological Systems*, Princeton: Princeton University Press.

Deleuze, G. (1994), *Difference and Repetition*, trans. P. Patton, New York: Columbia University Press.

Deleuze, G. (2004), 'Bergson's Conception of Difference', in *Desert Islands and Other Texts*, trans. M. Taormina, New York: Semiotext(e).

Deleuze, G. and F. Guattari (1987), *A Thousand Plateaus*, trans. B. Massumi, Minneapolis: University of Minnesota Press.

Edwards, S. (2000), *Swarming on the Battlefield: Past, Present, and Future*, Santa Monica: RAND.

Gordon, D. (2000), *Ants at Work: How an Insect Society is Organized*, New York: W. W. Norton & Company.

Hardt, M. and A. Negri (2004), *Multitude*, New York: Penguin.

Hobbes, T. (2003), *Leviathan*, Cambridge: Cambridge University Press.

Langton, C. (ed.) (1995), *Artificial Life: An Overview*, Cambridge, MA: MIT Press.

Levinas, E. (1989), 'Ethics as First Philosophy', in S. Hand (ed.), *The Levinas Reader*, New York: Routledge.

Marx, K. (1990), *Capital: Volume I*, trans. B. Fowkes, New York: Penguin.

Morton Wheeler, W. (1911), 'The Ant Colony as an Organism', *Journal of Morphology*, XXII: 301–25.

Plato (1997), *Parmenides*, trans. R. E. Allen, New Haven: Yale University Press.

Plato (2003), *The Republic*, trans. D. Lee, London: Penguin

Reynolds, C. (1987), 'Flocks, Herds, and Schools: A Distributed Behavioral Model', *SIGGRAPH '87/Computer Graphics*, 21 (4): 25–34.

Schmitt, C. (1996), *The Concept of the Political*, trans. G. Schwab, Chicago: University of Chicago Press.

Sleigh, C. (2003), *Ant*, London: Reaktion.

Thacker, E. (2004), 'Networks, Swarms, Multitudes' (parts one and two), *Ctheory*, May 18, 2004, www.ctheory.net

Thacker, E. and A. Galloway (2004), 'Protocol, Control, and Networks', *Grey Room*, 17: 6–30.

Thacker, E. and A. Galloway (2006), 'On Misanthropy', in Krisa Joasia (ed.), *DATA browser 03: Curating Immateriality*, Brooklyn: Autonomedia.

Wilson, E. O. and B. Hölldobler (1995), *Journey to the Ants*, New York: Belknap Press.

Notes

1. Most of these are found in Deleuze and Guattari's *A Thousand Plateaus* (1987), especially the chapters on 'The Geology of Morals' and 'Becoming-Animal', though the concepts of 'the machinic' and the 'body without organs' are first developed in *Anti-Oedipus*. Deleuze and Guattari make several references to the work in molecular genetics by François Jacob and Jacques Monod, who published a series of key papers in the 1950s and 1960s outlining the metabolism in the cell using the model of cybernetics. In addition, because *A Thousand Plateaus* spans a wide range of disciplines, it is tempting to place concepts such as 'nucleic acids of expression' and 'proteins of content' alongside developments in genetic engineering in the 1970s, which brought to public consciousness the possibility of engineering hybrid species.

2. The concern with 'concept' and 'life' is already present in Deleuze's early essay on Bergson: 'We are looking for a concept of difference that does not allow itself to be reduced to degree or intensity, to alterity or contradiction: such a difference *is* vital, even if the concept itself is not biological. Life is the process of difference' (Deleuze 2004: 39).

3. Indeed, in *A Thousand Plateaus* the concept of 'the molecular' tends to be more about physics and music than anything 'biological'. Thus the role of time, transformation and 'becoming' marks the molecular: 'Becoming is to emit particles that take on certain relations of movement and rest because they enter a particular zone of proximity' (Deleuze and Guattari 1987: 273).

4. On this see Camazine et al. (2001). This textbook contains a highly readable theoretical introduction, followed by a series of case studies exploring biological self-organisation in a number of insect species, birds, fish, and so on. Myrmecologist Deborah Gordon's book, *Ants at Work: How an Insect Society is Organized* (2000), also provides a clear account for the non-specialist of the 'bottom-up' organisation of ants.

5. This phenomenon can be witnessed on a smaller scale by anyone who has had to deal with an 'ant problem' in their own home. See Camazine et al. (2001: 257–83)

6. Already we can see that the scientific study of swarms brings with it a host of concepts, metaphors and worldviews that are much more than just scientific. As Charlotte Sleigh notes in her cultural study *Ant*, 'each myrmecologist has a behavior that, for him or her, defines the condition of being an ant. For Gordon, it is

working . . . For Wilson, it is fighting' (Sleigh 2003: 179). Such differences in views coexist with different methods for studying insect swarms, variously emphasising the (very anthropocentric) aspects of labour, reproduction, war or competition, and the domestic management of the brood.

7. It should be noted that this is already implicit in William Morton Wheeler's work in the nineteenth century. His inquiry into the mystery of what makes an ant colony a coherent whole prompts him to consider it a 'superorganism' or a kind of meta-organism. See his fascinating article 'The Ant Colony as an Organism' (1911).

8. For a more readable overview of the research, see Bonebeau and Théraulaz (2000: 72–9).

9. A more technical introduction is given in Bonabeau et al. (1999). In fact, in the late 1990s British Telecom hired swarm intelligence researchers to design a way to reroute telephone calls during emergencies.

10. The field of artificial life or 'a-life' has, for some years, taken inspiration from examples in nature and attempted to either generate or simulate them on the computer. For an overview of approaches and philosophies, see Langton (1995).

11. For a range of examples and viewpoints, see Arquilla and Ronfeldt (2001).

12. For instance, future military swarm units will require 'a mobile mesh communications network with high data throughput and survivability' (Edwards 2000: xvii).

13. In the first part of the dialogue, a youthful Socrates attempts to defend his notion of the Idea-as-One, while an elderly Parmenides patiently listens and then quickly points out the contradictions in Socrates' analogies. Socrates' analogies include the analogy of the sun (the One is like the sun, shining during a single day and in many places; the One is thus indivisible), and the analogy of the sail (the One is like a sail, each part of which covers every man; the One is thus divisible). The critique of Parmenides points to the so-called dilemma of participation in the theory of Ideas/forms, which has to do with part–whole relations: if actual objects a and b are related to Ideas X through participation, then either a and b participate in the whole of X, in which case X becomes divided from itself, or a and b participate in a part of X, in which case X is merely the sum of parts a and b (Plato 1997).

14. 'These elements must in effect be determined, but reciprocally, by reciprocal relations which allow no independence whatsoever to subsist' (Deleuze 1994: 183).

15. 'A multiple ideal connection, a differential relation, must be actualised in diverse spatio-temporal relationships, at the same time as its elements are actually incarnated in a variety of terms and forms' (Deleuze 1994: 183).

16. '. . .wherever there is a multiplicity, you will also find an exceptional individual, and it is with that individual that an alliance must be made in order to become-animal' (Deleuze and Guattari 1987: 243).

17. 'The anomalous, the preferential element in the pack, has nothing to do with the preferred, domestic, and psychoanalytic individual . . . The anomalous is neither an individual nor a species; it has only affects' (Deleuze and Guattari 1987: 244).

18. 'If the anomalous is neither an individual nor a species, then what is it? It is a phenomenon, but a phenomenon of bordering . . . there is a borderline for each multiplicity' (Deleuze and Guatari 1987: 245).

19. Critiques of Badiou's own critique of Deleuze have been many, from reactionary diatribes that faithfully hold to Deleuze's concepts, to border-policing in the space between philosophy and mathematics. An example is the special issue of *Futur Antérieur* (April 1998), which includes polemical replies by Arnaud Villani and José Gil. To be fair, it is worth noting that Badiou's reading of Deleuze is a very selective one. Arguably, Deleuze's concept of 'multiplicity' undergoes significant

changes between early works such as *Bergsonism*, the collaboration in *A Thousand Plateaus*, and later works such as 'Immanence: A Life'. To treat this debate fully, one would have to account for these changes, as well as Deleuze's own engagement with mathematics (which, as Manuel DeLanda points out, is rooted not in set theory but in differential geometry), as well as Deleuze's own philosophy of 'number' (for example his distinction between a 'numbered number' and a 'numbering number').

20. I have tried to elaborate these ideas in Thacker (2004) and, in collaboration with Alex Galloway, in Thacker and Galloway (2004).

21. On this point see also Thacker (2004) and Thacker and Galloway (2004).

22. For a variant on this argument, see Thacker and Galloway (2006).

Chapter 10

The Body Without Organs and Internet Gaming Addiction

Ian Cook

A man in his 20s who had been playing computer games continuously for over 50 hours died of exhaustion . . . [F]ired early last month over his frequent absences due to his game addiction, Lee had been coming to the PC café every day to play . . . The head of the mental health department at Daegu Fatima Hospital . . . said, 'Computer game addiction, just like alcohol and drug addiction, is a disease accompanied by withdrawal symptoms like anxiety, irritability and depression.' (English Chosun 2005)

. . . a couple in Incheon, South Korea, were arrested last week when their 4-month-old daughter died after being left alone by the couple [who] . . . lost themselves in playing Blizzard's massively multiplayer online PC game *World of Warcraft*, and returned to their home only to find [their only child] . . . dead from suffocation. (Gamespot 2005)

A variety of fears haunts the digitised imaginary: monstrous cyborgs, cyber-stalking paedophiles, digital pied pipers,[1] apocalyptic computer viruses, Y2Ks, panoptic surveillance devices that serve Big Brother or the Global Corporation. 'Internet addict' now belongs on this list. While some Internet addicts are addicted to webporn (Cook 2006), others are Internet gaming addicts. This chapter is an attempt to conceive the Internet gaming addict through Deleuze and Guattari's concept of the body without organs. Conceiving the Internet gaming addict in this way enables an explanation of Internet gaming addiction as an expression of a pathological predisposition to reform the assemblage, or configuration,[2] of Internet gaming.

The chapter consists of two parts. The first comprises an account of Deleuze and Guattari's concept of the body without organs in terms of three modes of emergence (organism, subjectification and significance). The second offers a view of Internet gaming addiction as a pathological impetus to reform particular modes of emergence that derives from the effects of striation, as habit, and intensity. The configurations that emerge from the body without organs, then, form pathological (molar) forms due to the combination of a predisposition to reconfigure, the formation of striations on the body without organs which cause attempts to produce the re-emergence of specific configurations, and the pursuit of intensity.

Conceiving the Body Without Organs

Internet gaming addiction represents a pathological predisposition to repeat a particular configuration. This impetus manifests in terms of the three forms of emergence of the body without organs identified by Deleuze and Guattari. These are organism, subjectification and significance. For Deleuze and Guattari, the body without organs 'is that glacial reality where the alluvions, sedimentations, coagulations, foldings, and recoilings that compose an organism – and also a signification and a subject – occur' (Deleuze and Guattari 1987: 159). They seek to analyse the emergences of the body without organs that form across 'the strata, organisms, State, family' (157). In order to do so, they attempt to account for 'the *surface* of the organism, the *angle* of significance and interpretation, and the *point* of subjectification or subjection' (159, emphasis added). The body without organs expresses what Spinoza called 'infinite substance'. As a result, the body without organs is in a constant state of formation and reformation that occurs across and between a myriad of planes that express totality. All emergences from the body without organs are effected and re-effected within infinite substance. Thus 'it is through a restriction, a blockage, and a reduction that the libido is made to repress its flows in order to contain them in the narrow cells of the type "couple", "family", "person", "objects"'. This is necessary because 'the libido does not come to consciousness except in relation to a given body, a given person that it takes as object' (Deleuze and Guattari 1983: 293).

The moment of 'object-choice', however, 'refers to a conjunction of flows of life and of society that this body and this person intercept, receive, and transmit, always within a biological, social, and historical field where we are equally immersed or with which we communicate' (Deleuze and Guattari 1983: 293). Ongoing interaction between these fields means that this is not a 'once and for all' moment, and all emergences from the body without organs will be done and redone, as none has permanence. The body without organs is 'the site of cultural inscription', as Fox notes, 'and is constructed and reconstructed (territorialised) continually' (Fox 2002: 352). Emergences from the body without organs result from effects on mental surfaces. The mind forms a surface upon which existential figures (or configurations) are produced.

Deleuze conceives of the brain 'in terms of the conversion of a cerebral surface into a metaphysical surface . . . "the brain is not only a corporeal organ but also the inductor of another invisible, incorporeal, and metaphysical surface on which all events are inscribed and symbolised"' (Bains 1997: 522).

None of the phenomena named in this discussion of the emergences from the body without organs have 'individuality', in the sense that this is normally understood in Western societies. As Bains points out, Deleuze and Guattari devoted much of their energy to the attempt to overcome the conception of 'the subject as the ultimate essence of individuation, pre-reflexively contemplating its own existence, and to develop a schizo-analytic subjectivity superposing multiple strata of subjectivation in a multi-componential cartography opposed to the Conscious–Unconscious dualism of the Freudian schema' (Bains 1997: 522).[3]

Organism

The configurations of organism reflect a connection between particular organs. Thus, it is 'the organisation of the organs we call the organism' (Deleuze and Guattari 1987: 160). The relationship between the organism and the body is not direct and it may well be that the word 'body' plays little role in a vocabulary derived from Deleuze and Guattari's works. 'Bodies are not the locus at which forces act, they are the production of the interaction of forces' (Fox 2002: 356).

For an individual, the organism is merely 'a chance overlapping of the energetic, molecular, and biological processes that produced it'. As a result, that which 'we may essentialise as the natural body for a species is . . . no more than an over-growth of "part-organs" on the surface of . . . the transcendental condition for any organic body . . . a "body without organs"' (Mullarkey 1994: 342). The organism, then, does not comprehend an entire 'body'. Instead, the organism 'is a stratum on the [body without organs] . . . a phenomenon of accumulation, coagulation, and sedimentation that, in order to extract useful labor from the body without organs, imposes upon it forms, functions, bonds, dominant and hierarchised organisations, organised tendencies' (Deleuze and Guattari 1987: 159).

Subjectification

For Deleuze, 'the Other is neither an object in the field of my perception nor a subject who perceives me: the Other is initially a structure of the perceptual field, without which the entire field could not function as it does' (Deleuze 1990: 307). Otherness, then, is an effect produced across a surface in which 'others' emerge in relation to 'others' (Jameson 1997: 406). The fact that the structure of the 'perceptual field' of otherness 'may be actualised by real characters, by variable subjects – me for you and you for me – does not prevent its pre-existence, as the conditions of organisation in general, to the terms which actualise it in each organised perceptual field – yours and mine' (Deleuze 1993: 59).

The crucial attribute of the otherness of subjectification is the enfolding of proximity. Proximity is conceived here in the same way that gravitons are conceived. That is, as effects transmitted between two points. The difference is that the distance between the two points affects the transmission of gravitons in a way that it does not affect the transmission of proximity. (Think of the couple in love, or the flirtatious couple, whose movements correspond or relate somehow, no matter how many people occupy the space between them.) Proximity travels between points of otherness. One of the effects of the transmission of proximity is to produce immediacy and discreteness with respect to otherness. The transmission of proximity results in otherness within which 'others' emerge. The Other must be understood as a structure and not as 'a particular "form" inside a perceptual field (distinct from the form "object" or the form "animal")'. For the Other is 'a system which conditions the functioning of the entire perceptual field in general'. This is the reason that Deleuze distinguished an 'a priori other' from a 'concrete Other'. The former designates the structure and the latter 'designates real terms actualising the structure in concrete fields'. The 'concrete Other' is, by definition, someone. 'The a priori Other, on the other hand, is no one since the structure is transcendent with respect to the terms which actualise it' (Deleuze 1993: 65).

Subjectifications emerge, as Ruthrof has pointed out, because an 'order of subjection' exists. 'Here Deleuze distinguishes subjectification as the formation and fixing of subjectivity from subjectivation, or the self-positing of subjectivity' (Ruthrof 1997: 565). Subjectification, then, is not individual self-creation, but a formation and form of containment that emerges upon and through a particular stratum (in this analysis the stratum of subjectification). 'We are continually stratified. But who is this we that is not me, for the subject no less than the organism belongs to and depends on a stratum?' (Deleuze and Guattari 1987: 159). Subjectification produces 'containment' because it produces configurations through which otherness (including ours) is held in place. For Deleuze and Guattari one of the questions that arises in this context is:

'how can we unhook ourselves from the points of subjectification that secure us, nail us down to a dominant reality?' (160). It is for this reason that subjectification manifests the form of proximity that emerges as relating to others. For subjectification allows us to react to events around us ('you have to keep small rations of subjectivity in sufficient quantity to enable you to respond to the dominant reality' (160)). More importantly, subjectification allows us to enfold as/with a communal configuration. 'You will be a subject, nailed down as one, a subject of the enunciation recoiled into a subject of the statement – otherwise you're just a tramp' (159).[4]

Signifiance

The emergences from the body without organs that manifest signifiance have little proximity, or significant remoteness, than those of subjectification. For the figures that emerge on this surface are held in place by more formal modes of differentiation. They are described here as 'remote' because the particularities that might be associated with bodily elements enfolded in the subjectifications are excluded from the configuration. The configurations that emerge from the body without organs conceived thus are those in which emergences enfold body parts and things, but these emergences are becomings- and beings-general, in which specificity is a sign of a failure in the process of enfolding associated with these configurations.

The remoteness associated with signifiance results in the formation of objects/points/othernesses less through bodily position than through social position. The names given to those who occupy such social positions – for example 'teacher', 'parent' or 'worker' – indicate 'a place in a certain arrangement of machines rather than an entity. It's a bit like a business card – it advertises what one can do, the prior connections and relations that are embedded within' (Brown and Lundt 2002: 15). From this perspective, 'territories and territorialisations may be not only physical but also psychological and spiritual: philosophy and ideology have historically reterritorialised land as "nations", Homeland or Fatherland' (Fox 2002: 353).

Signifiance, for Deleuze and Guattari, 'clings to the soul just as the organism clings to the body' (Deleuze and Guattari 1987: 160). Signifiance is a continuing process, however, and must be done and redone in light of prior signifiance. 'For the perpetuation of "signifiance" is secured in turn by *interpretance*, or infinite interpretation, forever feeding on earlier interpretations' (Ruthrof 1997: 566). Signifiance is produced through a plane or order of signification and that which emerges must partake of (and be captured by) a system of meaning. 'You will be signifier and signified, interpreter and interpreted – otherwise you're just a deviant' (Deleuze and Guattari 1987: 159).

Addiction as 'pathological' reconfiguration

Addiction, herein a pathological predisposition to reform a particular configuration, begins with a predisposition to reconfigure. The predisposition to configure reflects a (Nietzschean) drive to form, become or express. The occurrence of configurations affects infinite substance by producing striations, or effects on the surfaces of emergence, that make it highly likely that the same processes of configuration will recur. In short, habits form.

The discursive element 'addict', however, is enfolded with only some of these habits. That which differentiates the addict from the user is the enfolding of the element 'addict' with those elements that result in the emergence 'user'. Addict, crucially, functions as an effect of significance, and emerges in the addict–therapist configuration (that is 'treating' or 'treatment' in its verb form). Insufficient words are available for an adequate discussion of the ways in which Internet gaming addiction manifests a therapeutic configuration. As a result, I offer no discussion of the ways in which the emergence 'addict' requires a stratum upon which therapy occurs. Instead, this discussion follows the theoretical path from configuration to reconfiguration to a pathological impetus to reconfigure.

Configuration

From Spinoza we learn that 'everything that exists strives to persevere in its being' (Gatens 2000: 60). A predisposition to configure, then, dominates the body without organs. If nothing else, this predisposition satisfies the requirement that things be done. It is for this reason that the question that must be asked, as Buchanan notes, concerns what a body can do. For this is 'the critical means of finding out what masochists, drug users, obsessives and paranoiacs are actually trying to do. The question works by staking out an area of *what* a body actually can do' (Buchanan 1997: 79).

From a more explicitly Nietzschean perspective, configuring expresses will to power. Emergence extends (fractal-like) into the world in order to replicate its pattern to the nth degree. Deleuze accepted Nietzsche's approach to determining whether or not an action is good. In order to do so, we must ask ourselves whether we can see ourselves 'doing it an infinite number of times'. If we can, then this action can become a 'mode of existence'. When it comes to alcoholics who would like to drink, then, Deleuze challenges them to affirm that they would do so with a readiness to drink for eternity: 'You want to drink? Good, very well. If you drink, drink in such a way that each time you drink, you would be ready to drink, redrink, redrink an infinite number of times' (Deleuze 1980: 8).

Reconfiguring

Configurations do not form once and for all. Most configurations are repeated. The simplest explanation for this is the need to repeat certain actions regularly. Deleuze, however, posits a 'passion for repetition' (Deleuze 1994: 97–8). Indeed, 'for Deleuze the subject is produced as an effect of repetition' (Neil 1998: 420). This might explain why Deleuze and Guattari advise us to keep a little of the configurations of organism, subjectification and signifiance – for we will need them to act again (Deleuze and Guattari 1987: 160). It may also be why Deleuze believes that 'historical repetition is . . . above all a condition of historical action itself. . . . historical actors or agents can create only on condition that they identify themselves with figures from the past' (Deleuze 1994: 91). Configuration might emerge anew as each moment of becoming, but this is both difficult and unlikely. It is unlikely because of the familiarity and ease associated with re-forming configurations (relative to forming each configuration somehow for itself). Configurations produce striations, which means that the re-emergence of a given configuration becomes more probable than the formation of an entirely new configuration. Configuring anew in each moment is difficult, because to become anew requires escaping the effects of striation.

Configurations are their own attractors, in the sense that there is an attraction to reforming configurations that are easier to form (a process mediated by a variety of other factors). In this case, configuration develops it own dynamic, as 'satisfaction'. It is for this reason that Lambert describes an institution as 'an organised system of means to attain satisfaction'. Organisms enter 'the milieu of institutions' and the means by which they attain satisfaction are artificial. Living ceases to function as 'a state of satisfaction, but rather life itself is defined by the multiple degrees of intensity (quality) and by artificial states of satisfaction'. The result is that satisfaction is not that of addressing a 'natural' need but relates to the 'artificial means created to address an instinctual inclination, in the sense that a dish of poached salmon glazed in truffle oil does not resemble the hunger it is made to satisfy' (Lambert 2003: 183).

For Deleuze, traps lie in wait for becoming, and escaping these snares is difficult. 'For some people', Fox suggests, 'being a "patient" or receiving care . . . closes down possibilities creating a body-self trammelled by dependency' (Fox 2002: 359). This is the most significant of all of the explanations for reconfiguration, since it explains the formation of the molarities of existence. For, as has been noted, 'the Humean subject is merely an effect of repetition, a habit, "nothing but the habit of saying "I"' (Neil 1998: 429). This explanation for reconfiguration is also important because it is those configurations that endlessly and tirelessly (and tiresomely) re-emerge that reflect the molarities about which Deleuze and Guattari write. These molarities are associated with habits, and it is through habits that we maintain continuities. It is for this reason that 'habit, in the form of a passive binding synthesis, precedes the pleasure principle and renders it possible. The idea of pleasure follows from it in the same way that . . . past and future follow from the synthesis of the living present' (Deleuze 1994: 97). The crucial feature of these habits is that they express a necessary aspect of becoming and being. A habit is a 'contraction' that is contracted by a mind. A habit is not 'an instantaneous action which combines with another to form an element of repetition'. Rather it is 'the fusion of that repetition in the contemplating mind'. Deleuze argued that the heart, muscles, nerves and cells each have a soul 'but a contemplative soul whose entire function is to contract a habit'. A habit, then, 'concerns not only the sensory-motor habits that we are; the thousands of passive syntheses of which we are organically composed. It is simultaneously through contraction that we are habits, but through contemplation that we contract' (74).[6]

However, the requirements for, and ease of, reconfiguration are not the only, or in some cases the best, explanations for practices of reconfiguration. For one of the principal sources of the motivation to reconfiguration is an impetus to re-experience (perhaps increase) the pleasures, or better intensities, associated with a previous configuration. Intensity seems a more useful description than pleasure simply because 'intensity' refers directly to the flows that traverse the formations that emerge from the body without organs, whereas 'pleasure' leads us back to molarities and reterritorialisation. 'Pleasure is an affectation of a person or a subject; it is the only way for persons to "find themselves" in the process of desire that exceeds them; pleasures, even the most artificial, are reterritorialisations' (Deleuze and Guattari 1987: 156). It certainly seems easier to understand the base-jumper as recreating the intensity of this experience, rather than re-experiencing 'pleasure'. Indeed, the sense of fullness that derives from intense experiences seems, at least to me, to be a better explanation for a desire for reconfiguration than pleasure.

The masochist, in Deleuze and Guattari's rendering, manifests a predisposition to form particular configurations in order to fill themselves with higher levels of intensity. This, undoubtedly, is not a search for pleasure, since the masochist seeks neither pain nor pleasure (deferred or otherwise). 'The masochist is looking for a type of body without organs that only pain can fill, or travel over, due to the very conditions under which that body without organs was constituted' (Deleuze and Guattari 1987: 152). Colebrook continues to refer to pleasures in the following, but captures something of the motivation for reconfiguration nonetheless: 'The child's mouth . . . that has experienced pleasure at the breast comes to desire or anticipate the breast. In this expectation desire can produce an image or "investment"' (Colebrook 2002: 82). Deleuze and Guattari's 'masochist' also expresses the search for maximum intensity via the formation of flows that overtake the entire surface of the body without organs. The masochist seeks to form a body without organs 'in such a way that it can be occupied, populated only by intensities. Only intensities pass and circulate' (Deleuze and Guattari 1987: 153). Thus, in their view, 'the masochist has made himself a body without organs under such conditions that the [body without organs] can no longer be populated by anything but intensities of pain, *pain waves*' (152).

The crucial question, in this context, concerns the nature of the surface that forms. For producing a surface across which they can flow with the greatest intensity remains the masochist's goal (and the goal of drug addicts). Masochists seek 'a type of body without organs that only pain can fill, or travel over . . . Pains are populations, packs, modes of king-masochist-in-the-desert that he engenders and augments. The same goes for the drugged body and intensities of cold, *refrigerator waves*' (Deleuze and Guattari 1987: 152). While reconfiguration enables the re-emergence of intensity, it is highly likely that it will be for experiencing increasing levels of intensity. That is, an impetus arises to exceed the level of intensity experienced because of the formation of particular configuration. Colebrook has suggested that Deleuze takes desire to exceed the actual. In the case of the breast-feeding child, then, 'the mouth's past pleasure produces an idea or image of further pleasure . . . The breast becomes more than what it actually is (a body part) and takes on an added virtual dimension – the breast of fantasy, pleasure and desire' (Colebrook 2002: 82).[7]

'Pathological' reconfiguration

The motivation to reconfigure in order to re-experience a level of intensity or even an increase in a level of intensity are potential precursors to a tendency to practise pathological reconfiguration, whenever higher levels of intensity are sought through a mimicking of previously formed configurations. We might conceive this in terms of a 'tolerance', which causes people to experience less pleasure from later configurations. Experiencing one level of intensity through a particular configuration produces an impetus to form at a higher level, simply because this higher level of intensity produces deeper feelings of fullness or a total occupation in/as a configuration. If intensities result from one configuration, then we can assume an impetus to produce greater absorption and higher levels of intensity in a following configuration.

The preceding motivation to pathological reconfiguration may well be enough. Three other possibilities might explain pathological reconfiguration. One of these is that it can result in an emptying effect. Deleuze and Guattari refer to the emptiness of the body without organs of the masochist and drug addict. For them, 'the masochist and the drug user court these ever-present dangers that empty their [bodies without organs] instead of filling them' (Deleuze and Guattari 1987: 152). The pursuit of intensity, paradoxically, results in an emptying that reduces the level of intensity experienced that, in turn, causes an attempt to achieve fullness in the same way. It may be that only a 'religious experience', or some similar configuration, can cause an addict to form an impetus to engage another configuration in which intensity is experienced and through which the search for fullness continues.

An even more questionable explanation for pathological reconfiguration is to treat it as an attempt to escape the striations that result from repeated experience of high levels of intensity. The image that comes to me is of the 'burning' that can result when images remain too long on a screen. In this case, we might reconfigure as a drug user not to experience the fullness of being under the drug's influence but to shed the effects of the striations that resulted from previous configurations of drug-taking. One of the more likely scenarios, in this context, is the adoption of a different form of pathological configuration in order to reduce the effects of the striations associated with a preceding form of pathological reconfiguration. An obsession with jogging may result from an attempt to free ourselves from a predisposition to become a heavy drinker. Mouths fill continually in an attempt to overcome a predisposition to smoke (which might be an attempt to reproduce the breast-mouth-stomach configuration). The most extreme form of this emergence is in Artaud's work, in which a desire to escape the effects of the body leads to the positing of freedom as the body without organs.

The crucial point to bear in mind with respect to the preceding analysis is that the descriptions provided are merely one way to conceive and represent emergences from the body without organs and the forms of repetition that reflect processes of territorialisation, stratification and reconfiguration. Organism, subjectification and signifiance, conceived as they are here, do not represent three forms of emergence for three distinct effects, but three ways of looking at emergence. In many cases, the effects emerge in ways that bring several of them together. 'The individualising of pain and suffering by biomedicine (often with the collaboration of the human sciences) territorialises and limits the body without organs as organisms or bodies-*with*-organs, which are then the natural subjects for the expertise of medicine' (Fox 2002: 352).

The Body Without Organs and Internet Gaming Addiction

Both the 'body without organs' and 'Internet gaming addiction' divide infinite substance. To that extent, both fail to describe or ascribe. The body without organs fails because it divides the indivisible. It fails even more completely here, because the discussion produces no re-integration of the separate modes of emergence from the body without organs into an adequate description of a total process. While insights into Internet gaming addiction may arise from conceiving it through the three emergences from the body without organs presented above, no integration of these insights concerning Internet gaming addiction will be attempted here.

Internet gaming addiction fails to describe, in part, because it enfolds and elides an element that enables configurations of judgement in which a therapist-patient-psychology-diagnostic configuration produces a description/ascription of 'addiction'. The configuration that produces the diagnosis 'addiction' is undoubtedly important. This second part of the chapter, however, is devoted to the task of conceiving Internet gaming addiction through the analysis of the body without organs presented in the first part. It consists of three sections, dealing with Internet gaming addiction in terms of organism, subjectification and signifiance. The importance of the therapist-patient configuration to producing 'addiction' is that, while becoming is subject to constant and inescapable repetition, only some predispositions to repeat are named as pathological or as 'addiction'.

Organism and Internet gaming addiction

Organism directs attention to the organs configured as Internet gaming addiction. In the first instance, an emergence of organism produces a predisposition to reconfigure as this organism. Returning to sameness (even a different sameness) constitutes an attractor of the reconfiguration as a specific form. These attractors form part of a variety of configurations as Internet game player. Some of these configurations enfold bodily elements, but not all do so. Organism within Internet gaming addiction is also that of limitlessness and intensity associated with becoming in the context of Internet gaming.

An analysis of Internet gaming addiction in terms of striation begins with attention to the elements enfolded in using a computer or game console. The postures and other bodily positions associated with gaming become striations to which a return is easily available. Configuring the elements 'chair', 'desk', 'keyboard', 'VDU', 'joystick' and 'controller' produces game-play and can result in a predisposition to return to this form of organism. The longer the postures and other organism-configurations of gaming are maintained the greater the predisposition to return to them. Approaching gaming in this way helps to make some sense of the predisposition to reconfigure as, for example, *Pong*-player or *Tennis for Two*-player.[8] Neither was an Internet-based game, but both proved 'that there was something immensely satisfying about an interactive electronic game' (Chaplin and Ruby 2005: 46). Players' satisfaction came from 'the sudden gift of control, at the relationship that sprang into existence between themselves and this machine'. To understand this reaction to 'a little green blip bouncing between two lines on a five-inch screen' we must bear in mind that 'to the children of the first TV generation, controlling the image on the screen in front of them proved to be a wildly satisfying experience' (Chaplin and Ruby 2005: 35). The simplicity and capacity to reconfigure the gaming organism produces a predisposition to return to this configuration.

A predilection for returning to the gaming configuration is not merely a matter of reconnecting machine-body-assemblages, but also involves other configurations of organism. The return to a gaming-space is another reconfiguration of organism. For Nintendo's most famous designer, Miyamoto Shigeru, 'great video games are like favourite playgrounds, places you become attached to and go back to again and again. Wouldn't it be great to have a whole drawer full of "playgrounds" right at your finger tips?' (Miyamoto 1991). J, a self-confessed *Quake* addict, believes that problems arise for players when they 'need a safe place to hide, and the game becomes that place' (J 2004).

Organism is also present through the very processes of reconfiguration available. Gaming-spaces invoke infinite sameness. Configuration and reconfiguration are endless, but the elements from which they are formed remain limited and, as a result, familiar. Miyamoto, principal designer of *Super Mario Bros.* and *The Legend of Zelda*, and Will Wright, principal designer of *The Sims* and *Spore*, are among the best practitioners of the principle that 'the simpler the rules are, the larger the space that can . . . emerge from that, and the more elegant the game is' (Wright 2006). *Spore* expresses this principle. For the game's possibility space,[9] as Wright calls it, allows for the evolution of a single-celled organism into a society of beings. *Spore* is unique, according to Kosak, because it begins with a very limited goal (mere survival) but can lead to a player being 'turned loose with a UFO and the ability to simply play with whole species, worlds, and solar systems' (Kosak 2005: 5).

Gaming-space, in at least some of its manifestations, enables configurations of gaming that produce striations predisposing players to pathological reconfiguration, although the player may experience it as joy. In some games the point of the exercise is simply to be and to act in the gaming-space. *Zelda* is one example: here winning is not the point and, indeed, is not available. The joy experienced in playing the game derives from the connection to the world the player experiences. The difference between being stimulated and feeling connected is fundamental to Miyamoto's game design. For him, 'interactiveness is everything'. While he recognises that the player wishes to be stimulated, he

> would like the player to voluntarily feel it. For instance when Link from the *Legend of Zelda* pulls on a lever and a grand demo movie shows a door opening, I think this is a 'giving'. I would not make it so pressing a button pulls a lever, Link would merely hold the lever. Then the player can use the controller to 'pull' and open the door. I concentrate on this interactiveness the most. (Miyamoto 2001)

Wright echoes this view of gaming in the following passage: 'When I look at Lara Croft, I'm not really displacing my emotional state into her, but I'm feeling her as my agent in the world. The fact that I can have an agent, and manipulate and control the experience, is more of what games are based on' (Wright 2006).

While the joy felt by these gamers may be a reflection of intense feelings that derive from a sense of limitlessness, those who play first-person-shooter (FPS)[10] games provide a better illustration of the tendency to develop a pathological predisposition to reconfigure as the form of organism Internet gaming. Successful FPS games are highly immersive 'twitch games'. They are twitch games because of the rapidity of bodily configuration and reconfiguration *and* because of the additional organism-elements enfolded into them (sounds are one of the more significant of these). A variety of bodily and non-bodily elements enfold to produce the complex dance of organic and nonorganic elements that is game-proficient-controller-using.

These elements further enfold, however, within a gaming-space designed to produce 'immersion', which can only be understood as an emergence of organism. *Doom*, for example, produced the medical condition DIMS (*Doom*-induced motion sickness). Although other FPS games existed when *Doom* was released, *Doom* 'was awfully scary, exciting and simply incredible'. *Doom 3* goes further and has 'full surround-sound, cracking glass, bullets flying past your ears, and frightening monsters suddenly attacking you from behind' (Zimbabwe 2004). The designers of *Doom 3* were clearly successful. One *Doom*-player, who has created his own *Doom 3* webpage, has 'yet to play a game as immersive as *Doom 3*. You feel like you are part of the story. I found myself shaking at times, literally too afraid to enter the next room. It is intense! The scripted parts of the game add majorly [*sic*] to the experience of feeling part of it all' (Tim n.d.).

Subjectification and Internet gaming addiction

Internet gaming adds a crucial element to the surface of becoming: the element of otherness. Introducing this element enabled emergence through subjectification. While the first participants in Multi-User Dungeons (MUDs) enjoyed the role-playing game, this was not why some players logged on for hours at a time. Many found the game irresistible because they were interacting with real people. Joining a MUD, then, was not simply playing a game, it was playing a game that enfolded otherness.

> Each MUD served as the locus for a specific community, each bound together by the enjoyment their members derived from spending time together in an alternate world. Friendships and governments formed. The communities experimented with democracy, anarchy, and totalitarianism. They role-played duels and hung out in personally customised strings of text that described living rooms and castles and furniture, speaking to each other across huge geographical distances with their fingers, a keyboard, and their imagination. (Chaplin and Ruby 2005: 165)

One reason to believe that people are pathologically predisposed to reconfigure in Massive Multiple Online Role-Playing Games (MMORPGs), evident in this quotation, is that they enfold proximity. Indeed, advocates of MMORPGs argue that they enfold greater proximity than that experienced in face-to-face relationships. Raph Koster, of *Ultima Online* (UO), has defended 'playerkillers' because of their role in promoting community in MMORPGs. Without playerkillers, 'these places would not have acquired the sense of cultural identity that they now have. Bonds have been formed by struggling against a common Other that would otherwise have been cheaper, and easily earned' (Koster 1998). Koster and others have developed what they refer to as 'The Rules of Online World Design'. The first of these is that designers must understand that 'It's not Just a Game. It's a service, it's a world, it's a community.' These rules include a reference to 'The Schubert Triangle', whose three points are simulation, gameplay and community. The role of the designer is to achieve balance with respect to these points, for this will result in player-retention. 'Too much sim and the game will not be welcoming. Too much game and it will be shallow and not encourage community. Too much community, and your game becomes superfluous – they could get that in a chat zone after all' (Koster et al. n.d.).

The point that the authors of these rules are seeking to make is that MMORPGs persist when they provide a real sense of community. Ensuring that the community stays with your game becomes another problem for the designer – allowing players to modify elements of the game (mods) or to introduce new elements (or provide depth). Depth 'creates ongoing games and a new type of player community'. It also represents a barrier to exit from the game, as it creates a sense of ownership of the game amongst those playing. 'This is very important because there is emotional investment in what is built.' Creating an emotional connection to elements of the game, rather than the community that constitutes a surface for emergence, is crucial. For 'guilds and clans and friends are NOT enough, because entire guilds will defect (Air Warrior and Diablo guilds picked up wholesale to move to UO. . .)' (Koster et al. n.d.).

FPS gaming enfolds significant levels of proximity. Eighty per cent of the 751 FPS gamers who responded to a recent online survey were members of an FPS clan (Jansz and Tanis 2007: 135). The proximity felt in FPS games, then, is not with the figures shot at, but for the others with whom one must work to kill those figures. This focus on working with others leads designers and players of FPS games to reject the view that these games teach players to be killers. According to blindwisdom, only those who grew up with an FPS game would 'understand that the game promotes communication and team work' (blindwisdom 2007).

FPS gaming has spawned a number of tournaments in which teams compete against other teams. FPS clans have proliferated, with many requiring a considerable commitment of time and effort on the parts of their members. One of the more interesting of these is the Fraggot Clan. The name comes from a combination of frag (to kill) and faggott. According to its website, its founders 'want the gay gamer community to be a presence in the FPS world. There are several well established gay MMO guilds, why not an FPS clan?' Like all clans, the Fraggot Clan divides into sub-divisions, and 'if you want to be a part of a particular division you must apply in the Recruitment subforum' (Fraggot Clan 2006). At the time of writing, the following positions were open in the Breakfast of Champions Clan, which focuses on 'tactics, leadership, teamwork and accuracy': Air Traffic Control Specialist, Pilot and Sniper (Breakfast of Champions 2007).

FPS games also enfold proximity when conducted as LAN parties. LAN parties are events in which people create temporary local networks through which they play multiplayer computer games. The centrality of the gaming-space to the social bonds (subjectifications) formed is unmistakable. While LAN parties reduce lag, 'just as important is the special quality of trash-talking each other across the room while playing, and the instinctive social ritual of consuming vast amounts of food and drink together' (Raymond n.d.). Many who are unable to emerge through this configuration are likely to shake their heads at the pathology associated with people who are only able to have a party through (in) their computers.

Some MMORPGs introduced 'trade professions', allowing what might be thought of as different forms of subjectification to emerge. Trade professions represent a radically different form of subjectification from that otherwise available (especially in FPS games). Some see trades not only as legitimate ways to emerge, but value the form of subjectification that emerges from engaging in a trade or profession. *Ultima Online*'s Sonomoa Oasis militia sought support from those who shared

> the idealistic goal of most citizens of Oasis that one day the city will need few active guards, and the spotlight will rightfully fall on our tavernkeepers, smiths, tinkerers, seekers, innkeepers, chefs, tailors, beggars, alchemists, mages, bards, rogues, librarians, scholars, rangers, miners, assassins, diplomats, and tamers. (Koster 1998)

Signifiance and MMORPGAs

The emergence of trade professions also suggests effects of signifiance. This evidences the arbitrariness of the artificial separation of subjectification and signifiance practised herein. Effects of signifiance are important to an analysis of Internet gaming addiction, however, because less proximate forms of otherness constitute 'objects' that attract a pathological predisposition to reconfigure. Signifiance manifests in the various occupations and roles available within MMORPGs. In this case, signifiance emerges in recognition according to role, rank or other game-position designation. The leaders of warring clans, found in *Anarchy Online*, express signifiance and their occupation of this role produces a pathological predisposition to reconfigure on this form.

Manifesting as some abstract role, which lacks the specificity that derives from the proximity of the otherness of subjectification, is an attraction to reconfiguring within the game. *Ultima Online*, for example, is governed by game mechanics that 'do not only reward behaviour that considers the good of the many, they demand it'. As a result, the role of a player who seeks to function through the signifiance configurations of the game is to pursue governance. This is 'the process of developing into someone in the game context who seeks to emulate Lord British's goal of equitable governance'.[11] Those who manifest governance acquire political power. The designers' intentions in *Ultima Online* lead them to 'include a mechanism to reward those players who successfully survive and continue to success, by granting them greater power to govern others' (Koster 1998).

No matter what the source of satisfaction associated with the emergences of signifiance within the game, the crucial element is the capacity to increase status. For example, whatever level of minstrel emerges within *Lord of the Rings Online*, what it takes to attain a higher level of minstrel is evident. This direct relationship between achievement and status may explain the pathological predisposition to reconfigure through emergences of Internet gaming addiction. It may also explain the depth of resentment felt by those who earn wealth, objects or abilities within the game towards those who simply buy such advantages without earning them. Danny Peacock, a *Final Fantasy XI* veteran, feels that 'the ability for some hoity-toity punk with too much money to visit a website and trade his real money away for pretend money is appalling'. The problem, for Peacock, is that gaining game-money without effort results in 'no gain whatsoever and detracts so much from the game, not only for him/herself, but for anyone that plays the game as it was meant to be' (Karabinus 2005).

Chaplin and Ruby suggest other experiences of signifiance in their fascinating account of the experiences of a particular MMORPG user, David Reber. Reber began participating in *Anarchy Online* when one of his former colleagues sold him his software after his wife threatened him with divorce if he did not stop playing (Chaplin and Ruby 2005: 158). Reber was attracted to this world because 'he liked the logic of the rule-based game, the eloquence of decisions based on a dice roll, and he liked the escapism. He enjoyed making up characters and inventing backstories for them' (Chaplin and Ruby 2005: 157). Significance is also present here because one of Reber's goals was to match the actions of an avatar he created in this virtual world with the backstory he had invented for that character. This created a particularly interesting effect and one that indicates both significance and a pathological predisposition to reconfigure in particular forms. Reber created two alter egos in *Anarchy Online*. One of these, Brisbanevi, was 'greedy and cutthroat', and Reber believed this avatar was more like him. The other avatar, Twinke, was 'generous and kind'. Reber played both characters for some time, before he began devoting himself to Twinke. He did so because he 'wanted to show the world, or the world of Rubi-Ka at least, that there are good people out there, who are not out for blood, for lust, for money, always having to get something for something' (Chaplin and Ruby 2005: 160).

Reber's shift from Brisbanevi to Twinke is fascinating in this context. Chaplin and Ruby suggest that 'role-playing as Twinke has made him feel good. He's found himself enjoying her generosity of spirit, her openness. Role-playing Twinke has even made him "less of a dick at work," David says' (Chaplin and Ruby 2005: 161). Re-emerging or reconfiguring as Twinke, then, is something Reber is attracted to because of the effects he can produce through this avatar in terms of the emergence of doing-good. This might explain why some 'online players are quite sensitive when it comes to what they perceive as fair and unfair, elevating matters of entertainment to issues of justice and desert' (181).

Conclusion

Internet gaming is of infinite substance. The separation of organism, subjectification and significance is by nature arbitrary, and the emerging configurations that are here associated with Internet gaming addiction are both multiple and unitary. Conceiving Internet gaming addiction in terms of the multiplicity organism-subjectification-significance allows an unpacking of the various elements – both human and non-human, physical and mental – that may combine to form a mechanic-organic-imaginative configuration resulting in a pathological predisposition to repeat or to reconfigure. In this way, an explanation for the attractors, striations and sources of intensity associated with Internet gaming addiction can be traced.

References

Bains, P. (1997), 'Subjectless Subjectivities', *Canadian Review of Comparative Literature*, 24/3 (51): 511–28.

blindwisdom (2007), 'MSNBC BLASTS Jack Thompson For Blaming VT Shootings on Video Games', http://digg.com/gaming_news/MSNBC_BLASTS_Jack_Thompson_For_Blaming_VT_Shootings_on_Video_Games

Breakfast of Champions FPS Clan (2007), 'What Makes Us Special', http://www.freewebs.com/boc-clan/aboutus.htm

Brown, S. D. and L. Lundt (2002), 'A Genealogy of the Social Identity Tradition: Deleuze and Guattari and Social Psychology', *British Journal of Social Psychology*, 41 (1): 1–23.

Buchanan, I. (1997), 'The Problem of the Body in Deleuze and Guattari, Or, What Can a Body Do?', *Body & Society*, 3 (3): 73–91.

Chaplin, H. and A. Ruby (2005), *Smartbomb: The Quest for Art, Entertainment, and Big Bucks in the Videogame Revolution*, Chapel Hill: Algonquin Books.

Colebrook, C. (2002), *Gilles Deleuze*, London: Routledge.

Cook, I. (2006), 'Western Heterosexual Masculinity, Anxiety and Web Porn', *Journal of Men's Studies*, 14 (1): 47–63.

Deleuze, G. (1980), 'Spinoza 09/12/1980: Power & Classical Natural Right', trans. S. Duffy, http://www.webdeleuze.com/php/texte.php?cle=20&groupe=Spinoza&langue

Deleuze, G. (1990), *The Logic of Sense*, trans. M. Lester with C. Stivale, ed. C.V. Boundas, New York: Columbia University Press.

Deleuze, G. (1993), *The Deleuze Reader*, ed. C. V. Boundas, New York: Columbia University Press.

Deleuze, G. (1994), *Difference and Repetition*, trans. P. Patton, London: Athlone Press.

Deleuze, G. and F. Guattari (1983), *Anti-Oedipus: Capitalism and Schizophrenia*, trans. R. Hurley, M. Seem and H. Lang, Minneapolis: University of Minnesota Press.

Deleuze, G. and F. Guattari (1987), *A Thousand Plateaus: Capitalism and Schizophrenia*, trans. B. Massumi, Minneapolis: University of Minnesota Press.

English Chosun (2005), 'PC Game Addict Drops Dead After Marathon Play', http://english.chosun.com/w21data/html/news/200508/200508080012.html

Fox, N. J. (2002), 'Refracting "Health": Deleuze, Guattari and Body-self', *Health*, 6 (3): 347–63.

Fraggot Clan (2006), 'Welcome to the Home of the Fraggot Clan', http://www.frgt-clan.net/e107/news.php

Gamespot (2005), 'Couple's Online Gaming Causes Infant's Death', http://au.gamespot.com/news/6127866.html

Gatens, M. (2000), 'Feminism as "Password": Re-thinking the "Possible" with Spinoza and Deleuze', *Hypatia*, 15 (2): 59–75.

J (2004), 'Tuesday, April 6th 2004', *Everquest Daily Grind: MMORPG Infinity (no beyond)*, http://eqdailygrind.blogspot.com/2004_04_01_archive.html

Jameson, F. (1997), 'Marxism and Dualism in Deleuze', *The South Atlantic Quarterly* 96 (3): 393–416.

Jansz, J. and M. Tanis (2007), 'Appeal of Playing Online First-person Shooter Games' *CyberPsychology & Behavior*, 10 (1): 133–36.

Karabinus, A. (2005), 'Real Money for Virtual Goods in Online Games?', *Blogcritics Magazine*, Eric Olsen, http://blogcritics.org/archives/2005/12/05/170450.php

Kosak, D. (2005), 'Will Wright Presents *Spore* . . . and a New Way to Think About Games – GDC 2005', http://au.gamespy.com/articles/595/595975p1.html

Koster, R. (1998), 'What Rough Beast? – May 6th 1998', http://www.raphkoster.com/gaming/essay2.shtml

Koster et al. (n.d.), 'GDC Presentation: The Rules of Online World Design', http://www.raphkoster.com/gaming/gdc.html

Lambert, G. (2003), '*Une Grande Politique*, or the New Philosophy of Right?', *Critical Horizons*, 4 (2): 177–97.

Miyamoto, S. (1991), 'May 1991, Mario Mania Players Guide Interview', A. Robinson and C. Johnson, http://www.miyamotoshrine.com/theman/interviews/0561.shtml

Miyamoto, S. (2001), 'January 2001, Nintendo Power Interview', A. Robinson and C. Johnson, http://www.miyamotoshrine.com/theman/interviews/010704.shtml

Mullarkey, J. (1994), 'Duplicity in the Flesh: Bergson and Current Philosophy of the Body', *Philosophy Today*, 38 (4): 339–55.

Neil, D. (1998), 'The Uses of Anachronism: Deleuze's History of the Subject', *Philosophy Today*, 42 (4): 418–31.

Raymond, E. S. (ed.) (n.d.), 'LAN party', *The Jargon File*, http://www.catb.org/jargon/html/L/LAN-party.html

Ruthrof, H. (1997), 'Deleuze and the Body: Eluding Kafka's "Little Death Sentence"', *The South Atlantic Quarterly*, 96 (3): 563–78.

Tim (n.d.), 'A Briefest of Brief Review', http://members.iinet.net.au/~tmorrow/doom3/doom3.html

Wright, W. (2006), 'Thinking Big', http://www.gamesindustry.biz/content_page.php?aid=19489

Zimbabwe (2004), '*Doom 3* Overview on Facts & Speculation', http://doom3.filefront.com/info/Overview

Notes

1. 'Young ROTCs with bright cheeks, tucked into their stiff, green uniforms, are lining up to play *America's Army* and *Full Spectrum Warrior*, just like people lined up to play Willy Higinbotham's *Tennis for Two* nearly fifty years ago. They're a little glassy-eyed and utterly delighted, like you can imagine the children who followed the Pied Piper into the ocean might have been' (Chaplin and Ruby 2005: 196).

2. To me, 'configurations' seems preferable to 'assemblages' in order to avoid the implication of agency; that is, the suggestion that emergences might form according to the will of agents with a pattern in mind (for which parts have been readied 'for assembly').

3. See also Deleuze (1994: 152).

4. Also see Fox (2002: 353) on this.

5. It might be more correct to refer to this as quasi-reconfiguration, in that no two configurations can be identical. In this case, subsequent configurations follow the form of preceding configurations.

6. See also Deleuze (1994: 75).

7. Colebrook (2002: 82). Another motivation for reconfiguration is to produce different effects than those experienced from previously formed and reformed configurations. In this case, the reconfiguration of emergences of higher intensity is to resolve problems that resulted from that previous configuration. The reconfiguration of configurations of domestic violence, for example, may be a result of the striations that make this an easier configuration to form and of the intensities that resulted from it. A crucial question in this context concerns why those who have experienced domestic violence seem to have a predisposition to

reform configurations that produce domestic violence (more often than not, this configuration is something to which they return). One answer is that of habit or striation, but another is that it involves an attempt to arrive at a different intensity. We recreate these configurations in order to overcome them. In this case the desire produced may not be for the repetition or increase of a previously experienced intensity, but for a different affect altogether. Reconfiguration here is in order to resolve effects that have resulted from intensities produced in a previous configuration.

8. *Tennis for Two* was one of the first video games (invented in 1958). It simulated tennis or table tennis and 'consisted mostly of resistors, capacitors and relays, but where fast switching was needed . . . transistor switches were used'. See the Wikipedia entry for 'Tennis for Two'; see also http://www.pong-story.com/tennis1958.htm

9. 'Every player has the opportunity to go off in different directions, have a different experience, basically control their own story. And this is what I call the possibility space of a game' (Wright 2006).

10. 'FPS' indicates that the player's being-in-the-game is as a gun barrel pointing 'into' the gaming-space.

11. 'Lord Cantabrigian British is the name of the ruler of Britannia, kingdom of the fictional world of Sosaria, created by Richard Garriott for his computer game series *Ultima*. Lord British is also a nickname for Garriott himself.' See the Wikipedia entry for 'Lord British'.

Chapter 11

Deleuze's Concept in the Information-Control Continuum

Horst Ruthrof

How can we best locate the Deleuzian notion of the concept in the larger field of conceptuality and its theorisation and how does such an orientation affect our understanding of Deleuze and Guattari's contribution? Taking a broad view of Deleuze's remarks on signification, meaning and the concept as they appear across his writings, we cannot but note a certain tension between an early formalism and a more 'corporeal' approach under the later influence of Guattari (Ruthrof 1997b: 563). It would be wrong, however, to suggest that the way the two thinkers present the notion of the concept in *What Is Philosophy?* (Deleuze and Guattari 1994b) allows for a corporeal reading in any perceptual or quasi-perceptual sense. The concept remains a *syneidetic*, rather than becoming a *synaesthetic*, composite.

Having said this, the Deleuzian approach to the core of meaning, the concept, is a powerful and intriguing way of reformulating the description of an historically rich and still fiercely contested topic. In this chapter I discuss the Deleuzian concept in light of its formal traces, providing a briefly sketched overview of the current debate in the analytical philosophical paradigm, with an emphasis on Jerry Fodor's 'atomistic concept', the redefinition of the concept in corporeal pragmatics, and the concept in the 'information-control continuum' – a semiotic spectrum stretching from pre-perceptual information processing by the human organism, perception, and perceptual experience to natural language, technical sign systems, formal logic and the digital code. My excuse for such an assembly of diverse vistas is Deleuze's own approval of philosophical *collage*. But perhaps a more appropriate justification for comparing the Deleuzian picture of the concept with other theorisations of conceptuality is that the former sharply deviates from the tradition and in so doing puts the discussion on an entirely new footing. It is no exaggeration to say that the way Deleuze and Guattari argue for their notion of the concept very much illustrates what they mean by *deterritorialisation* and *reterritorialisation*. In shifting the concept into a narrow band of philosophical creativity they deterritorialise standard descriptions and reterritorialise the field of conceptuality. The degree of difference introduced by Deleuze and Guattari can be appreciated best if we consider mainstream arguments as well as some other 'deviant' positions.

How then does Deleuze proceed from his early descriptions of sense to the notion of concept as creative construct in *What Is Philosophy?* And how, if at all, is the tension between formal description and the commitment to corporeality resolved or resolvable? In *The Logic of Sense* Deleuze insists that to function at all, sense has to be instantiated by being 'incarnated', though it cannot be said to have either 'physical' or 'mental existence'; it merely 'inheres or subsists'. Sense is an in-between entity being 'both the expressible or the expressed of the proposition, and the attribute of the state of affairs'. As 'exactly the boundary between propositions and things' (Deleuze 1990: 20–2) sense is a virtual entity, a 'neutral' something that 'can be only indirectly inferred' (123). This suggests a notion of sense as stipulated and so highly abstract if not formal. At the same time, clear intimations of corporeality are already present in this early work: neither states of affairs associated with death nor the concept of mortality as a 'predicate of signification' are able to acquire sense unless they include 'the event of dying as that which is actualised in the one and expressed in the other' (145). This 'sous-sense or *Untersinn*', a sense underlying signification, appears to reinforce the express conviction that 'everything is body and corporeal' (136). This is indeed the case if we accept, as I think we should, the observation made in *What Is Philosophy?* that we cannot 'escape the ignoble' but must 'play the part of the animal (to growl, burrow, snigger, distort ourselves)'. In other words, 'thought itself is something closer to an animal that dies than a living, even democratic, human being' (Deleuze and Guattari 1994: 108).

The tension between the formal and quasi-perceptual or corporeal couldn't be starker, especially if we recall Deleuze's embrace of structuralist syntactic circularity carried over into as late a work as *A Thousand Plateaus*. Here Deleuze and Guattari reintroduce the notion of an 'infinitely circular' network of signs in which 'every sign refers to another sign, and only to another sign, ad infinitum', an idea, I suggest, that retains respectability only if we extend the notion of the sign beyond the linguistic to include nonverbal sign systems (Deleuze and Guattari 1987: 112–13). For only if we break the Saussurean syntactic circularity by including *Untersinn* in human semiosis in both its verbal and nonverbal forms are we able to account for perceptual grasp and its mental modifications in *Vorstellung*. Only then does it make sense to say, as they do, 'representations are bodies too' (Deleuze and Guattari 1987: 86). However, this requires a reformulation of what they call the 'amorphous atmospheric continuum' that functions as the signified but which 'continually glides beneath the signifier'. What is needed, I argue, is the specification of this 'medium' or 'wall' in terms of nonverbal, iconic signs, that is, olfactory, gustatory, haptic, emotive, somatic, tactile, aural, visual and other readings. That such a *corporeal* transformation is compatible with Deleuze's position is supported by his definition of 'recognition' as the 'harmonious exercise of all the faculties upon a supposed same object: the same object may be touched, remembered, imagined or conceived' (Deleuze 1994: 133). I will return to this intersemiotic theme below under the heading of *corporeal pragmatics*.

The Concept in *What Is Philosophy?*

Contrary to the tradition of defining the concept as a general, regulative feature of language and perception, the concept undergoes a radical transformation in Deleuze and Guattari's late collaborative work *What Is Philosophy?* The radicalness of their reformulation alone justifies a description of their position, something I will attempt in this section in a summary fashion. The concept is not only regarded by the authors as a special tool in the intellectual armoury of philosophical writings, it is made the central feature that defines the very purpose of philosophy. From the outset philosophy is characterised as 'the art of forming, inventing, and fabricating concepts'. Nor do concepts stand on their own as part of a mere technical apparatus; they are intricately woven into the process of theorising philosophically by their dependence on 'conceptual personae that play a part in their definition'. The philosopher is 'the concept's friend', personifying as he or she does the 'potentiality of the concept'. The very object of the discipline of philosophy is no more, nor less, than '*creating* concepts'. The only requirement for the friends of the concept to do their job is to make sure that the concepts they are creating 'are always new' (Deleuze and Guattari 1994: 2).

Other traditional activities of a philosophical kind such as contemplation, reflection or communication are no longer seen as disciplines but as machines for 'constituting Universals'. Unlike concepts which, in the revised sense, have been granted considerable explanatory force, universals 'explain nothing but must themselves be explained'. Philosophy creates knowledge via the fabrication of 'pure concepts', with the philosopher functioning as the point of convergence where creative thought and concept become one. What then does this new concept look like? According to Deleuze and Guattari, it is 'autopoietic', that is, self-creating, composite, with an 'irregular contour' resulting from the 'sum of its components'. As a fragmentary whole, the concept 'totalises its components'. On account of its complexity, Deleuze and Guattari's concept stands in the sharpest possible contrast to such a notion as, for example, Fodor's 'atomistic' concept (Fodor 1998a, 1998b). I will return to this point in more detail below. Here we need to stress that although Deleuze sees a singularity in the moment of concept creation, what is so created is never one-dimensional. As the authors put it bluntly, 'there are no simple concepts' (Deleuze and Guattari 1994: 15). Whenever a new concept is created it cuts up our knowledge of the world in a novel way requiring other concepts to be likewise 'reactivated or recut' (18).

In addition to its constitutive features, the concept also has a temporal dimension in the sense that it 'has a *becoming* that involves its relationship with concepts situated on the same plane' (Deleuze and Guattari 1994: 18). The notion of plane here refers to a level where comparisons, interaction between concepts, competing articulations from within the same philosophy, can take place. When a concept interacts with other concepts in this way the authors speak of a 'junction of problems' where conceptual coexistence is possible. At this point in the argument Deleuze and Guattari draw the reader deeper into the complexities of their analysis. The concept is now described by way of three important distinctions. (1) Every concept is relational in that it always points back to other concepts as a result of the conceptual character of its constitutive components. (2) The concept is characterised by a double consistency: endoconsistency and exoconsistency. Endoconsistency describes the internal consistency of the concept, the fact that its components though heterogeneous are inseparable and yet share partial overlaps allowing something undecidable to 'pass from one to other'. As the authors put it, 'zones and bridges are the joints of the concept' (20). (3) The concept has a unifying singularity, which the authors describe as the 'conceptual point' that continuously moves among the concept's components holding together their various 'intensive features'. This movement they refer to as a 'traversing' and 'survey' which ensures the immediate co-presence and dynamic stability of the conceptual components in an 'order without distance' (20). Though instantiated in corporeality, the concept itself is 'incorporeal'. Instead of spatial and temporal coordinates, the concept is determined by 'intensive ordinates'. This proviso separates the concept from the states of affairs to which it may refer and 'in which it is effectuated'. The kind of event the concept articulates is thus not contaminated by particulars; rather the concept speaks the hecceity of the 'pure Event', which the authors call 'the event of the Other or of the face' (21). But now the reader is returned to an earlier conviction in the writings of Deleuze, the formal notion of 'infinite speed' as a determinant of the concept: 'The concept is defined by *the inseparability of a finite number of heterogeneous components traversed by a point of absolute survey at infinite speed*', whereby 'survey' (*survol*) or the tracing of the contours of conceptual components is defined as 'the state of the concept' characterised by a special kind of infinity (21).

Unlike in Deleuze's *Logic of Sense*, the 'infinite speed' of the concept is now qualified by the notion of 'specific infinity', according to which the state of the concept may vary between 'greater or lesser speed' according to the quantity of its concepts and the degree of interaction between its components. This leads the authors to stipulate that concepts are absolute in terms of their condensation of conceptual components and the work they perform in reterritorialising established philosophical thought. At the same time, concepts are said to be relative in terms of their fragmentary internal assemblage of components. In short, the concept 'is *infinite through its survey or its speed but finite through its movement that traces the contours of its components*' (Deleuze and Guattari 1994: 21).

Now the authors draw a sharp distinction between what philosophy and its concepts are in relation to other disciplines and human creative activities. Neither the concept nor philosophy as a whole is seen to be discursive. This, Deleuze and Guattari argue, is the result of the dependence of discursive formations on the relational structures of propositions. This looks like a rebuke of analytical philosophy which, from Frege to Quine and Davidson, has placed propositions at the centre of its activities. Later in the book the authors observe that by having turned the concept into a function Frege and Russell led philosophy down a non-philosophical path, for logic is not accidentally reductionist but necessarily so (Deleuze and Guattari 1994: 135). Philosophy in the Deleuzian picture does not work with propositions at all but with sentences. Why would the authors wish to hold what looks very much like a *tour de force* position? It seems that having rarefied the notion of the concept the way they have, and given its stipulated endoconsistency and exoconsistency, Deleuze and Guattari are now committed to permit only sentences rather than propositions as philosophy's proper forms of expression. Once this is done, there is no room for variables, which are necessary components of propositions. As Deleuze and Guattari insist, 'the *independence of variables* in propositions is opposed to the *inseparability of variations* in the concept' (23). If propositions were allowed into philosophy, the idea of concepts as centres of vibration would be violated.

The three major pursuits of knowledge – philosophy, science and art – are aligned with one another by the process of *extraction*. They are differentiated by the kinds of 'things' aimed at in this process. Philosophy extracts concepts which constitute pure events; science extracts prospects articulated in the form of propositions; and art extracts percepts and affects composed into blocs of sensations or monuments. Science sticks out here because it is not at all self-evident that there is no role for concepts in scientific endeavour; at least, a special kind of argument has to be advanced to make this distinction convincing. Even when science deals with the same portion of the world, such as objects, on the Deleuzian view there are no concepts involved (Deleuze and Guattari 1994: 33). Rather, the evidence is transformed into a series of propositions as functions operating in a discursive system. While philosophy does its work on a plane of immanence, science requires a 'plane of reference', a kind of 'freeze-frame' in which objects are viewed as functions (117–18). Another important alignment and difference between philosophy and science concerns reason and its use. In philosophy reason is contingent, in science it is necessary. The former produces 'inseparable variations', the latter 'independent variables' (126). A further major difference between the two activities lies in their mode of enunciation: whereas science actualises reference by determining states of affairs, philosophy lends consistency to virtuality by inventing a new conceptual order (133).

The pure event instantiated by the concept in philosophy is contrasted sharply also with the work of art in which sensations as a composite of percepts and affects are the defining characteristics. As a 'bloc of sensations' the work of art replaces language by monuments. Creativity in philosophy and art thus work in distinctly different ways: in philosophy creativity produces concepts; in art it organises percepts and affects into a being of sensation. As a result, Deleuze and Guattari insist, the sole definition of art is composition (Deleuze and Guattari 1994: 163–99). All three pursuits are consistently yet very differently organised by an 'omnitude' and an all-encompassing perspective. In Deleuzian language, they operate on different planomena: science on the plane of reference; art on the plane of sensations; philosophy on the plane of conceptual constructivism. The plane of philosophy is a 'reserve of purely conceptual events' (36).

The Plane of Philosophy

If the notion of 'plenomenon' introduces us to the general principle of planes which organise the activities of science, art and philosophy in fundamentally different ways, then the plane of philosophy circumscribes the typical way in which the concepts of any specific philosophy are generated and organised. It is the identifiable plane selected by a philosopher that allows us to recognise their concepts as forming a coherent way of rethinking the tradition. Or, put differently, we are able to abstract a philosophical plane from the consistency of its concepts. Once a plane is recognised as such, we can decide the magnitude of a philosophical contribution by measuring 'the nature of the events to which its concepts summon us or that it enables us to release in concepts' (Deleuze and Guattari 1994: 34).

Perhaps Deleuze and Guattari are overstating the randomness of the creation of concepts when they call concepts the 'outcome of throws of the dice' on a plane of immanence. After all, philosophy is described as a 'constructivism' in the sense of the creation concepts and at the same time the 'laying out of a plane'. In guiding the reader towards a more precise grasp of their notion of the plane the authors tell us both what the plane is and what it is not. The plane is neither a programme nor a design nor an end nor a means. The plane is not a concept; nor is it a contingent feature of the neuron functions of the brain. Put positively, the plane is the 'reservoir' and 'reserve of purely conceptual events', a 'desert' populated by concepts. The plane 'secures conceptual linkages' and as such functions like a transcendental condition, a 'pre-philosophical' and implicit presupposition of concepts. As such, 'concept creation' and the institution of a plane are mutually interdependent processes of philosophy. Because of the work of deterritorialisation performed by concepts on a plane of immanence, the plane is also called an 'absolute ground of philosophy' (Deleuze and Guattari 1994: 35–42).

Just as concept and plane presuppose each other, so too do both depend on their creation by a conceptual persona. In Deleuze and Guattari's universe only those who 'renew the image of thought' are philosophers; those who do not are mere 'functionaries'. In renewing the image of thought, philosophers create new concepts and so instantiate a new plane of immanence. In so doing, they become 'conceptual personae' whose role it is to *show thought's territory, its absolute deterritorialisations and reterritorialisations*. Philosophers become conceptual personae by virtue of their creation of concepts and planes of immanence. Even though concepts cannot be deduced from the plane, conceptual personae and planes of immanence presuppose each other in the sense that once concept creation has occurred we can no longer separate conceptual personae from their concepts and plane (Deleuze and Guattari 1994: 51–69).

The Concept in the Literature

Having reterritorialised the field of conceptuality in this way, how does the Deleuzian concept compare with standard accounts in the literature? Only the briefest sketch of a few selected positions can be given here. A helpful recent summary of some of the dominant discourses on the concept can be found in a collection by Laurence and Margolis (Laurence and Margolis 1999: 3–81). Broadly, and contrary to Deleuze and Guattari, the concept has been and still is being theorised as a ubiquitous feature of both natural and technical languages (Villanueva 1998). As such, it is generally regarded as a regulatory feature of the meaning of words and expressions. Where the various approaches to the concept differ is in the degree of definitional tightness or relative fuzziness of the concept. Laurence and Margolis give an indication of where we have gone since John Locke, who regarded complex concepts as the 'aggregate' result of 'simple Ideas', the latter being 'united together in an unknown substratum' (Locke in Laurence and Margolis 1999: 9). On the recent cognitive view of conceptuality (Fauconnier and Turner 2002; Gallese and Lakoff 2005; Janssen and Redeker 1999; Lakoff 1994; Lakoff and Johnson 1999; Verhagen 2005) we could articulate Locke's 'substratum' now as a double neural input, physical reality made readable by our brains on the one hand and, on the other, the most primitive base of such readings, such as 'mappings' (Fauconnier and Turner 2002) or 'iconic realisations' (Ruthrof 1997a, 2000). Concepts, then, would have evolved as *economising quasi-perceptual schematisations*, a picture built up from iconicity to concepts, the signified and the linguistic sign, with feedback to allow for Kant's relation of receptivity and conceptual spontaneity. Unlike the Deleuzian account, this revision of the Lockean concept has in common with most of the current research that it applies generally to natural language.

The literature distinguishes the *concept* from *concept acquisition* and *concept possession* (Margolis 1999). The notion of concept possession is a mainstay in the *typicality* approach to the concept. Regarding concepts as types or typifications rather than as definitionally controlled entities is one of the ways in which theorists have tried to escape the methodological stranglehold of analytical and formal, definitional approaches to the topic. With no commitment to strict categorisation, concepts here appear to be akin to something like Wittgenstein's 'family resemblances' to which language users have non-identical but intersubjectively shared access, allowing for a degree of difference and overlap. *Prototype theory* is another candidate vying for explanatory power in concept research. As the term suggests, concepts here are regarded as clusters of types related to a prototypical concept by analogy. While avoiding the unattractive stipulation of definitional boundaries, prototype theory lacks an explanation as to the mental-material ingredients that are generalised to form a conceptual prototype and how this abstractive process works. A similar criticism can be levelled at the *theory-theory* approach which looks at concepts in their relation to the larger conceptual frames within which they function. Again what is missing is an argument for the genesis of concepts out of their pre-conceptual state, for the kinds of ingredients of which they are made up and what kind of interpretive labour is involved in their use (Laurence and Margolis 1999).

When the machinery of post-Fregean philosophy is applied to the domain of mental events, as it is by Bealer in 'A Theory of Concepts and Concept Possession' (1998), we find 'understanding a concept' defined as 'determinate concept possession' in the sense that concepts are 'irreducible entities comprising the ontological category in terms of which propositions (thoughts in Frege's sense) are to be analysed' (Bealer 1998: 270, 261). As is the case with set theoretical assumptions, on this view the concept, its acquisition and possession are subject to the constraints of strict sense. What renders this and many similar approaches unsatisfactory is that they take for granted the possibility of describing concepts in positivist isolation without a comprehensive picture of natural language beyond propositional convictions (Peacock 1992; Putnam 1975, 1988). As Ray Jackendoff notes, 'the notion of a concept cannot be explicated without at the same time sketching the background against which it set' (Jackendoff 1999: 305). Such a background would have to view natural language concepts at the very least within a pragmatic context if not also in their relation to perception and perceptual experience. As we have seen, the Deleuzian concept sharply deviates from such accounts in that it bars the propositional path altogether. Once we formulate reality in terms of propositions and variables we are doing science and not philosophy.

If we are looking for a notion of the concept at the furthest remove from the Deleuzian position, Jerry Fodor's conceptual atomism looks like a suitable candidate (Fodor 1998a). In Fodor's *informational semantics* concepts reflect mind–world relations and so escape definitional analyticity. His atomism allows for such concepts as brown, cow, or 'browncow', but not brown cow. For Fodor, informational semantics is the answer to the metaphysical question of meaning in the sense that 'semantic access' is the precondition for both epistemic access and our capacity 'to think about things' (Fodor 1998a: 78). In atomistic informational semantics, 'concepts are individuated by the properties they denote', just as their 'properties are individuated by their necessary relations to one another' (74). Here 'concept individuation' can be understood as conceptual performance in contrast to 'concept possession' or conceptual competence. In conceptual performance, our descriptions 'pick out unnamed individuals by reference to their properties' (99). In 'cluster concepts' with lots of criteria, as against Putnam's 'one-criterion concepts', the compositionality of mental representations rests largely on the observation of the ubiquity of its traces. Fodor sharply distinguishes such concepts from names because names do not decompose into identifiable properties (99–100). This is not entirely convincing since in a name such as 'the Iron Curtain' the metaphoric 'iron' does indeed contribute to the concept, a criticism to be resumed more generally below. Fodor abandons the idea that concepts could be prototypes because they 'don't compose'. He likewise rejects the statistical notion of concepts as 'stereotypes', while retaining the term 'stereotype' for concepts as 'databases for fast recognition procedures' (139). Fodor speaks of 'compositionality of conceptual repertoires' but jettisons iconicity as inapplicable to higher-level concepts, such as animals or furniture (110). Instead of some kind of perceptual ingredient or iconicity, Fodor fills the theoretical vacuum with 'nomic, mind–world relations' (121) and offers a shortcut heading under the term of 'properties' to which humans 'lock'. Unfortunately, Fodor's description of concept possession as 'being locked to a property' and 'having a disposition' remains vague (126). 'With doorknob as with red, all there is to being it is how things tend to strike us' (141). Sure, but how and with what do we fill in his empty schema? Neither Fodor's conceptual atomism nor the current discourses on the concept, nor indeed the Deleuzian rarefied concept, permits any such explanation. We need to look elsewhere. One very different approach to the topic that does address concept constitution and possession can be found in neurological research and cognitive linguistics (Lakoff and Johnson 1999). Another approach is via corporeal pragmatics, to be introduced below.

The Deleuzian concept differs from the majority of such theorisations in that it does offer a detailed account of concept constitution and function. More importantly, it shrinks the arena of investigation to a high level of abstraction: philosophical concepts; and second, given this difference at the level of generalisation, the Deleuzian concept may be said to operate at a meta-level if compared with dominant forms of concept research. While this affords Deleuze and Guattari a certain advantage in focus, this seems to be outweighed, as I shall argue below, by the degree of rarefication they have introduced to the topic. Perhaps the most dissatisfying feature of the entire literature on the concept is its failure to come to grips with a problem raised by Kant under the notion of 'spontaneity', and sharply brought up to date by Sellars under the heading of 'the Myth of the Given'. Simply put, the phrase refers to the assumption that humans have access to what is given in nature without the interference of conceptual processes. What is missing then in the theorisation of the concept is a normative 'space of reasons' within which the process of feedback between concepts and experiences can be placed (Sellars 1956: 298–9; Davidson 1984). A very different approach to the theorisation of the concept is needed to resolve the important question of how our concepts fit into the way humans experience the world, from non-conscious perception to perceptual experience, natural language, philosophical abstractions and other technical forms of signification. Enter corporeal pragmatics.

Corporeal Pragmatics

Corporeal pragmatics offers a perspective from which the Deleuzian position takes on a somewhat different appearance. That a comparison is warranted at all is suggested by Deleuze and Guattari's puzzling observation that 'the concept of a bird is found not in its genus or species but in the composition of its *postures, colors, and songs*: something indiscernible that is not so much *synaesthetic* as *syneidetic*' (Deleuze and Guattari 1994: 20, my emphasis). This remark appears to offer a double message, one which suggests both that ordinary concepts are still within the purview of Deleuze and Guattari's project after all, and that the initial promising emphasis on the corporeality of the concept is seriously undercut by a Husserlian turn to ideation. Nonetheless, even a rejected synaesthetic form of conceptuality locates the Deleuzian concept at least in the vicinity of a perceptually oriented paradigm. To prepare the ground for a comparison with the Deleuzian position a brief introduction of the main 'corporeal' principles is needed. In sum, on the corporeal pragmatic view of language, meaning occurs when language users, under community guidance, associate arbitrary signifiers with non-arbitrary signifieds made up of iconic materials regulated by concepts. The deep conviction driving this approach to natural language is that our dominant explanations fail to account for a fundamental aspect of language, namely its relation to perception. Corporeal pragmatics aims to redress this imbalance by exploring the hypothesis that the signifiers of natural languages become meaningful only when they are activated by such nonverbal signs as olfactory, gustatory, haptic, emotive, somatic, tactile, aural, visual and other readings of the world. In other words, linguistic meaning is essentially *heterosemiotic* and *intersemiotic*. This emphasis favours a *synaesthetic* characterisation of the theorisation of meaning and the concept in contrast with Deleuze's declared *syneidetic* preference.

Taking on board Kant's idea of the concept in the *Critique of Pure Reason* as a rule rather than a signified, and the somewhat wobbly character of the empirical concept (Kant 1965: A727–730/B755–758) and its function as a 'container' of sensations (A50/B74) as well as condensation of perception (A722/B750), I propose to collapse sensations and *Anschauungen* into Peircean iconic ingredients of the signified. This allows us to say that concepts are regulatory formations selecting and imposing order on quasi-perceptual materials, that is, on iconic nonverbal signs. From a broad semiotic vista, we can speak of a progression from highly perceptual signifieds to general as well as formal signs. We could say then that natural language signifiers such as 'beer', 'greeting', 'to run', 'voting', or 'body' amount to linguistic signs whenever they are combined with a signified consisting of an iconic quasi-perceptual content regulated by a concept whose boundaries are flexible to a certain degree and whose analysis is infinite in principle. In contrast, formal signs could be characterised as signifiers (x, y) whose signifieds lack iconic materials and thus are perceptually empty or, one could say, are determined only by their relations to other signifiers. In other words, in formal sign systems, where the concept has nothing to rule, the signified collapses into the signifier. As a result, and reserving Gödel's critique for another discussion, formal systems can be defined as self-sufficient syntactic sets. This view can be made compatible with the Deleuzian distinction between empty functives, or propositions, which in science are employed to refer, and philosophical concepts embedded in sentences, which generalise with the help of contingent reason.

Suppose we describe the signified as consisting of two components, one summed up under the notion of quasi-perceptual iconic materials, the other identified as a regulatory concept. Now we need to specify how the concept typically regulates those materials. I suggest that we distinguish four conceptual functions. (1) A *directional* function in that the concept points our mental states in a certain direction whenever we recognise a signifier; (2) a *qualitative* function in that the concept determines the *kind* of mental materials to be activated; (3) a *quantitative* function in that the concept tells us how much iconic material is required and suffices in response to a signifier; and (4) the function of determining the *degree of schematisation* to which the language user subjects the quasi-perceptual materials to be activated. Summing up, we can say that the fourth function of concept as regulator, determining degrees of *schematisation* of mental material content, is significant both in terms of positioning any specific language use in a broader picture of semiosis and pointing to the *kinds* of concepts we have.

It would seem that the signifieds of natural languages themselves are not homogeneous as far as their concepts are concerned, but that they contain fundamentally different kinds. For simplicity's sake we can distinguish three main types: a relatively small number of concepts governed by actual definitions; the vast majority of natural language concepts that are not so governed; and a small number of theoretical but not strictly formal concepts. Accordingly, we can draw the following triple distinction. We can speak of *hard-edged concepts*, characterised by firm definitional boundaries. Their task is to conceptualise the formal features of natural language and technical languages, such as numbers, geometrical terms, temperature, DNA relations and other scientific and technical terms. Typically, such sign systems leave their origins in natural language behind, tending to evolve within the parameters of their specific axiomatic rules. In Kant's terms they would be 'arbitrarily invented concepts', the only concepts characterised by definitions (Kant 1965: A729/B757). Following Husserl, we could call such concepts *eidetic*. Examples would include 'circle', '24 degrees Celsius', 'CO_2', or 'SS316'. In natural language, by contrast, we encounter *soft-core concepts*, characterised by a reasonably well-determined centre within horizons of diminishing definitional force. They could be called *quasi-perceptual schematisations*, because they derive their character from perceptual experience and perception, retaining traces of those origins. *This group forms the vast bulk of natural language concepts.* Their boundaries are wobbly and forever contested, as Kant and later also Russell noted, and greatly depend on the discursive context in which they appear. Using the Deleuzian vocabulary we could also call them *synaesthetic* concepts (Deleuze and Guattari 1994: 216). Examples of *soft-core concepts* include 'tree', 'bush', 'running', 'house', 'slow', 'home', 'body', 'object', 'love', 'freedom', 'green', 'democracy', and so on. We also have to distinguish a middle group of concepts that look like hard-edged concepts, but are so only superficially. Let us call them *soft-edged concepts*, because their descriptions look like definitions by which we attempt to set them off sharply from other concepts. However, in spite of this definitional intent such concepts reveal their different character by the fact that they remain contested and 'drift' pragmatically under pressure from competing concepts. This is why Kant aligned such *a priori* concepts as 'substance, cause, right, equity, and so on' with empirical concepts in the sense that they too, 'strictly speaking', cannot be defined (Kant 1965: A728/B756). All non-formal, theoretical concepts could be regarded to belong to this group. Examples could include the concepts of the signifieds of 'noema', 'noesis' (Husserl), 'enunciative modalities' (Foucault), *'différance'* (Derrida), *'differend'* (Lyotard), 'public sphere' (Habermas), 'reflective equilibrium' (Rawls), 'embodied realism' (Lakoff and Johnson), and all other concepts defined in theoretical, but not formal, contexts.

As even this briefest of outlines of the corporeal pragmatics project makes clear, the concept in Deleuze and Guattari differs from this project as much as it does from Fodor's and those discussed in standard accounts. To get a better grip on where to locate the Deleuzian concept in relation to other theorisations it may help to place it in a broad spectrum of semiosis stretching from the human organism's uptake of electro-magnetic radiation to perceptual experience, language and artificial sign systems. I call this spectrum the 'information-control continuum'.

The Information-Control Continuum

In light of recent findings in the theory of perception, the neurosciences and cognitive linguistics, standard language philosophy and linguistics, would do well to radically review their premises, approaches and findings. Perhaps the most compelling message to come out this new research is that the bulk of information that constitutes our object world is non-conscious (Fauconnier and Turner 2002; Gallese and Lakoff 2005; Lakoff and Johnson 1999; Maud 2003). This has serious implications for our understanding of natural language. In particular, we need to ask now how language relates to perception and pre-perceptual information processing. To schematise this problematic, let us imagine a spectrum stretching from the way the pre-linguistic hominid organism evolved to be able to select from an abundance of electro-magnetic radiation what was useful for survival, to conscious perception, to the evolution of natural language, and further to technical languages, formal sign systems and the digital code. In this schematisation we note a hiastic double movement. One movement can be observed from the massive information available to the non-conscious, pre-perceptual organism to the minimal information per byte in the digital bitstream. A counter-movement in the same spectrum can be noted if we look at it from the perspective of control, a movement from minimal control to the maximisation of control in the Boolean code. Importantly in this scenario, natural language is sandwiched between perception and artificial sign systems and yet the relation between perception and human speech largely remains a taboo in the theorisation of language. On the assumption that this relation is crucial to an appropriate grasp of how language functions, the question becomes legitimate as to what degree the various theories of the concept are able to acknowledge the special position natural language occupies in the information-control continuum. This provides a platform for analysis of how well various theories are able to account for remnant perceptual ingredients in language as well as the vicinity of language to artificial languages and at the same time its distance from them. As we have seen, the majority of theories of the concept have nothing to say about the former while leaning strongly towards a formal perspective on natural language. Fodor's conceptual atomism is remarkable for its radical break with anything that precedes language. The Deleuzian concept, though anything but atomistic, also occupies a narrow niche in natural language, namely, philosophical abstraction. Since it is regarded as syneidetic rather than synaesthetic, it is deliberately distanced from the perceptual side of the spectrum. Against the background of alternative perspectives on the theorisation of the concept and my initial summary of the Deleuzian concept, I now offer the following critique.

Ten Critical Remarks

1. Deleuze and Guattari have so rarefied the concept such that only a small segment of what is commonly regarded as concepts can legitimately be regarded as the conceptual domain. This would appear to disqualify the Deleuzian concept from functioning in a general pragmatics.
2. The Deleuzian concept looks elitist in the sense that only the highest intellectual endeavour qualifies for its creation. This flies in the face of the more 'democratic' notion of the concept in the literature.
3. One could argue that by accepting only a certain narrowly defined kind of concept, Deleuze and Guattari have (deliberately) committed the fallacy of composition, conflating a part of the semantic scope of 'concept' with its 'total' range.

4. Deleuze and Guattari's strategy in defining the concept is reductive in the sense that they have disqualified disciplines other than philosophy from being able to have concepts. In the wake of this reductionism, other disciplines are left to redefine what they used to call 'concepts'.

5. One result of this reductive procedure is the elimination of iconicity from the concept, its quasi-perceptual ingredients that distinguish concepts from the components of formal languages such as symbolic logic, chemical formulae and Boolean code. In other words, the Deleuzian concept is too formal, or at least too eidetic.

6. The notion of infinite speed ('more or less') as a fundamental feature of the concept likewise shifts it into the domain of formal signification, since what the concept, broadly understood, embraces (con-capere) resists the elimination of the temporal dimension of language.

7. What distinguishes sentences from propositions is precisely their quasi-perceptual ingredients (what something feels like, tastes and smells like, looks like), linking all concepts from ordinary language to technical (but not formal) languages, including philosophical discourse. Infinite speed and the elimination of iconicity suggest that Deleuze and Guattari are conflating two fundamentally different processes: generalisation and formalisation.

8. In the literature on the concept, the Deleuzian variety can be identified as one of three radically different notions, the other two being Fodor's atomistic concept and the concept as it functions in corporeal pragmatics. What distinguishes the Deleuzian concept from Fodor's most sharply are its compositionality, abstraction and restriction to philosophy. Compared to the concept in corporeal pragmatics, the Deleuzian notion differs above all by its syneidetic rather than synaesthetic generalisation and its confinement to a narrow bandwidth in the semiotic spectrum.

9. Given both the narrowing of the scope of what counts as a concept and the level of abstraction it undergoes in Deleuze and Guattari's description, it would seem that the Deleuzian concept occupies a meta-level if compared with the way concepts have been described in the literature. Stipulated as radically and creatively innovative, the Deleuzian concept governs all other concepts in the sense that once in place it requires at one stroke the fundamental reorientation of what are ordinarily called concepts. The regulatory function of concepts as defined in the literature is thus generalised to a meta-function.

10. It is its meta-function that empowers the Deleuzian concept to effect a radical *deterritorialisation* of the existing landscape of concept descriptions and a *reterritorialisation* of the literature from the perspective of the so revised notion of the concept and the plane of immanence it establishes. The Deleuzian meta-function of the concept may permit the interpretation that ordinary concepts nevertheless qualify as concepts so long as they are reworked from a radically new philosophical perspective.

Conclusion

What would we have to do if in the face of such critical remarks we were to accept Deleuze's concept? Would we have to invent a new term and definition for what has traditionally been called the 'concept'? Or is there a way of finding a place for the Deleuzian concept in the larger scheme of general conceptuality? I conclude by suggesting that such an accommodation is indeed both possible and useful. As their example of the redefinition of the concept of 'bird' demonstrates, it can be argued that the Deleuzian concept applies not only to philosophy but to all language and perception. What Deleuze and Guattari have emphasised in *What Is Philosophy?* is a rearticulation of the concept at its most creative: a meta-concept able to provide an emptied body of thought with new organs. Infertile terrains well-ploughed by intellectual functionaries are refertilised by the philosopher as conceptual persona. When new concepts in the Deleuzian mould are thrown into the arena of habitual thought they do more than merely replace old ones; they establish an entirely new way of viewing a discursive field; they create a new plane of conceptualising the world. The Deleuzian concept both speaks a new language and demonstrates its own operation; it acts as both example and meta-term. In this respect, Deleuze and Guattari's contribution amounts to a fundamental revitalisation of thinking. Not unlike Heidegger's observation that ordinary language is a 'forgotten and used up poem', Deleuze and Guattari show us how to rediscover the philosophical potential of habitual language and thought.

References

Bealer, G. (1998), 'A Theory of Concepts and Concept Possession', in E. Villanueva (ed.), *Concepts*, Atascadero: Ridgeview.

Davidson, D. (1984), 'On the Very Idea of a Conceptual Scheme', in E. LePore (ed.), *Inquiries Into Truth and Interpretation* (Oxford: Clarendon Press).

Deleuze, G. (1990), *The Logic of Sense*, trans. M. Lester with M. Stivale, ed. C. V. Boundas, New York: Columbia University Press.

Deleuze, G. (1994), *Difference and Repetition*, trans. P. Patton, New York: Columbia University Press.

Deleuze, G. and F. Guattari (1987), *A Thousand Plateaus: Capitalism and Schizophrenia*, trans. B. Massumi, Minneapolis: Minnesota University Press.

Deleuze, G., and F. Guattari (1994), *What Is Philosophy?*, trans. H. Tomlinson and G. Burchell, New York: Columbia University Press.

Fauconnier, G. and M. Turner (2002), *The Way We Think: Conceptual Blending and the Mind's Hidden Complexities*, New York: Basic Books.

Fodor, J. (1998a), *Concepts: Where Cognitive Science Went Wrong*, Oxford: Clarendon Press.

Fodor, J. (1998b), 'There Are no Recognitional Concepts; Not Even Red', in E. Villanueva (ed.), *Concepts*, Atascadero: Ridgeview.

Gallese, V. and G. Lakoff (2005), 'The Brain's Concepts: The Role of the Sensory-motor System in Reason and Language', *Cognitive Neuropsychology*, 22: 455–79.

Jackendoff, R. (1999), 'What Is a Concept That a Person Can Grasp It?', in E. Margolis and S. Laurence (eds), *Concepts: Core Readings*, Cambridge, MA: MIT Press.

Janssen, T. and G. Redeker (eds) (1999), *Cognitive Linguistics: Foundations, Scope and Methodology*, Berlin: Mouton de Gruyter.

Kant, I. (1965), *Critique of Pure Reason*, trans. Norman Kemp Smith, New York: St. Martin's Press.

Lakoff, G. (1994), 'What Is a Conceptual System?', in W. F. Overton and D. S. Palermo (eds), *The Nature and Ontogenesis of Meaning*, Hilldale: Lawrence Erlbaum.

Lakoff, G. and M. Johnson (1999), *Philosophy in the Flesh: The Embodied Mind and Its Challenge to Western Thought*, New York: Basic Books.

Laurence, S. and E. Margolis (eds) (1999), *Concepts: Core Readings*, Cambridge, MA: MIT Press.

Margolis, E. (1999), 'How to Acquire a Concept', in E. Margolis and S. Laurence (eds), *Concepts: Core Readings*, Cambridge, MA: MIT Press.

Maud, B. (2003), *Perception*, Chesham: Acumen.

Peacock, C. (1992), *A Study of Concepts*, Cambridge, MA: MIT Press.

Putnam, H. (1975), *Mind, Language and Reality*, Cambridge: Cambridge University Press.

Putnam, H. (1988), *Representation and Reality*, Cambridge, MA: MIT Press.

Ruthrof, H. (1997a), *Semantics and the Body: Meaning from Frege to the Postmodern*, Toronto: University of Toronto Press.

Ruthrof, H. (1997b), 'Deleuze and the Body', *South Atlantic Quarterly*, 96 (3): 563–78.

Ruthrof, H. (2000), *The Body in Language*, London: Cassell.

Sellars, W. (1956), 'Empiricism and the Philosophy of Mind', in Herbert Feigl and Michael Scriven (eds), *Minnesota Studies in the Philosophy of Science*, Minneapolis: University of Minnesota Press.

Verhagen, A. (2005), *Constructions of Intersubjectivity: Discourse, Syntax, and Cognition*, Oxford: Oxford University Press.

Villanueva, E. (ed.) (1998), *Concepts*, Atascadero: Ridgeview.

Chapter 12

Illusionary Perception and Cinema: Experimental Thoughts on Film Theory and Neuroscience

Patricia Pisters

> Thus, in the vanguard of the practical, *technical invention* only crowns an obsessive dream. All great inventions are preceded by mythical aspirations, and their novelty seems so unreal that trickery, sorcery, or madness are seen in them. (Morin 2005: 209)

> Rich artistic effects have been secured, and, while on stage every fairy play is clumsy and hardly able to create an illusion, in the film we really see the man transformed into a beast and the flower into a girl. There is no limit to the trick pictures which the skill of the experts invent. . . . Every dream becomes real, uncanny ghosts appear from nothing and disappear into nothing, mermaids swim through the waves, and little elves climb out of the Easter lilies. (Münsterberg 2002: 61)

At the end of the nineteenth century and the beginning of the twentieth, cinema was often connected to stage illusionism, to the mysteries of technological inventions and to intuitions about the working of the human mind. In 2006 two films set around the turn of the nineteenth to twentieth century – *The Illusionist*, directed by Neil Burger, and *The Prestige*, directed by Christopher Nolan – point towards a renewed interest in cinema's relation to perceptual illusions through the stories of professional conjurers.[1] The simultaneous appearance of these films also points to a renewed theoretical interest in the luring powers of the screen and the tricks it can play with the brain. Early theoretical visions on cinema's connection to the operations of the mind, such as Hugo Münsterberg's *The Photoplay: A Psychological Study*, were not fully integrated into modern film theory as it developed as an academic discipline from the 1950s onwards.[2] When in 1956 Edgar Morin, as one of the last of 'early film theorists', published his book *Le Cinéma ou l'Homme Imaginaire* film theory was about to enter its ideological phase where film scholars, drawing on structural linguistics and psychoanalysis, started to seek for academic legitimacy by beginning to 'treat the radically debiologised [sic] subject/spectator as an effect of the film text, all (unconscious) mind, stripped of flesh, poetry, scepticism and imagination' (Mortimer in Morin 2005: xi). Morin's ambitious project to question cinema in all its complexity in relation to the mysteries of the human mind did not get recognition and was even scorned as a mystification of popular cinema's alienating power in service of capitalist ideology. Morin considered a person's reality as semi-imaginary and cinema as the technology that allows us to see how a person and the world are interpenetrated. The cinema, according to Morin, is the world half assimilated by the human mind:

> All the things that it projects are already selected, impregnated, blended, semi-assimilated in a mental fluid where time and space are no longer obstacles but are mixed up in one plasma. All the diastases of the mind are already in action in the world on the screen. They are projected into the universe and bring back identifiable substances from it. *The cinema reflects the mental commerce of man with the world.* This commerce is psychological-practical assimilation of knowledge or of consciousness. The genetic study of the cinema, in revealing to us that *magic* and, more broadly *magical participation* inaugurate this active commerce with the world, at the same time teaches us that the penetration of the human mind in the world is inseparable from an imaginary efflorescence. (Morin 2005: 206)

Münsterberg's and Morin's sensitivity to the ambiguous relationships between cinema, reality and the mind seems to be much better understood at the beginning of the twenty-first century. In this essay I argue that the re-appreciation of the magical qualities of cinema and the illusionary quality of perception can be rethought interdisciplinarily by relating film theory to certain developments in neuroscience. Deleuze's cinema books, *The Movement-Image* (1986) and *The Time-Image* (1989), are central to this re-appreciation of mental-materialist film theory in at least two ways. First, with his principle that 'the brain is the screen' Deleuze has invited film scholars to go beyond ideological, linguistic and psychoanalytic models and methods and turn to neurosciences. When his cinema books appeared in the 1980s Deleuze was asked on what basis we can assess film; he answered with remarkable premonition:

> I think one particularly important principle is the biology of the brain, a micro-biology. It's going through a complete transformation, and coming up with extraordinary discoveries. It's not to psychoanalysis or linguistics but to the biology of the brain that we should look for principles, because they don't have the drawback, like the other two disciplines, of applying ready made concepts. . . . The whole of cinema can be assessed in terms of

cerebral circuits, simply because it's a moving-image. Cerebral doesn't mean intellectual: the brain is emotive, impassioned too . . . You have to look at the richness, the complexity, the significance of these arrangements, these connections, disjunctions, circuits and short-circuits. . . . Creating new circuits in art means creating them in the brain too. (Deleuze 1995: 60)[3]

Deleuze himself rarely explicitly referred to the neurosciences, but the film-philosophical concepts he developed in the *Movement-Image* and *The Time-Image* do relate the brain and the screen in an immanent way, mainly due to the Bergsonian inspiration of these books. In this chapter I take Deleuze's suggestion literally and propose some experimental thoughts of interdisciplinary connectivity that move between neurobiology and film-philosophy, where I will focus on the phenomenon of visual illusions or illusionary perception.[4]

The second way in which Deleuze's cinema books are central concerns the Deleuzian concept of the powers of the false, which allows for a new evaluation of illusions, magic and the possibilities of fraud and trickery. Therefore, at the end of this chapter I will move from film-philosophy to neurobiology to look at some philosophical implications of the proposed principles of the brain as screen. Throughout my discussions I will refer very specifically to *The Illusionist* and *The Prestige* to indicate how these films, set in Vienna and London respectively around 1900, relate to contemporary questions in neuroscience and film-philosophy.

New technologies play an important though not always foregrounded role here in two ways. In cinema technologies, it is not surprising that, given the impact of digital technology in the twenty-first century, cinema is returning to its beginnings and investigating its original fascination with visual perception, illusion, truth and the stimulation of the mind. New visual technologies are also important in the neurosciences: with the possibility of visualising the brain in EEG, PET, MRI, fMRI and MEG scans, pictures of the brain are highly influential in neuroscientific research and they raise questions that travel back into popular culture and philosophy.[5]

Visual Illusions: Magic, Cinema and the Neurosciences

On the DVD commentaries of their films, both Neil Burger and Christopher Nolan indicate that as filmmakers they are attracted by the world of magic of the late nineteenth century because cinema is so closely related to conjuring, playing with the mind and creating visual illusions. The Musée de la Magie in Paris presents magic tricks and automatons from France's most well-known magician Jean Eugene

Robert-Houdin (1805–71).[6] Robert-Houdin was the first to perform magic tricks on stage in his theatre on the Boulevards des Italiens in Paris that he opened in the 1860s. The theatre's last owner before its destruction in 1927 was George Meliès, the famous film pioneer who combined cinema and stage illusions. In *The Illusionist* and *The Prestige* some of Robert-Houdin's tricks are performed again, like the Orange Tree (an orange tree that seems to grow on stage in *The Illusionist*) and the Bullet Catch (the magician catches a bullet fired at him with his hand in *The Prestige*). Robert-Houdin also experimented with electricity, a connection between technological inventions and magic that in *The Prestige* is addressed by the great and mysterious inventor Nicolas Tesla, who in the film invents a machine for teleportation by electricity.[7] In *The Illusionist* phantasmagoric projections of images on smoke screens and mirror images become very realistic apparitions of the dead. Magic and cinema technology have been connected since the nineteenth century and keep on surprising our minds.

Visual illusions play a key role in this relationship between magic and cinema, and the Musée de la Magie has a number of them on display.[8] These visual illusions are like magic in themselves and indicate how the brain can see the same image in two different ways (as for instance in the famous Duck or Rabbit Drawing), or how it can be fooled by the visual data, for instance seeing motion where there is none (as in the Rotating Snake Illusion). Visual illusions have not only fascinated magicians and filmmakers, but also philosophers, psychologists and more recently neuroscientists. Some visual illusions are very old, such as the Waterfall Illusion of Motion after-effect mentioned by Aristotle.[9] In the nineteenth century many geometric illusions (such as the Muller Illusion or the Zollner Illusion) were discovered and in recent decades computer technology has added new illusions (for instance Hybrid Images which are images seen differently at different spatial distances).

Visual illusions seem to indicate truths about our perceptual system and the functioning of the brain and have therefore provided a rich source for neurobiological experiments (Eagleman 2001: 920–6). Visual neuroscientists see three general reasons to study visual illusions. First, such illusions are 'particularly good adaptations of our visual system to standard viewing situations. These adaptations are "hardwired" into our brains, and thus can cause inappropriate interpretations of the visual scene. Hence illusions can reveal mechanisms of perception' (Bach and Poloschek 2006: 20). Second, visual illusions can be caused by certain clinical conditions, such as psychoses, epilepsy and migraine that can cause visual hallucinations, which are basically illusions created by the brain itself with less (or no) connection to perceptual reality. And third, our brain is constantly looking for known patterns in random structures with low information content, called pareidolia, which makes phenomena like visual illusions an interesting area of investigation (Bach and Poloschek 2006: 20).

In what follows I will focus on the first reason for investigating visual illusions: the ways in which they can reveal mechanisms of normal perception to such an extent that they 'challenge our default notion that what we see is real' (Bach and Poloschek 2006: 20). There are many different types of visual illusions and different ways in which our perception might be illusory, each having different implications for the ways in which our perceptual system functions in relation to our cognitive skills and consciousness. But I will first look at the meta-theoretical insight that visual illusions challenge our basic assumptions of the relation between perception and reality.

Everything You Have Seen is a Trick: Perception as Mental Operation

In *The Photoplay*, published in 1916, Hugo Münsterberg (1863–1916), who was a professor of Experimental Psychology at Harvard, was already referring to visual illusions to get a better understanding of what film does to the brain. Münsterberg considered cinema a new art form that heralded new ways of perceiving the world. He was particularly interested in the relations between the screen and the brain. As a neurobiologist *avant la lettre* he studied visual illusions and discovered some new ones himself, such as the Münsterberg Checkerboard Illusion. He argued that such tricks of perception illustrate that

> Since we cannot be sure that movement *really* takes place in objective reality, the perception of movement may well be mental, an operation of the mind. . . . Optical illusions throw perception into question, they prove that perception, at least in some cases, is a mental act and has only a partial relation to 'reality'. (Langdale 2002: 15–16)

In a similar way, cinema is a mental act with a partial relation to reality. Arguably, in his cinema books, Deleuze elaborates these ideas more systematically. He emphasises that cinema, through its particular audio-visual quality, gives us subjective perceptions (a character's spatial or mental point of view) as objective observations (the camera's point of view, presumably giving a picture of reality). In this way cinema catches us in 'a correlation between a perception-image and a camera-consciousness which transforms it' (Deleuze 1986: 74). Subjective and objective images become like 'communicating vessels' which makes it in many cases difficult to distinguish objective reality from subjective imagination.

Before turning in the next section to focus on specific neuroscientific findings, here I would like to address this more general question of the ways in which cinema is related to the mind by considering stories presented through the cinema in a 'semi-subjective' ('semi-imaginary' or 'free indirect') way that allows visual illusions to play an important role.[10]

In *The Illusionist*, the story of Eisenheim – the illusionist of the title – is actually seen through the eyes of the character of chief inspector Uhl, who arrests Eisenheim at the orders of Crown Prince Leopold. The latter thinks Eisenheim is a fraud and a charlatan. The film starts with inspector Uhl who speaks in voiceover about what he knows (through investigation) of Eisenheim's youth, while the images become flashbacks. In many scenes throughout the story Uhl is participating or witnessing (such as the scenes where he visits Eisenheim's stage performances or investigates the murder of Sophie, the crown prince's fiancée who loves Eisenheim). But in many other scenes the camera wanders off on its own, giving us images that Uhl has certainly not actually seen, nor even could have (such as those involving the conversations between Sophie and Eisenheim during their childhood friendship, or the love scene between them when they are adults). The status of these images is unclear. Perhaps Uhl imagines these scenes and they are all in his mind; but the camera renders all images in an objective way. In any case *The Illusionist* shows very clearly how cinema in general has this 'specific, diffuse and supple status' (Deleuze 1986: 72) between subjective and objective.[11] Neil Burger, on the DVD commentary, similarly mentions the confused status of the image between subjective and objective, between imaginary and real. When we see the film's ending, we can think (with inspector Uhl) that we have figured out how Eisenheim has played tricks on everybody's minds to get Sophie back. But we cannot be sure. As Burger comments:

> It may be exactly how he is imagining or it may be just that, his imaginings. The movie is told from Uhl's point of view and he does not know everything. He thinks he has it but does he really? Or is it just something he chooses to believe? The whole movie is about perception, how we see the world, how we see in general. What we believe, what we won't believe, what we take on faith. For Uhl this is what he chooses to believe or what the audience chooses to believe, and maybe it's true, maybe it isn't. (Burger 2006)

In a different way *The Prestige* also presents its events semi-subjectively. It is the story of a rivalry between two magicians in Victorian London,

Robert Angier and Alfred Borden. The narration is more complicated than in *The Illusionist* since there are two criss-crossed points of view: that of Angier, who is reading Borden's notebook in the past, and Borden's perspective, as he reads Angier's diary in the present. The story also addresses other layers in time, and these interwoven temporal perspectives add another complication to the narrative. But in this film too, subjective and objective images are heterogeneously combined, and many questions concerning tricks and truth remain unresolved. Although the end of the film reveals the ultimate secret of Borden's magical disappearances and reappearances, the mysteries of the scientific powers of electricity of the machine designed by Nicolas Tesla, and of Angier's doubling, remain utterly puzzling. In the DVD interview, Christopher Nolan admits that these mind-games are his main motivation for making films: 'I would hope people would walk away having been entertained by the story but that there would also be all kinds of resonances and, I don't know, interesting thoughts banging around their brains' (Nolan 2006). As neuroscientists with different means, illusionist filmmakers show us how the nature of the brain and the nature of the filmic image call perception's relation to reality into question. Vision is a mental operation with all kinds of resonances and it is ambiguous in itself.[12]

Watch More Closely: Attention and Awareness

Illusionists and filmmakers also play in other ways with aspects of perceptual illusion. It is a well-known fact that many conjuring tricks (be they performed by illusionists, conmen or filmmakers) are based on a playing with our attention and awareness that guides what we actually and consciously see. In *The Prestige* Angier creates a stage act called 'The Transported Man' where he leaves the stage by one door and immediately enters again through another door at the other end of the stage. The film shows how Angier does the trick by using a lookalike. This works very well because the audience fails to pay attention to the differences between the two men, who are dressed identically, have the same haircut and make the same gestures in catching their top hat (it's the hat that receives more attention than the person catching it). The trick is revealed to the audience when the lookalike becomes increasingly drunk, starts behaving unpredictably and moves his body differently to Angier. Finally Borden intrudes onto the show, taking the place of Angier's double and making the audience aware of all the tricks in the act. In another scene, Borden, in prison after having been accused of the murder of Angier, distracts the attention of a guard by pretending he is too clumsy to perform a trick with a red ball and drops it, so that the guard does not notice Borden chaining him to a table. Magicians and filmmakers alike play with the audience's attention and awareness.

Münsterberg also emphasised the central function of attention in film viewing. Beyond the first sense impressions of perception (which, as we have seen, can in itself be illusionary), attention plays a key role for creating meaning out of what we see on the screen. As Münsterberg argues:

> The mere perception of the men and women and of the background, with all their depth and their motion, furnishes only the material. The scene which keeps our interest alive certainly involves much more than the simple impression of moving and distant objects. We must accompany those sights with a wealth of ideas. They must have a meaning for us, they must be enriched by our own imagination, they must awaken the remnants of earlier experiences, they must stir up our feelings and emotions, they must play on the suggestibility, they must start ideas and thoughts, they must link in our mind with the continuous chain of the play, and they must draw attention constantly to the important and essential element of the action. An abundance of such inner processes must meet the world of impressions and the psychological analysis has only started when perception of depth and movement alone are considered. . . . The chaos of the surrounding impressions is organised into a real cosmos of experience by our selection of that which is significant and of consequence. . . . Our attention must be drawn now here, now there, if we want to bind together that which is scattered in the space before us. Everything must be shaded by attention and inattention. (Münsterberg 2002: 79–80)[13]

Münsterberg identifies several characteristics of attention: it is something that comes into the centre of consciousness; it makes other impressions fade away to the point that we don't see them; it adjusts the body of the perceiver to the perception; and it groups ideas, feelings and impulses around the object of attention (Münsterberg 2002: 85–6).[14] He also identifies a range of filmic effects (such as lighting, speed or repetition) that steer our attention. The filmic close-up, which eclipses literally all other objects from the scene, is the technique that emphasises most clearly the effects of attention: 'the close-up has objectified in our world of perception our mental act of attention and by it has furnished art with a means which far transcends the power of any theatre stage' (87). Münsterberg gives the example of a locket hung on the neck of a stolen or exchanged infant, shown in close-up, that will guide our attention and tells us that everything will hinge on this locket twenty years later when the child is grown up.

Münsterberg's observations are rather impressionistic but the issues he raises about perception as partly illusory and directed by attention are pertinent. For Münsterberg attention equals conscious perception that makes us unaware of other objects in the perceptive field. In this way he expresses the classic psychological insight 'that even though we think we see everything that is in front of us, we actually have very limited conscious representation of the outside world' (Lamme 2003: 12). The question now is whether contemporary neuroscience can provide more refined insights into the ways in which our perception is coloured by and limited to what catches our conscious attention.

Neuroscientists today have very sophisticated technology at their disposal which makes it possible to observe and measure processes taking place in the brain when we perform all kind of tasks (like watching and seeing). In respect to the question of attention, neuroscientific experiments have now indicated that it is useful to re-evaluate the classic distinction between the conscious (attention/awareness) and the unconscious (inattention/unawareness) and make a new distinction between attention and awareness. In respect to consciousness, which is traditionally related not only to attention but also to reportability (we can tell what catches our attention, respond to what we are aware of), neuroscientific observations of the brain tell us that even objects that are not consciously reported, remembered, or compared to other objects can still be registered in a conscious mode, albeit a more restricted level of consciousness. Neuroscientists Victor Lamme and Pieter Roelfsema have introduced a distinction between different modes of vision in order to understand the division between unconsciousness and consciousness in a more differentiated way:

> An analysis of response latencies shows that when an image is presented to the visual system, neuronal activity is rapidly routed to a large number of visual areas. However, activity of cortical neurons is not determined by this feedforward sweep alone. Horizontal connections within areas, and higher areas providing feedback, result in dynamic changes in tuning. (Lamme and Roelfsema 2000: 571)

This brain activity called feedforward sweep ensures that we immediately distinguish form, colour, shape, movement and other large visual categories like faces, animals, and so on. This process – which makes us, for instance, jump away from a falling object – is largely unconscious. Feedback processing refers to the processes that take place one tenth of a second later and are called recurrent interactions or resonances. Here consciousness starts to emerge and we can relate what we see to other experiences, memories, emotions, and so on. However, the circuit of recurrent consciousness can be restricted (P-conscious) or elaborate (A-conscious) (Lamme 2006: 35). If something does not catch our attention (in the sense that we cannot report on it) this may be because (unconscious) feedforward processing gets stuck, or because (conscious) recurrent processing is not elaborate enough. This would imply that not everything we cannot report on is unconscious, but that there is conscious experience that exists independently from reportability (Lamme 2006: 29). To elaborate on this insight, Lamme proposes to distinguish between attention and awareness:

> Instructing to focus attention (either in man or monkey) almost invariably leads to enhanced neural responses through the brain . . . Typically, the neural responses are enhanced right from the outset, which indicates that the attention works on the feedforward sweep. . . . From the combined neural and psychological perspective, attention thus is a rather different phenomenon than awareness. It is best described as a set of mechanisms that enable the better routing of sensory inputs towards the executive systems of the brain. Attention is selection. . . . The way in which we have defined awareness at the neural level is rather different. As soon as visual input undergoes recurrent processing of some (as yet not precisely defined) critical mass, awareness arises. This could work for attended as well as unattended stimuli. (Lamme 2000: 399)

This definition of attention as belonging to immediate feedforward processing challenges the idea that attention would be part of consciousness (Münsterberg's classic psychological insight). Attention according to this definition belongs to unconscious processes. On the other hand, objects that we do not attentively see (or can report on) are not automatically relegated to the unconscious but can be part of conscious experiences that remain stuck somewhere in the network of resonances. The implications of this insight remain to be analysed more fully but perhaps a return to cinema can provide some preliminary thoughts for further reflection.

The Secrets of a Locket

I would like to return to the example of the locket – and object around which the whole narration of *The Illusionist* is in fact constructed. At the beginning of the film Eisenheim as a young boy fabricates a locket for Sophie. When he gives her the locket, we see in close-up how it has a secret opening mechanism. At several key moments in the narrative the locket turns up, until the very end of the film where it is shown again in close-up in Sophie's hand – a repetition of the image at the beginning but now with the whole story having given it full significance. On one level the locket is thus indeed a visual narrative device that (consciously) steers our attention in the classic psychological way described by Münsterberg. But on another level, when we take into account both the ways in which cinema presents a semi-subjective reality and the neuroscientific distinction between attention and awareness, we can nuance this analysis.

As already indicated, *The Illusionist* is told from inspector Uhl's perspective, but the images are presented objectively and often give us sometimes more information than he can possibly know. Many of the scenes with the locket are presented in this ambiguous way, caught between objective and subjective. During the course of the film Uhl will slowly find out what the viewers have already seen. For instance, the viewer knows from the start how the locket can be moved into a heart shape that reveals a picture of the young Eisenheim, and has seen that Sophie secretly still wears the locket after fifteen years. These scenes are revealed in close-up, but with an objective camera and without any eyewitness report from Uhl. We can see here how this one visual object, a locket, is presented in a semi-subjective way that indicates the ambiguous relation of perception to reality. We don't know if it happened as we have seen it happen, or if it was all a projection of Uhl's mind.

If we now consider all these close-ups of the locket not as conscious attention, as Münsterberg assessed it, but as objects of automatic (unconscious) feedforward recognition, we can then start to investigate whether the film also distinguishes moments of restricted and elaborate resonance. On an aesthetic cinematographic level, the locket in close-up has indeed become part of habitual recognition, a cliché that does not necessarily resonate with deeper levels of our imagination, memory or emotions. And yet the locket in *The Illusionist* does not give us the pure and automatic cliché. How does the film trace resonating circuits in the brain? Let's look at it closely once more.

Towards the end of the film, the narrative perspective of the locket scenes is more clearly subjectively restricted to inspector Uhl's actual observations. When Sophie is conjured as an apparition on stage, she mentions the locket, saying that she was wearing it at the moment of her death. It's not a remark that is particularly emphasised, just one element in the mesmerising event of her apparition on stage. When inspector Uhl a moment later searches Eisenheim's workplace, he finds a notebook entitled 'Orange Tree'. When he opens it, he does not find the secret of the growing orange tree illusion, as he had hoped, but a drawing of the locket. Disappointed that the notebook is not about the orange tree Uhl puts it back on the desk. But then he hesitates, and we notice he has second thoughts: the drawing of the locket begins to resonate with previous events and thus moves into his field of awareness (we have to remember that Uhl, because of the semi-subjective narration, has actually not yet seen the locket in the way the viewers have). He suddenly seems to recall Sophie's words on stage, and then remembers something that vaguely caught his attention earlier on when he began the investigation into her murder – something he saw from the corner of his eye in the stable where Sophie could have been murdered; something, indeed, in the back of his mind, as Burger comments on the DVD. And yes, when he returns to the stable he finds the locket in the hay, next to a gem stone from the crown prince's sword, providing enough evidence to arrest the prince for murder. We could thus conclude that the cliché of a locket in close-up that catches our immediate attention surpasses the status of habitual recognition and becomes an object of awareness when it enters resonant circuits of the brain (of the character in the film and the viewer alike).

Münsterberg's observations about attention are still valuable, but can be made more precise by referring to neurobiological insights. Questions of stereotypical representation and complex narration could benefit from these neuroscientific principles. With respect to Deleuze's cinema concepts, the difference between attention and awareness could also provide new insights into the relation between movement-images (which are sensori-motor images) and time-images (which relate to various levels of the virtual, time and imagination), but this remains to be developed.

F for Fake: Powers of the False and Decisive Will

The final question I would like to address relates to the philosophical and ethical implications of illusionary perception and questions of attention and awareness. In *The Time-Image* Deleuze develops the concept of a 'power of the false' which he relates to the cinema of Orson Welles, arguing that *F for Fake* is the manifesto of Welles' work and his reflection on cinema. Not surprisingly, Welles presents himself in this film as a magician. Deleuze relates Welles' fascination for conjuring to a fundamental aspect of modern cinema of the time-image in which truthful narration (where we could still believe our eyes) has been replaced by falsifying narration (where nothing is what it seems). The forger becomes *the* character of the cinema, Deleuze argues, 'not the criminal, the cowboy, the psycho-social man, the historical hero, the holder of power, and so on, as in the action-image, but the forger pure and simple, to the detriment of all action' (Deleuze 1989: 132). What the forgers in Welles actually show us is that the truth always refers to a system of judgement, which is shattered in a regime of falsifying narration. Welles' cinema shows that the 'truthful man' in fact wants nothing other than to judge life on the basis of preconceived principles. But in Welles' cinema, the system of judgement falls apart and is replaced by a power of the false. In *F for Fake* the famous art forger Elmyr de Hory demonstrates that he can forge a Picasso in ten minutes that no expert can distinguish from the original. In all his films Welles proposes a whole range of forgers, of whom the artist has the most generous creative powers of creating the truth. But other types of forgers, less generous, less creative, even more deadly, exist as well. Deleuze mentions Nietzsche's truthful man (the frog) and the sick man (the scorpion) who embody the spirit of revenge in various ways. According to Deleuze the image's relation to a power of the false, in normal perception as well as in cinema, indicates that

> it is not a matter of judging life in the name of a higher authority which would be good, the true; it's a matter, on the contrary, of evaluating every being, every action and passion, even every value, in relation to the life which they involve. Affect as immanent evaluation, instead of judgement as transcendent value. (Deleuze 1989: 141)

Obviously, the question now is, how exactly does this Deleuzian 'power of the false' relate to the problems and questions concerning visual illusion addressed above? First of all, if cinema is a semi-subjective way of storytelling that has an inherently ambiguous relation to reality and the truth, and if perception itself is a mental operation that only partly relates to reality, then obviously the false is not inherently bad or wrong (illusion or falsity is no longer an error if reality is ambiguous). But it truly becomes a power. Falsifying narrations and visual illusions, whether in phenomenal reality or screen reality, all start operating in the world and at the same time they create new circuits in the brain. The power of the false therefore becomes a power of the will – or, in Nietzschean terms a will to power: 'Neither true nor false, an undecidable alternative, but power of the false, decisive will' (Deleuze 1989: 145).

With respect to the problem of attention and awareness several aspects are worth further reflection. According to Münsterberg, film is a wonderful and manipulative art form that steers the attention of the viewer and is able to create the most powerful emotions, but also with potential dangerous effects. In 1917, in a posthumous publication, he asked: 'how can we make sure that this eagerly sought entertainment is a help and not a harm to young minds?' (Münsterberg 2002: 191). If we now refine Münsterberg's insight with neuroscientific knowledge of how the brain actually processes visual information, we can understand that the power of the false can work on three levels: on the unconscious level of automatic processing of habitual sensori-motor images; as non-reportable but nonetheless (restricted) conscious resonances (perhaps it is here that intuition or pre-monitions are situated?), and in elaborate feedback circuits. The powers of the false probably have different effects on different levels, and this remains to be investigated. But most importantly the question is no longer 'is Eisenheim tricking the audience or are these real spiritual phenom-ena?', but 'why is he doing this?', or 'what will make him decide to create this truth?' To answer these questions we could evaluate and compare his conjuring powers to a whole range of forgers, and thus investigate the motives of anyone who wants a certain image to be true (as for Eisenheim's story, inspector Uhl decides it doesn't matter if it's a trick or true; Eisenheim is doing it to be with Sophie).

One final aspect of visual illusions that can be related to the powers of the false could be signalled here. If the screen is a manipulative force that has the power to create (new) circuits in the brain, then the brain itself has some controlling power as well. Neuroscientists have conducted experiments with visual illusions to investigate whether the brain has the voluntary control to choose between different ways of seeing. In the Wagon Wheel Illusion, for instance, the brain can decide to rotate the wheel to the left or to the right. Raymond van Ee and others have analysed how, in watching rivalry stimuli like the Necker Cube, subjects have 'to a considerable extent control over the reversal rate – and all in a similar way – of either of the two competing Necker Cube percepts' (van Ee et al. 2006: 3129). When we cannot know for sure what proper-ties of the image are true, our brain has to decide and make a choice. Although again, while the wider philosophical implications of this neu-roscientific finding are not at all fully clear, it seems that this too is an important insight. If the forger (artist or idiot) can create new circuits in the brain by creating new images with a partial relation to reality, it is also true that on the reception side of the screen not everything is decided or predictable beforehand, and here too there is a decisive will at work to process the images in different ways.

Conclusions

Returning to *The Illusionist* and *The Prestige* we can draw two possible conclusions. Although the films both deal with visual illusions, magic and the powers of the false, each of them seems to have a slightly differ-ent attitude towards the art of conjuring. Neil Burger says at the end of his commentary:

> How do you make your way in a world where you are unable to pin down what really is true whether that be on a political level or on a spiritual one?

> Are there powers that can't be explained? Does the universe make moral
> sense? We probably never know. That's the story of *The Illusionist*.
> (Burger 2006)

He says this at the moment where Uhl decides that he has figured out
how Eisenheim performed his magic and that he knows what really happened. At that moment it is no longer important whether it was actually
true or whether it was a trick because 'he did it all to be with her' (Burger
2006). The affective dimension of the evaluation that Deleuze relates to
the powers of the false is subscribed to by *The Illusionist*. In *The Prestige*
the stakes are rather different. Here the emphasis is not so much on the
fact that we have to decide what is true (based on alternative principles
of ethical evaluation), rather, the film enhances the idea that we, the
viewers, *want* to be fooled. When Angier comes up with a performance
that is no trick but actually really mysterious (Tesla's electric transporta-
tion machine) the theatre owner tells him: 'It's very rare to see *real*
magic. Dress it up, disguise it. Give them enough reason to doubt it.' The
audience actually knows they are being fooled but that is precisely what
they want. 'The world is solid', Angier says. Making people wonder is
the highest ambition a magician and filmmaker can have. But whether
visual illusions tell our brain that we really can't tell the truth and thus
have to decide what we believe to be real, or whether we really want to
be fooled because reality is actually solid, it doesn't matter. The mysteries of the brain and the magic of the screen ask us to watch more closely
and to perceive differently every time we look again.

References

Anderson, J. (1996), *The Reality of Illusion: An Ecological Approach to Cognitive
Film Theory*, Carbondale: Southern Illinois University Press.
Bach, M. and C. Poloschek (2006), 'Optical Illusions', *ACNR*, 6 (2): 20–1.
Burger, N. (2006), 'Special Features', *The Illusionist*, DVD, directed by N. Burger,
Yari Film Group Release and Twentieth Century Fox Home Entertainment.
Deleuze, G. (1986), *Cinema 1: The Movement-Image*, trans. H. Tomlinson and B.
Habberjam, London: Athlone Press.
Deleuze, G. (1989), *Cinema 2: The Time-Image*, trans. H. Tomlinson and R. Galeta,
London: Athlone Press.
Deleuze, G. (1995), *Negotiations*, trans. M. Joughin, New York: Columbia
University Press, 1995.
Deleuze, G. (2000), 'The Brain is the Screen', in G. Flaxman (ed.), *The Brain is the
Screen: Deleuze and the Philosophy of Cinema*, trans. M. T. Guirgis, Minneapolis:
University of Minnesota Press.
Dumit, J. (2004), *Picturing Personhood: Brain Scans and Biomedical Identity*,
Princeton: Princeton University Press.
Eagleman, D. (2001), 'Visual Illusions and Neurobiology', *Nature Reviews
Neuroscience*, 2 (12): 920–6.

Epstein, J. (1946), *L'intelligence d'une machine*, Paris: Les Editions Jacques Melot.

Gregory, R. (1997), 'Knowledge in Perception and Illusion', *Philosophical Transactions: Biological Sciences*, 352 (1358): 1121–7.

Lamme, V. A. F. (2000), 'Neural Mechanisms of Visual Awareness: A Linking Proposition', *Brain and Mind*, 1 (3): 385–406.

Lamme, V. A. F. (2003), 'Why Visual Attention and Awareness are Different', *Trends in Cognitive Sciences*, 7 (1): 12–18.

Lamme, V. A. F. (2006), 'De geest uit de fles', *Psycholoog*, 41 (4): 186–92.

Lamme, V. A. F. and P. Roelfsema (2000), 'The Distinct Modes of Vision Offered by Feedforward and Recurrent Processing', *Trends in Neuroscience*, 23 (11): 571–9.

Lamme, V., H. Supèr, and H. Spekreijse (1998), 'Feedforward, Horizontal, and Feedback Processing in the Visual Cortex', *Current Opinion in Neurobiology*, 8 (4): 529–35.

Langdale, A. (2002), 'Editor's Introduction', in H. Münsterberg, *The Photoplay: A Psychological Study and Other Writings*, New York: Routledge.

Mather, G., F. Verstraten and S. Anstis (eds) (1998), *The Motion Aftereffect: A Modern Perspective*, Cambridge, MA: MIT Press.

Morin, E. (2005), *The Cinema, or The Imaginary Man*, trans. L. Mortimer, Minneapolis and London: University of Minnesota Press.

Münsterberg, H. (2002), *The Photoplay: A Psychological Study and Other Writings*, ed. A. Langdale, New York: Routledge.

Nolan, C. (2006), 'The Director's Notebook: The Cinematic Sleight of Hand of Christopher Nolan' and 'The Art of The Prestige Gallery', *The Prestige*, DVD, directed by C. Nolan, Touchstone Home Entertainment.

Pisters, P. (2006), 'Arresting the Flux of Images and Sounds: Free Indirect Discourse and the Dialectics of Political Cinema', in I. Buchanan and A. Parr (eds), *Deleuze and the Contemporary World*, Edinburgh: Edinburgh University Press.

van Ee, R., A. J. Noest, J. W. Brascamp and A. V. van den Berg (2006), 'Attentional Control Over Either of the Two Competing Percepts of Ambiguous Stimuli Revealed by a Two-Parameter Analysis: Means Do Not Make the Difference', *Vision Research*, 46 (19): 3129–41.

Notes

1. The plot summary of *The Illusionist*, according to the DVD cover: 'The acclaimed illusionist Eisenheim (Edward Norton) has not only captured the imaginations of all Vienna, but also the interest of the ambitious Crown Prince Leopold (Rufus Sewell). But when Leopold's new fiancée Sophie (Jessica Biel) rekindles a childhood fascination with Eisenheim, the Prince's interest evolves into obsession . . . and suddenly the city's chief inspector Uhl (Paul Giamatti) finds himself investigating a shocking crime [the murder of Sophie]. But even as the inspector engages him in a dramatic challenge of wills, Eisenheim prepares for his most impressive illusion yet.' The plot summary of *The Prestige*: 'Two young, passionate magicians, Robert Angier (Hugh Jackman), a charismatic showman, and Alfred Borden (Christian Bale), a gifted illusionist, are friends and partners until one fateful night when their biggest trick goes terribly wrong [Angier's girl-friend drowns]. Now the bitterest of enemies, they will stop at nothing to learn each other's secrets. As their rivalry escalates into a total obsession full of deceit and sabotage, they risk everything to become the greatest magicians of all time. But nothing is as it seems, so watch closely.'

2. I will return to Münsterberg's work below. One of the first contemporary film theoreticians who acknowledges Münsterberg's insights for (re)new(ed)

developments in film theory is Joseph Anderson (1996). Another example of early film theory that addresses the magical (and poetic) qualities of the screen is Jean Epstein's *L'intelligence d'une machine* (1946).

3. See also Deleuze's 'The Brain is the Screen' (Deleuze 2000).

4. I refer to 'illusionary perception' and 'visual illusion'. Sometimes the term 'optical illusion' is used. Strictly speaking, 'optical illusions' refer to illusions or distortions of vision in the outside world, or related to the retinal system. Visual illusions refer to illusions caused by processes in the brain because the imput is ambiguous. But very often both terms are used.

5. See also Dumit (2004), who focuses on PET scans. PET scans are tomographic images that measure chemical processes in the brain through radioactivity. EEG technology (Electro Encefalo Gram) measures brain activity through electrodes. MRI (Magnetic Resonance Imaging) is a scanning technology based on a strong magnetic field and radiowaves that capture cross sections of the brain (or other parts of the body); fMRI measures not only structures of the brain but also activity. MEG (Magnetic Encefalo Gram) can measure the speed of neural processes through magnetic signals. See for instance http://www.ru.nl/fcdonders/general/introduction.

6. See http://www.museedelamagie.com

7. Nicolas Tesla (1856–1943), played by David Bowie in the film, was a US inventor and electrical engineer whose work proved critical for much of the electronic technology we make use of today, including radio, telephone and television. For more information on him and the impact of his work see http://www.electrical-ternative.com/tesla.htm

8. For a presentation of visual illusions see http://www.michaelbach.de/ot. See also http://www.visual-media.be for an overview of an archaeology of media technology and visual illusions.

9. For an historical overview of this effect and its significance for modern neurosciences, see Mather et al. (1998).

10. Deleuze refers to this semi-subjective quality of cinema as 'free indirect discourse'. For an elaborate discussion of cinema and free indirect discourse see Deleuze (1986: 72–5); see also Pisters (2006).

11. Deleuze (1986: 31–2) relates this characteristic to what he calls the 'perception-image', which is both a specific image type but also the 'zeroness' of all images, a sort of 'degree zero' at the basis of all cinematographic perception (which will find its full realisation in the time-image).

12. See also Gregory (1997).

13. In a nutshell Münsterberg (2002: 79–80) here gives a summary of the elements that he discusses in relation to film. After perception and attention he also discusses memory, imagination, suggestion and emotion.

14. Münsterberg differentiates between voluntary attention, in which we actively seek something, and involuntary perception which begins from something external. It is this type of attention that Münsterberg relates to cinema. But in both cases Münsterberg relates attention to consciousness.

Chapter 13

Surface Folds: The Archival Events of New Medialised Art

Timothy Murray

How might a turn to philosophy enable the analysis of the impact of digital technologies on the parameters of the artistic archive and its transformations of the conventions of curatorial practice, art criticism and aesthetics? Over the past decade, I have combined academic research and writing on performance, cinema and video with curatorial projects in new media art. Deeply influencing my understanding of contemporary art and critical practice has been my work on a number of extensive projects.[1] These experiences in curating a wide range of new media art have prompted me to refine the sense of authorship, performance, subjectivity and archivisation that inform my prior monographs. My collaborations with new media artists and artworks has led to transformative thinking about (1) the artistic and cultural challenges posed by archival advances in mobile technologies, biotechnologies and security systems; (2) the global fluidity, flexibility and accessibility of the digital archive and its impact on humanistic conventions of preservation and research; and (3) the digital network as an affirmative, evolving event that loosens institutional boundaries of artistic creation, exhibition and critique. Fundamental to the project is a consideration of the shifts that occur when the archival meets the virtual, when the singularity of the archival object blends into the plurality of the digital network, and when humanistic research responds to the urgent, interdisciplinary imperatives of digital culture. In an effort to reflect on the undisciplined knowledge of international new media practices, I am now working on a broad philosophical and curatorial project that dwells on the cultural transformations wrought by the 'immaterial archive'.

It easily could be argued that one need not have awaited the arrival of new media art, a term that gained currency in the early nineties, to engage in reflections on the 'immaterial archive'. In 'The Archive and the Instant', the film theorist Mary Ann Doane argues, in an excellent chapter in *The Emergence of Cinematic Time: Modernity, Contingency, the Archive* (2002), that archival immateriality constitutes the very stuff of cinema. For Doane, film's potentiality is aligned with a contingency that is particularly archival. On the one hand, 'what film archives', she insists, 'is first and foremost a "lost" experience of time as presence, time as immersion' (Doane 2002: 221–2). On the other hand, because Doane appreciates film's capabilities 'of registering and recording singularities', which she aligns with contingencies, film confronts her with 'the specter of an archive of noise, linked to issues of legibility, cataloguing, and limitless storage' (222). Indeed, her book's thesis is framed by the alignment of the rise of cinema with the interrelated ghostings of the photographic after-image, on one side, and the rise of the temporal irreversibility of thermal dynamics and the contingencies of the logic of statistics, the other. The thesis to which she returns throughout is 'that an indexical ensured contingency played a major role in thinking about the cinema as the archival representation of time' (229).

What I find interesting in the context of the ensured contingency of knowledge is how Doane frames her thesis regarding the purity of cinema's 'record of time' (Doane 2002: 229) by contrasting it with her presentation of what she calls the generalised notion of power associated with the later Foucault. She contests not only the drive of the hegemony of power, but also the implications of Foucault's notion of 'the surface effectivity of discourse' for its refusal of both the unconscious and the possibility of 'a subject explicable as a subject of desire, pleasure, anxiety, and lure' (239). While I share Doane's commitment to the cinematics of desire (what I have articulated as a psycho-philosophical approach to new media art), I want to reflect on the paradox, which goes unnoted in her book, that Foucault emphasises and elaborates on the valence of 'the surface effectivity of discourse' not simply in the interviews on power (published in English in the 1980 collection *Power/Knowledge*, from which Doane quotes), but most specifically and contextually in his elaborations on enunciation and the archive in *L'Archéologie du savoir* (1969). Precisely in response to his contestation of a delimiting notion, tradition and practice of the archive, Foucault argues already in 1969 (hardly the 'late Foucault') for the discursive potential of something of an immaterial archive. This is where he articulates an archival praxis of difference in which

> The archive dissipates the temporal identity from which we like to admire ourselves to conjure the ruptures of history; the archive breaks the lineage of transcendental teleologies; and there, where anthropological thought interrogates the being of man and his subjectivity, the archive explodes the 'other' and the 'outside'. (Foucault 1969: 172)

At the same time as he argues for a generalised archival discourse of difference, Foucault gestures to the promises of institutionally specific practices that might profit from the very 'surface effectivity of discourse' in the expansion and accumulation of the archival event. Foucault sees in the institutional commitment to expanding resources, open archives and limitless storage (all in the age preceding 'open-source' archiving) something different from the legacy of 'legibility' that Doane appears to align with early twentieth-century procedures of cataloguing. For it is precisely the surge of accumulation, the continual surprise of informational texture, and the layers of enunciational multiplicity that lend to the archive its enunciational power. The archive, Foucault writes, is the horizon of *enoncés* marked by their 'thickness of accumulation' which never cease 'to modify, to change, to disturb, to upset, and sometimes to demolish' (Foucault 1969: 164). Such multi-layered thickness, which we might envision today as a fractal conglomeration of accumulated data, is what constitutes the lively energetics of the archive's 'surface effectivity of discourse'.

Rather than grounding the specter of noise in conventions of archival legibility, I have found myself attracted in my work as a curator and theorist of the archive to artistic and critical projects that capitalise on the expansiveness of the digital and immaterial surface to confront the user with the realities of undisciplined knowledge. Undisciplined, that is, once we embrace it from within the legacy of ruptured teleologies or even, to shift the terrain to the contestational Derridean project, from within the force field of the *différance* of archival fever.

Instead of quibbling with Foucault's translated essays of the 1980s, Doane might just as easily have dialogued with a curatorial project of the same period, one that openly confronted the ontology of cinema with the immateriality of the electronic archive. How might her approach to 'the surface effectivity of discourse' have been influenced by consideration of Jean-François Lyotard's curation in the early 1980s of *Les Immatériaux* for the Centre Pompidou. This 1985 exhibition featured a wide range of artistic, musical and architectural works whose primary materials were immaterial – emanations from electronic and digital sources. Based on artworks of an almost virtual kind, the show was driven by the philosophical imperative of 'immaterials' that challenge or question the modern philosophical confidence in the subject's analytical control over objects in time and space. Lyotard's ambitious exhibition generated both guarded enthusiasm and vociferous critique from critics, curators, and philosophers. Many critics voiced deep suspicion of the aesthetic merits of electronic art, not to mention the endorsement of electronic media by philosophers and theoreticians. And most sceptics shared an anxiety over the looming threat of the emergent techno-culture on humanistic practice, artistic convention and archival organi-sation. A passionate concern was voiced by Lyotard himself, who fretted that seductive developments in computing and techno-science might render their users indifferent to the nuances of difference and divergence that empower the most creative of information sciences: 'I see in its dis-position the sign that techno-science inures thought to the neglect of the differend essential to it' (Lyotard 1988: 29).[2] He joined the voices of his colleagues Foucault and Derrida who urged, albeit differently, a serious reflection on the cultural transformation of the archive, as both an insti-tutional practice and a critical procedure in the age of new technology.

It might now be argued that curatorial sensibilities that began with *Les Immatériaux* have nurtured the deep commitment of digital art to the thought of memory, the archive and the place of interactive media in global culture. Engaging their users in the dynamics of new combina-tions of code and content, the artists of the new media experiment with the nature of the archival base. At issue is less the history of the artist's oeuvre than the place of memory in the work of art itself and its problematic, if not ambivalent, dependency on technology. Working under the collaborative umbrella of the digital enterprise, which includes theorists, programmers and curators, new media artists engage the viewer in an interactive encounter that extends the archive from the public parameters of art history and university library to the personal depths of autobiography, cultural politics and coded data. An emphasis on memory, self-representation and the historical archive has been pro-nounced not only in the creation of digital art but also in the responsibil-ity assumed by a new generation of international curators for the theorisation and exhibition of the new media. In so doing, these practi-tioners and thinkers return to many of the archival paradoxes and dilemmas that Foucault articulated in *L'Archéologies du savoir* (1969), and to which Derrida responds indirectly in *Mal d'archive* (1995).

Immaterial Archive

My efforts to curate exhibitions and to build an international archive of multiple formats and content have been guided by Lyotard's call for sensitivity to the 'differend' inherent in the medium. Responding curato-rially to the conceptual and formal frameworks of the art itself, my exhibitions have been oriented around metacritical reflection on the media (Murray 1999; Murray, Kroker and Kroker 2003) 'The Art of

CD-Rom', 'NetNoise', and on social issues generated by the technosocial networks of digital culture (Murray 1999, 2001; Murray, Kroker, and Kroker 2002; Murray, Shevorym and Zimmerman 2006), 'Digital Terror and Ethnic Paranoia', 'Ecopoetics', 'Contact Zones', 'Tech Flesh'. Concurrently, the growth in the Goldsen Archive of special collections that highlight national difference, generic divergence, and well-founded technoparanoia has tempered my initial glee in the global techno-culture of the 1990s. Having written a book that addresses broad issues of digital memory, cultural retrospection and new media's inscription in cinema, *Digital Baroque: New Media Art and Cinematic Folds* (2008), I am now profiting from the lessons of 'curatorial instabilities' to think more broadly about the 'Immaterial Archive' writ large. I wish to address through close reading and institutional analysis how particular applications of technology and digital exhibition impact the organisation of the archive, its influence on the humanities, and its contribution to artistic and cultural conditions of stability and instability. Crucial to this research project is analysis of intersecting zones of institutional parameters that expand our sense of the cultural impact of the archive,[3] and related developments in digital technology and culture that inform procedures of social organisation and cultural practice (machineries of digital scanning, mapping and tracking; genome technologies; blogging as archival practice; mobile media and political cartography). Building on the studies and theories of the archive already mentioned, I mean to link the digital network to the archive as an extensively fibrous web of critical practice.

In reflecting on broad international (and yet particular) scenarios that link digital and networked artworks, exhibiting institutions, cultural paradigms and theoretical premises, I have come to focus broadly on what I call the Digital Archival Event. The result should provide a narrative counter, for example, to Doane's stellar account of the rise of the archive in the shadow of cinema: 'the archive preserves and perpetuates the aura of the original. . . . Hence, archival desire is an attempt to halt the vertiginous movement of mechanical and electronic reproduction' (Doane 2002: 222). It is precisely vertiginousness that has fueled expansion of the Goldsen Archive, rendering me sensitive to the incorporation of data, networks and mobile technologies into artistic practice and daily cultural encounter, and prompting the suspicion of political authorities concerned with matters of digital security.

The critical promise of this notion of the digital archival event results in a shift of balance between, say, artist or author and receiver or viewer. The Italian philosopher, Mario Perniola, contests the premise of individuality in a cultural environment in which 'the library, the archive, the mediatheque, the collection are situated in a horizon of the virtuality of moral intention' (Perniola 1995: 85). In his 1990 book, *Enigmes: le moment égyptien dans la société et dans l'art*, Perniola muses subtly on his approach to understanding a growingly complex culture in which the library, the computer and the archive have teamed up to displace the centrality of the facile world order of mass media and commodity. The result of what he lauds as the return of the centrality of the library is that

> The humanist vision that had conferred to the subject an ontological meaning has since disappeared . . . What's essential comes not from the depths of the soul, but from the extraneity of writing, the book, the computer. . . . The information society seems to propose a model of knowledge that is not answerable to the activity of the subject. (Perniola 1995: 86)

Perniola invites us to profit from the informational interconnectivity of networks, libraries and archives in order to dislodge the making and reception of text from its modernist dependence on strictly Cartesian and Hegelian paradigms. His argument positions the production of knowledge as an enigmatic activity of 'cross-culture'. It is in something like the development of the emergent, digital archive that

> two crucial and seemingly opposed critical orientations become connected and enfolded: one directed toward the most advanced developments of technology, the technical reproducibility of the work of art, the videographic and the electronic; the other, in contrast, directed toward the most emotional dimensions of experience, toward the ethnology and the phenomena of possession. (Perniola 1995: 110)

Perniola would caution us to remain wary, however, of the ease with which the technological can become embedded with the phenomena of possession. Fueling utopian thinking about digitality in the 1990s, the uncritical merging of technology and possession is what prompted Richard Coyne's insightful critique of 'technoromanticism's trajectory toward a transcendent disembodied reality' (Coyne 1999: 280), or Scott Durham's cautionary tale of the postmodern 'desire for the simulacrum: as an unrealizable desire for possession or as an unthinkable utopian desire for metamorphosis' (Durham 1998: 45). Crucial to my approach to a psycho-philosophical approach to new media art is an added emphasis on 'the surface effectivity of discourse' through which Deleuze and Foucault were thinking the archive already in 1969. Foucault focused his attention on the phantom of archivisation itself when he entered into dialogue with Deleuze's *Logique du sens* (1970). If we turn our attention to Foucault's exceptional essay on Deleuze, 'Theatrum Philosophicum'

(1997), we will come to appreciate the complex debt of his writings on archivisation to Deleuze's spectral musings on the surface in *Logique du sens*. Permit me to cite a rather long passage from the early pages of this essay as a means of performing what might now be widely forgotten as Foucault's enthusiastic incorporation of the Deleuzian surface:

> We should be alert to the surface effects in which the Epicureans take such pleasure: emissions proceeding from deep within bodies and rising like the wisps of a fog – interior phantoms that are quickly reabsorbed into other depths by the sense of smell, by the mouth, by the appetites; extremely thin membranes, which detach themselves from the surfaces of objects and proceed to impose colors and contours deep within our eyes (floating epiderm, visual idols); phantasms created by fear or desire (cloud gods, the adorable face of the beloved, 'miserable hope transported by the wind'). It is this expanding domain of intangible objects that must be integrated into our thought: we must articulate a philosophy of the phantasm that cannot be reduced to primordial fact through the intermediary of perception or an image, but that arises between surfaces, where it assumes meaning, and in the reversal that causes every interior to pass to the outside and every exterior to the inside, in the temporal oscillation that always make it precede and follow itself – in what Deleuze would perhaps not allow us to call its 'incorporeal materiality'. (Foucault 1997: 218)

Of interest to me, then, whether in Foucault's early essays on the archive or in this encomium of Deleuze, is precisely his fascination with the eventfulness of the archive, with its immateriality as the expanding field of discourse whose phantom arises between the surfaces of what he prefers to call 'incorporeal materiality'.

Archival Surface

My approach to writing about 'immaterial archives' in the contexts of technology, cinematics and new media has thus been increasingly informed by my thinking about the complexity of the archival surface. As Foucault suggests, any thought of the surface in dialogue with Deleuze first requires a shift of focus away from the surface's philosophical subordination in the binary structure of depth and surface. Deleuze is insistent in *Logique du sens* that the surface needs to be thought as other than the mere support of mimesis, in contrast to the entrance to the dark cave of representation or the supporting frame of the dark chamber, or even as the cinematic screen that merely receives or serves as the agent for the complexities of perspectival or cinematic projection. To consider what it might mean to foreground the surface, or to give ground to the surface, it might prove helpful to give further consideration to what Deleuze calls the 'paradoxes of surface effects'. In *Difference and Repetition*, Deleuze articulates the philosophical role of surface as something distinct from its Platonic and Neoplatonic subservience to depth and profundity. In the Platonic construct, surface functions always in the subsidiary role of *technê*. Surface is merely the insufficient support of the copy which always stands as an insufficient supplement in relation to the original, to Idea. At best, the surface serves the function of craft as the medium that provides only for copies of copies (think of the print or of the architectural blueprint) and their continuous degradation of the original. In contrast, in *Logique du sens*, Deleuze turns to the Stoics for whom the surface is less a disappointing result of representation than the empowering event of the frontier of the present-past and the future-past, as the stretching or elongation of the event of becoming. 'The highest term', writes Deleuze, 'is not Being, but *je ne sais quoi* (aliquid), insofar as it subsumes being and non-being, existence and inherence. . . . the characteristics of the Idea are relegated to the other side, that is to this impassive extra-. . .'. 'Becoming unlimited', he continues, 'comes to be the ideational and incorporeal event, with all of its characteristic reversals between future and past, active and passive, cause and effect, more and less, too much and not enough, already and not yet. The infinitely divisible event is always *both at once*' (Deleuze 1990: 10). When we think of the surface as event, rather than merely as insufficient support, we can begin to integrate into the thought of new media and architectonic performance Deleuze's insight, already mentioned above by Foucault, that 'events, differing radically from things, are no longer sought in the depths, but at the surface, in the faint incorporeal mist which escapes from bodies, a film without volume which envelopes them' (Deleuze 1990: 12).

In order to think the surface as digital event, we must consequently embrace technology as a way of revealing the surface. In *Logique de sens*, Deleuze aligns the structural ground of what I'm calling the archival event with the reorganisation of ideals of economic and political totality in relation to technological progress. In contrast to the technocrat who is the natural agent of holistic thought, the rise of computers, and the possessiveness of dictatorship, the revolutionary is one who inhabits the Deleuzian surface between technological progression and social totality (Deleuze 1970: 64). Whether or not we wish to adopt Deleuze's avant-gardist embrace of 'the revolutionary', an approach to the digital archival event necessitates a critical awareness of the grounding of the technological framework in the discourse of the rise of twentieth-century intellectual formations and architectonic structures. That is, to repeat the premise informing my research, to think the surface as digital event, we must consequently embrace technology as a way of revealing the surface.

This thesis stretches the philosophical thought of the surface even a little further back in time, to Martin Heidegger's 1955 lecture, 'The Question Concerning Technology'. It is here that Heidegger argues vociferously for the eventfulness of craft, of technology, of *technê*. In also referring back to the Platonic tradition that distinguishes the original from the copy, Heidegger emphasises that '*technê* is the name not only for the activities and skills of the craftsman, but also for the arts of the mind and the fine arts. *Technê* belongs to bringing-forth, to *poiesis*; it is something poietic. . . . It is as revealing, and not as manufacturing, that *technê* is a bringing-forth' (Heidegger 1977: 13). What I find myself wondering is how we might rethink this notion of *technê* within the new world of techno-culture, of medialisation, in which communications systems, data banks, wireless networks and techno-fantasies merge in a new skin of fibrous event. Were we to consider provocative examples of electronic architectural skin, for example, we could reflect on examples that combine models of the economic, the archival and the digital from the practice developed by the German firm, ag4 Mediatecture. The design commitment of ag4 to 'architectural medialisation' works to transform the architectonic surface into an archival display of medialisation.[4] I would like to contrast two ag4 projects as a means of positioning this work within the context of rethinking the archival surface.

First is the T-Mobile headquarters in Bonn, realised in 2004, for which ag4 built what it claims to be the world's first transparent media façade. This is a horizontal panel construction covering some 300 square metres which is attached to the actual glass façade. The panels have integrated LEDs through which surface literally becomes medial event. Not limited to the skin of the building itself, the square in front of the T-Mobile façade is transformed into an interactive playground where a camera recording of activities on the square is incorporated into the media display (where surveillance becomes product becomes pleasure). The façade's basic self-generating program is complemented by single 'auto-active films' that advertise current events on the T-Mobile campus. Ag4 is most enthusiastic about what it calls 'the transparency which can be perceived from both the inside and the outside [which] is responsible for the special kind of magic of the transparent media façade' (ag4 2006: 25). Of course what we discover in considering the content of this structure's media presentation is that magic here seems to be far removed from the

Deleuzian surface event of *je ne sais quoi* and much more a function of what Marx called the magic of commodity fetishism. This is because the façade serves here as little more than the screen of corporate self-promotion, which is far removed, of course, from displaying the means of production, on one side, or the thought of *technê*, on the other. As ag4 proudly boasts to potential corporate clients: 'the potential of the transparent media façade has surpassed T-Mobile's greatest expectations: not only does the façade animate the company's logo, but the entire brand is staged by means of moving images and videos' (ag4 2006: 25).

Much more complex and theoretically promising is ag4's 2004 design concept, 'Fata Morgana', for the main railway station in Cologne. As described by ag4, this design is imagined much more as a medialised surface of the interrelated events of time and movement:

> The architecture of Cologne's main railway station with its large scale glass façade enables a clear view from the inside of the building onto the city's landmark – Cologne Cathedral. An area dedicated to transit, the main railway station is a hub for arrivals, departures and through-journeys. The central idea of the concept envisages to greet the traveller with the place of his or her departure as he or she arrives. This is made possible by a transparent media façade which is installed in front of the entire glass façade and faces the station's main arrival and departure hall. The media façade consists of panels with built-in LEDs with a vertical clearance of ten centimetres. The traveler will experience a complete media image from as little a distance as 10 metres. As she or he approaches the media image will begin to make way to the space behind the façade – the forecourt of Cologne Cathedral. (ag4 2006: 42–50)

The images on display interact with the arrival of the main-line trains. When a main-line train arrives, the announcement on the media façade communicates the train's arrival and its station of departure. This is followed by a live film of the latter station's foyer – for example, the forecourt of Frankfurt's main railway station. The arriving passenger enters the main foyer in Cologne, and suddenly feels they are back from where they came. The place of origin travelled with them as a memory and appears as an after-image, as a mirage. As the traveller approaches the exit this mirage becomes fainter and fainter while the point of arrival – Cologne – starts to dominate and becomes real. For those people waiting in the main foyer the media façade creates the vision of the main station as a hub for international transit (ag4 2006: 44).

This proposal inscribes the time and memory of travel itself into the medialised façade of a building that serves as the hub of transit and tourism (commerce and pleasure) in Cologne. As the bearer of the

after-image, the medialised surface here serves as the incorporeal materiality of the phantasm of travel itself. There are many ways in which
what ag4 calls the *vision* of transit can thus be understood as a design
paradigm of the Deleuzian event of the surface, particularly when we
remember what Deleuze calls 'the ideational and incorporeal event, with
all of its characteristic reversals between future and past, active and
passive, cause and effect, more and less, too much and not enough,
already and not yet. The infinitely divisible event is always both at once'
(Deleuze 1990: 8).

Surface Folds

Still, ag4 sometimes seems almost constitutionally incapable of thinking
the surface outside of its sense of the *vision* of the media façade, thus
aligning the façade with phenomenologies and technologies of vision
that are anchored in Platonic and Euclidean paradigms of depth, profundity and projection. An alternative approach to new media and the
immaterial archive might provide a means with which to distinguish
between the visual procedures of projection/profunding and the archival
practices of scansion and registration.

This is the distinction that lies at the core of my analyses in *Digital
Baroque* (2008). At issue is a deeply significant, archeological shift from
critical emphasis on perspective and projection to artistic experimentation with fold and surface that is emphasised, if not wholly embodied,
by the digital condition. In contrast to models of knowledge and representation derived from single-point perspective and systems of projection (the stuff of the cogito and the cinematic apparatus), the fold
embodies the elasticity of seriality and the continuous labyrinth of single
points (1s and 0s) that expand infinitely along the surface in all directions, rather than definitively in the shape of a cone, line or sight that
culminates in a single, utopian point or subjectivity. Such a concept
turns around the disturbance of confident paradigms of projection, dialectics and philosophical teleology by those of the accumulation, divergence and fractal simultaneity that I have been arguing to be constitutive
of the immaterial archive.

While Deleuze's embrace of the fold has become the centerpiece of
recent appropriations of the Baroque, including my own, it could be
aligned just as well with the 'surface effectivity of discourse' constitutive
of the archive in the digital age. At issue here remains something of an
archeological shift away from perspective and the very procedures of
corporate display that so readily identify T-Mobile as the penultimate

brand of ag4's complex engagement in medialised architecture. Indeed, Deleuze's allusion to the phantasm of the fold in *Logique de sens* could easily have been appropriated by ag4 as a much more productive description of the archival eventfulness of 'Fata Morgana' in Cologne, if not its broader artistic practice. We could easily say, of 'Fata Morgana', that the haunting possessions of the surface lend the energetics of archivisation to the otherwise merely medialised display of the passage through Cologne. Ironically, the designers of 'Fata Morgana' could easily have appropriated Deleuze's description of the surface membrane in their presentation of the import of the Cologne project. 'Independent of distance', Deleuze writes, 'surface membranes place in typological contact both interior and exterior space' (1970: 126). 'Fata Morgana' could be said to open the medialised surface to the effectivities of discourse through which the legibility of electronic data gives way to divergent, heterogeneous series of events that envelope 'corresponding singular points in the same aleatory point or space' (Deleuze 1970: 125).

The surface effectivity of the fold certainly fits with the artistic and critical vision of ag4's medialised Aspire Tower, which was constructed in 2006 for the Asian Games in Doha, Qatar. This 300-metre tower is covered in a stainless steel mesh that doubles as an almost surreal projection screen via the interplay between the reflective mesh and 4,000 tri-color LED luminaries which were individually addressed to permit animated patterns to dance across intersecting vertical and horizontal vectors. The performative result is something of an architectonic electro-fractal. During the Asian Games, spectres of the Olympic rings ascended the Tower; videos of celebratory sports moments were broadcast around an 8-metre section of the tower; and variably amped LEDs showered the city with medialised fireworks. It's almost uncanny how the Aspire Tower distributed the singularity-events, as Deleuze might say, in sync with the energetic potentiality of the heterogeneous series of the Asian Games. In contrast to solely individual and personal instantiations of subjectivity (the stuff of perspective and projection), Deleuze would suggest that the multimedia singularities of archival eventfulness itself always haunt the medialised surface.

This haunting might be even more pronounced when shifted to the smaller medialised screen of the even broader surface of the Internet. I would like to conclude by turning to a body of art work that exemplifies the new dynamics of archivisation, as a new ontological configuration of thought, medialisation and poetics. Collaborating for fifteen years as Out-of-Sync, the Australian artists, Maria Miranda and Norie Neumark, engage in just such performative explorations of archival eventfulness via intersecting new media interfaces, sound, CD-Rom, installation, video, Internet and graphics.⁵ Wishing to bring the touch of the human – its skin, organs and emotions – directly into the mix of computing culture, they have systematically developed artistic projects that inject the messiness of feeling, sound, trauma and delay into the digital frontier's paradigms of efficiency, speed and cognition. They initially set out by combining Miranda's digital imagery with Neumark's experimental sounds to investigate the unpredictability and confusion of human communication, as enhanced by digital sound and image. More recently, interdisciplinary experimentations with video installation, Internet art and mobile computing have extended the international reach of their studios in Coogee Beach and Sydney.

Out-of-Sync first received international acclaim following the 1997 release of their award-winning CD-Rom, *Shock of the Ear*, authored by Neumark with visuals by Miranda.⁶ In interacting with the CD-Rom, visitors scroll across archival traces of various scenarios of 'shock': shock treatment, electrocution, torture, car accident trauma and the linguistic confusions of polyglossia. The work's lyrical and melodic soundtracks of beckoning whispers, synthesised chords and natural sounds work marvellously to situate retroactive narratives of shock in a curiously kinesthetic environment. The artists' creative experimentation with the suspended time and eerie tranquility of shock set the stage for subsequent pieces whose blends of installation, Internet art, sound and video mine the convolutions of sensation in the digital network. These prescient new media artists recognised early on in the burgeoning Australian digital art scene how they might blend various platforms of interactivity to explore the energetic fields of trauma, corporeality and affect inherent in cultural and computing archives.

They have been particularly successful at seizing upon configurations central to computing, such as archival data, networked systems and coded bodies, as a means of raising playful questions about the human-computing interface. *The Museum of Rumour* is an Internet archive of contemporary rumour – its mnemonic remnants of media bits and historical account playfully extend the rumours of mass culture, from the appearance of The Virgin Mary outside the artists' flat at Coogee Beach to the Australian imaginary of gigantic feral cats roaming the landscape, something like those feline spectres so upsetting to Freud. Another fictional, Internet archive, *The Perpetual Emotion Project*, also blends installation and art for the Internet to present the ongoing research activities of Doktor Rumor and Professore Rumore who oversee the Institute for the Study of Perpetual Emotion. This deeply layered and parodic project on emotion in digital culture includes 'Séance – A Networked Glossalalia', which stages a 'pataphysical' experiment on the relays of perpetual emotion on the Internet, and 'The Dog Files', which charts the emotional relays between dogs and their humans.

The artists enhance the link between the body and its phantasms in *Machine Organs* (1999), a lyrical Internet commentary on the shared conventions of genetics and computing. Included in the *CTHEORY Multimedia* issue on the Human Genome Project, this piece follows its originary installation, 'Dead Centre: The Body with Organs', that puns on 'the digestion process' of scanning and coding, one whose perform-ance is rendered by Out-of-Sync as being as messy and noisy as it is stable and machinic. *Machine Organs* extends this performative exploration of computers as organs of digestion and excretion, transmission and emis-sion, by confronting users with the parallel of cultural fables and phan-tasms of corporeal organs that complicate the clarity of the body's cognitive mapping in the information age. In this piece, the body is not only the biological material of DNA but also the cultural stuff of fable (the French liver) and the carrier of emotive relations (breath, sound and the traces of culture).[7] Key to the inventive, conceptual projects of Out-of-Sync is thus the staging of the centrality of emotion, memory and affect in the hard-wired network of speedy machines, computing systems and genomic tracking. Miranda and Neumark thus extend the parame-ters of the digital archival surface by foregrounding the relationality of aesthetics within the psycho-corporeal zones of new media art.

The affective wizardry of their work always seems to involve a rethinking of the role of the information archive in artistic and net-worked culture as a fluid space of interactive reflection and sentiment. For their latest piece of art for the Internet, 'The Fourth Floor :: *Le Quatrième étage*', which was the inaugural commission for the relaunch of the online journal, *Metamute*,[8] Neumark and Miranda found them-selves contemplating the paradox of creating online art at a moment when they were hearing artistic declarations of the death of 'net.art'. Attempting to explore possibilities beyond the 'canon' of 'net.art', they aimed to craft a piece of interactive art made for the net, while wishing to tamper with the predictable seductions of flash and animation, which capitalise on the cultural equation of speed and digitality. Visitors to 'The Fourth Floor :: *Le Quatrième étage*' will find themselves confronted by the slowness of their art and by the pensiveness of the digital pause within the variations of each link. In creating the piece, the artists wanted to turn their attention to a project that highlights the Internet as a spirited place of 'expanded' reading, as a place where the intimacy of reading is maintained within the public folds of the blog. Users will find in this piece a surface of variations that encourage critical reflection on digital difference and repetition rather than a venue for rapid channel changing and nervous surfing.

'The Fourth Floor :: Le Quatrième étage' stages the interpellation of the new media archive and its enigmatic disruption of critical dependency on the narrative of history, the psychology of identification, and even the heroics of artistic authorship (indicative perhaps of the authors' casting aside of the proper name in favour of something of a marker of eventfulness, Out-of-Sync). The piece traces a moment in the life of a fictional blogger after s/he took up residency in a studio in Paris' Cité International des Arts (a little biographical teasing by the Australian duo who resided in that same space). There the blogger was faced with the enigmatic pull of two DVDs containing 4 gigabytes of unedited video, labelled 'rue Simon-Crubellier', which s/he found abandoned in a cupboard. Struck by the uncanny return of 'rue Simon-Crubellier', which is the street central to Georges Perec's Life: a User's Manual (1978), the book read by the blogger during sleepless nights, s/he begins a quest not only to organise and log the raw video material, but also to search through the streets and archives of Paris for the virtual place without a site, rue Simon-Crubellier.

The result is a blog in which the orphaned video clips are categorised in drop-down menus not by subject matter but by spatial relation, attesting to virtuality's inscription in the deferrals of presence and proximity: with, between, behind, front, inside, outside, far, near, above, below. The drop-downs provide access to video clips of Parisian sites and sights, accompanied by blog entries across a seemingly arbitrary field, from sequences of 'waiting/alone/studio' to 'stairs/intently/counter'. Frustrating the archival dependency on the grid or tableau, the vertical series of pop-up lists never appear simultaneously along the horizontal access. Nor do sequences related to space, time and perception ('out there/blur/perhaps') lend any phenomenological or cognitive stability to more conventionally empirical groupings ('windows/train/pair'). Within each entry, the user finds gridded video stills whose apparent organisation is then thrown topsy-turvy by the roll or click of the mouse, leading to parodic reversals, anamorphic extensions, graphic indications, erasures, colour variations, etc. The artists also provide users with the option of viewing the video clips in two other variations, in multiple compositions of small videos or in 'micro moments' of a single large frame. Each variation is accompanied by variant blog reflections and citations from Perec and others, as well as sounds whose hearing does not necessarily match the sight, thus troubling the videomatic relation, as the artists say, between 'hear and there'.

Such disjunction between phenomenological and haptic space turns the construction and reception of 'The Fourth Floor :: *Le Quatrième étage*' into a project of artistic re-search. Here the happy event of reading and thinking on the net is metacritically reflected by the protagonist's entries about the delightful and frustrating events of thinking, reading and creating in response to the enigmatic signifiers of the digital archive and the quest for the virtual place. To Out-of-Sync, the artistic blog lends itself to a similarly expanded surface of reading, one in which perceptions of intimacy and documents of facticity are rendered variable by the creative event of archival art on the Internet.

As a site of archival writing, their bilingual project in English and French displays the double 'hand' of the art blog. It performs the ephemeral *main-tenant*, the 'now', of the comment and the deliberate *maintenance*, the 'archive', of the flow of time's commentary. Its conceit is to sensitise the user through fiction and art to the incremental power of the archive as the performative place permitting its user to receive the imprint of digital culture as an interactive event. No longer in accord with the conventional truth-value of the archive where the certainty of fact can be discovered as if embalmed, the fluid archive of the network thus empowers the user to respond to enigmatic traces of coded facticity through the intense creativity of fabulation and the excessive affect of thought.

References

ag4 (2006), *Media Facades*, Cologne, London, New York: daab.

Coyne, R. (1999), *Technoromanticism: Digital Narrative, Holism, and the Romance of the Real*, Cambridge, MA: MIT Press.

Deleuze, G. (1970), *Logique du sens*, Paris: Editions de Minuit.

Deleuze, G. (1990), *The Logic of Sense*, trans. M. Lester with C. Stivale, ed. C.V. Boundas, New York: Columbia University Press.

Deleuze, G. (1994) *Difference and Repetition*, trans. Paul Patton, New York: Columbia University Press.

Derrida, J. (1995), *Mal d'Archive*, Paris: Galilée.

Doane, M. A. (2002), *The Emergence of Cinematic Time: Modernity, Contingency, the Archive*, Cambridge, MA: Harvard University Press.

Durham, S. (1998), *Phantom Communities: The Simulacrum and the Limits of Postmodernism*, Stanford: Stanford University Press.

Foucault, M. (1969), *L'Archéologie du savoir*, Paris: Gallimard.

Foucault, M. (1997), 'Theatrum Philosophicum', trans. D. F. Bouchard and S. Simon, in T. Murray (ed.), *Mimesis, Masochism, and Mime: The Politics of Theatricality in Contemporary French Thought*, Ann Arbor: University of Michigan Press.

Heidegger, M. (1977), *The Question Concerning Technology and Other Essays*, trans. W. Lovitt, New York: Harper and Row.

Lyotard, J-F. (1988), *L'Inhumain: Causeries sur le Temps*, Paris: Galilée.

Lyotard, J-F. (2006), 'L'art interactif dans l'âge des stratégies post-révolutionnaires', in J-P. Balpe and M. de Barros (eds), *L'art-t-il beson du numérique, Colloque de Cerisy*, Paris: Hermes.

Murray, T., curator (1999), *Contact Zones: The Art of the CD-Rom*, Cornell University, http://contactzones.cit.cornell.edu

Murray, T. (2000), 'Digital Incompossibility: Cruising the Aesthetic Haze of the New Media', *CTHEORY*, a078, http://www.ctheory.net/articles.aspx?id=121

Murray, T., curator (2001), 'Tech Flesh: The Promise and Perils of the Human Genome Project', *CTheory Multimedia*, http://ctheorymultimedia.cornell.edu/issue2/issue_main.htm

Murray, T. (2006), 'L'art interactif dans l'âge des stratégies post-révolutionnaires', in Jean-Pierre Balpe and Manuela de Barros (eds), *L'art-t-il beson du numérique, Colloque de Cerisy*, Paris: Hermes.

Murray, T. (2008), *Digital Baroque: New Media Art and Cinematic Folds*, Minneapolis: University of Minnesota Press.

Murray, T., curator, with A. Kroker and M. Kroker, curators (2002), 'Wired Ruins: Digital Terror and Ethnic Paranoia', *CTheory Multimedia*, http://ctheorymultimedia.cornell.edu/issue3

Murray, T., A. Kroker and M. Kroker, curators (2003), 'Netnoise', *CTheory Multimedia*, http://ctheorymultimedia.cornell.edu/four.php

Murray, T., T. Shevory and P. Zimmermann, curators (2006), 'Ecopoetics', *Rose Goldsen Archive of New Media Art*, Cornell University Library, http://goldsen.library.cornell.edu/internet/ecopoetics.php

Perniola, M. (1995), *Enigmas: The Egyptian Moment in Society and Art*, trans. C. Woodall, London: Verso

Notes

1. From the international exhibition 'Contact Zones: The Art of CD-Rom' (see http://contactzones.cit.cornell.edu) and the Internet art exhibition space, *CTHEORY Multimedia* (see http://ctheorymultimedia.cornell.edu), to the creation and curatorial direction of the Rose Goldsen Archive in New Media Art in the Cornell Library (see http://goldsen.library.cornell.edu).

2. At the time Lyotard was curating *Les Immatériaux*. Moreover, he expressed to me his ardent resistance to writing on a computer, since he thought it would alter his relation to the figurality of his discourse.

3. See, for example, the institutionalised practices evident at ZKM, University of Paris 1 Anarchive project, Daniel Langlois Foundation, Cornell's Goldsen Archive, etc.

4. Ag4 stands for *Arbeitsgemeinschaft für vierdimensionales Bauen* (Working Group Four-dimensional Construction). Information on ag4's architectural practice can be accessed on its website: http://www.mediafacade.com. A broader set of examples of medialised architecture can be found on the site of the Media Architecture Group: http://www.mediaarchitecture.org

5. An initial version of these remarks on Out-of-Sync were published as 'Thinking Blogging Out-of-Sync' which is my curatorial note accompanying their piece, 'The Fourth Floor', commissioned for online exhibition on Metamute.org: http://www.metamute.org/en/out-of-sync.

6. See my more detailed analysis of this piece in Murray (2000).

7. I provide a more detailed reading of *Machine Organs* in Murray (2006).

8. Out-of-Sync, 'The Fourth Floor', http://www.metamute.org/en/out-of-sync.

Afterword

Mark Poster

As William Bogard admits in his chapter in this volume, Deleuze did not theorise technology. Even worse from the standpoint of investigating new media, Deleuze not only does not theorise media, he rarely mentions the term. Nowhere in his considerable corpus does one find a sustained interrogation of the media, despite its increasing prominence in the social world. From radio, film and television to telephone, communications satellites and the Internet, media have become ubiquitous in daily life. In fact, France was the first nation to experiment on a broad scale with Internet communications in the form of the Minitel in the early 1980s. After its outdated and inefficient telephone system of the 1970s, France in the 1980s was a pioneer of new media technologies. In other words, the 'context' was there for theorists to examine the implications of what would shortly become a media culture. Search as one might – from Foucault, Derrida and Deleuze to Balibar and Lacan – one finds few French theorists taking the question of technology seriously.[1] Some exception would have to be made for Baudrillard and Lyotard, but in general the story is not bright. And yet the question of new media, and of media in general, is central to an understanding of Deleuze's concept of 'control society'. Perhaps because of its marginal position in Deleuze's work, this essay has gained enormous attention from theorists, as is evident from the great interest shown in it by the contributors to this volume. I shall briefly examine the 'Postscript on Societies of Control' here, to see what light it might shed on digital media culture.

It might be noted that, as Buchanan points out in these pages, Deleuze and Guattari's work, especially *A Thousand Plateaus*, has been very important to the theorisation of networked computing. It is quite common to find – as one does in Tauel Harper's chapter – a turn to the concept of the rhizome when theorising the Internet.[2] As a figure for a moving, heterogeneous, multiple phenomenon that resists identity and stability, the rhizome is a compelling concept for students of digital culture. It is worth citing again Harper's epigram from *A Thousand Plateaus* to underscore the basic sympathy of Deleuze and Guattari for the capacity of resistance deeply articulated in Internet architecture:

> Some people invoke the high technology of the world system of enslavement; but even, and especially, this machinic enslavement abounds in undecidable propositions and movements that, far from being a domain of knowledge reserved for sworn specialists, provides so many weapons for the becoming of everybody/everything, becoming-radio, becoming-electronic, becoming-molecular . . . Every struggle is a function of all of these undecidable propositions and constructs *revolutionary connections* in opposition to the *conjugation of the axiomatic*. (Deleuze and Guattari 1987: 473)

As we look with a critical gaze on 'Postscript for Societies of Control', we need to bear in mind Deleuze and Guattari's insight into media as potentially oppositional.

In the 'Postscript', Deleuze emphasises the absence of confining spatial arrangements in the exercise of domination afforded by the use of computer technology. In the formulation of Deleuze's argument by Hardt and Negri, 'What has changed is that, along with the collapse of the institutions, the disciplinary dispositifs have become less limited and bounded spatially in the social field. Carceral discipline, school discipline, factory discipline, and so forth interweave in a hybrid production of subjectivity' (Hardt and Negri 2000: 330). Beyond the negative trait of the absence of 'organising major sites of confinement' (Deleuze 1995: 177), control societies are, in Deleuze's text, maddeningly undefined. He discusses the control society again in 'Having an Idea in Cinema', but is once more both brief and vague, only adding to his previous discussion that, since 'information is precisely the system of control', 'counter-information' becomes a form of resistance (Deleuze 1998: 17–18). All of which suggests to me that Deleuze's understanding of networked digital information human–machine assemblages remains rudimentary. It is hard to imagine what 'counter-information' might be, for example. Does he mean that critical content is resistance? Or does the form of the critical content constitute resistance?

It might seem logical to conclude from his contrast between societies of discipline and societies of control that Deleuze is positioning himself against Foucault, or at least going beyond him in identifying forms of domination unexamined by the historian of the Panopticon. Yet this is not at all the case. Instead, Deleuze proclaims his agreement with Foucault, citing William Burroughs again as the fulcrum of the matter.

Deleuze writes: 'Foucault agrees with Burroughs who claims that our future will be controlled rather than disciplined' (Deleuze 1992: 164). But Deleuze provides no evidence that Foucault anticipated a transformation to societies of control, relegating discipline to the garbage can of history. It would appear that Deleuze was unwilling to position himself as the thinker who went beyond Foucault even as, in the same paragraph cited above, Deleuze compellingly characterises the break between the two orders of domination. In the following passage Deleuze insists that Foucault adopts the notion of societies of control: 'the disciplines which Foucault describes are the history of what we gradually cease to be, and our present-day reality takes on the form of dispositions of overt and continuous *control* in a way which is very different from recent closed disciplines' (Deleuze 1992: 164).

Deleuze's stadial theory, moving from discipline to control, is also far too linear in character. Elements of 'control' existed in Europe in the early modern period as the state hired spies to keep track of suspected miscreants. Equally, forms of 'discipline' proliferate in the twenty-first century as the United States, for example, erects more and more prisons under the so-called 'get tough' policies of recent administrations. The shift from discipline to control is also Eurocentric, overlooking the very different disposition of these state strategies in the southern hemisphere. François Vergès points out, for example, that 'In postcolonial Reunion, these two strategies have concurrently occurred. New types of sanction, education, and care have constructed a web of control around the Creoles, and along with the creation of a vast social network of control, there has been a multiplication of prisons, a criminalisation and psychologisation of politics' (Vergès 1999: 219). Deleuze's model of control as the next stage after discipline thus contains problems at numerous levels.

What is lacking in Deleuze's understanding of the move from discipline to control is precisely an analysis of the media as technologies of power. Surely media are different from prisons, education, and so forth, but one must understand the specificity of the media as structuring systems, as well as pay attention to the difference of media from one another. Television, print and the Internet are each disciplinary institutions, different from each other but also, in this sense, similar to prisons in that they construct subjects, define identities, position individuals and configure cultural objects. True enough, media do not require spatial arrangements in the manner of workshops and prisons, but humans remain fixed in space and time, at the computer, in front of the television set, walking or bicycling through city streets or on a subway with headphones and an mp3 player or a mobile phone. I refer to this configuration of the construction of the subject as a 'superpanopticon', to indicate its difference from modern institutions (see Poster 1990). The term 'control society' has the disadvantage of losing an ability to capture the new technologies of power, the media.

At heart Deleuze adopts a limited view of digital culture as simply 'control'. He writes in the 'Postscript': 'The digital language of control is made up of codes indicating whether access to some information should be allowed or denied' (Deleuze 1995: 180). Here the digital is always already 'control'. While this is in part true, it is equally the case that the digital is always already 'freedom', as Wendy Chun (2006) and Alexander Galloway (2004) rightly point out. Just as the culture industries are able to trace, through control mechanisms, users who download their music, so those users continue to download music files, to the consternation of the RIAA. Digital culture moves in two opposite directions at the same time: towards control and towards freedom from control. Admittedly Deleuze does acknowledge 'the passive danger' in computer technology of 'noise' and 'the active danger' of 'piracy and viral contamination' (Deleuze 1995: 180). But he does not go far enough in specifying the qualities of the digital that make both options possible. After disciplinary society, what might emerge is societies of control and freedom in a mixture that only political action – and this at a global level – can decide.

At a more general level, what stands in the way of an approach to media theory for Deleuze is his understanding of film as art. From *Difference and Repetition* in 1968 to the cinema books of the 1980s, Deleuze frames cinema only as art. When he recognises the altered sphere of everyday life as steeped in audio and visual technologies, he finds in art a liberatory escape from the quotidian: 'The more our daily life appears standardised, stereotyped and subject to an accelerated reproduction of objects of consumption, the more art must be injected into it in' (Deleuze 1994: 293). One cannot come near the problem of media with a view of the everyday as degraded, debased and baleful. It seems that Deleuze would have done well to heed the work of cultural studies, from Stuart Hall to Michel de Certeau, on the limits of modernist art theory, as well as the debate in postmodern theory over the merging of 'high' and 'popular' cultures. In that case, the persistence in Deleuze's work of art as revolutionary would have been mollified, opening a turn to a more general theory of media as culture. Lacking such a turn, Deleuze's view of control systems dependent on computing lacks the dimension of new media's potential for resistance to commodification and especially its potential for facilitating new forms of global politics. The becoming-machinic inherent in networked computing offers a new direction for political formation just as it contains the danger of control by Big Brother. Only a theorisation of media that takes both, drastically divergent options into account can serve well the purposes of critical theory.

References

Chun, W. H. K. (2006), *Control and Freedom: Power and Paranoia in the Age of Fiber Optics*, Cambridge, MA: MIT Press.

Deleuze, G. (1992), 'What is a *Dispositif?*', in F. Ewald (ed.), *Michel Foucault: Philosopher*, New York: Routledge.

Deleuze, G. (1994), *Difference and Repetition*, trans. Paul Patton, New York: Columbia University Press.

Deleuze, G. (1995), *Negotiations*, trans. M. Joughin, New York: Columbia University Press.

Deleuze, G. (1998), 'Having an Idea in Cinema', in E. Kaufman and K. Heller (eds), *Deleuze and Guattari: New Mappings in Politics, Philosophy, and Culture*, Minneapolis: University of Minnesota Press.

Deleuze, G. and F. Guattari (1987), *A Thousand Plateaus: Capitalism and Schizophrenia*, trans. B. Massumi, Minneapolis: University of Minnesota Press.

Deleuze, G. and F. Guattari (1994), *What Is Philosophy?*, trans. H. Tomlinson and G. Burchell, New York: Columbia University Press.

Derrida, J. and B. Stiegler (2002), *Echographies of Television*, London: Polity.

Galloway, A. (2004), *Protocol: How Control Exists After Decentralisation*, Cambridge, MA: MIT Press.

Hardt, M. and A. Negri (2000), *Empire*, Cambridge, MA: Harvard University Press.

Poster, M. (1990), *The Mode of Information: Poststructuralism and Social Context*, Chicago: University of Chicago Press.

Rodowick, D. N. (2001), *Reading the Figural, or, Philosophy After the New Media*, Durham: Duke University Press.

Vergès, F. (1999), *Monsters and Revolutionaries: Colonial Family Romance and Métissage*, Durham: Duke University Press.

Notes

1. Look, for example, at the discussion between Derrida and Stiegler on the question of technology (Derrida and Stiegler 2002). One finds occasional mention of computers in Deleuze, but only in passing (for example, Deleuze and Guattari 1994: 207).
2. See also, for example, Rodowick (2001).

Notes on Contributors

William Bogard

William Bogard is Deburgh Chair of Social Sciences and Professor of Sociology at Whitman College, Washington. He is the author of *The Simulation of Surveillance* (Cambridge University Press, 1996), as well as articles on Panopticism, Deleuze and Social Control.

Abigail Bray

Abigail Bray is a Postdoctoral Research Fellow in the School of Social and Cultural Studies and the Center for Women's Studies at the University of Western Australia. The author of *Hélène Cixous: Writing and Sexual Difference* (Palgrave Macmillan and St Martin's Press, 2004), she also published *Body Talk: A Power Guide for Girls* (Hodder Headline, 2005) with Elizabeth Reid Boyd. She is currently working on projects involving the cultural politics of child sexual abuse and post-structuralism and sexual difference.

Ian Buchanan

Ian Buchanan is Professor of Critical and Cultural Theory at the University of Cardiff, Wales. He is the founding editor of the *Deleuze Studies Journal* and series editor of the *Deleuze Connections* series. The author of numerous journal articles on Deleuze, Jameson, Žižek and de Certeau, his books include *Deleuze and Guattari's Anti-Oedipus* (Continuum, 2008) and *Deleuzism: A Metacommentary* (Edinburgh University Press, 2000).

Verena Andermatt Conley

Verena Conley is Visiting Professor of Comparative Literature and of Romance Languages and Literatures at Harvard University. She is the author of a number of texts concerning critical and cultural theory, ecology and gender studies and twentieth-century French literature, including *Littérature, Politique et communisme: Lire 'Les Lettres françaises,' 1942–1972* (Lang, 2004) and *The War with the Beavers: Learning to be Wild in North Wood* (Minnesota, 2003; 2005).

Ian Cook

Ian Cook is Programme Chair for the Politics and International Studies Programme in the School of Social Sciences and Humanities, Murdoch University. He is the author of *Government and Democracy in Australia* (Oxford University Press, 2004) and *Reading Mill: Studies in Political Theory* (Macmillan, 1998). His research interests concern political theory, politics and the Internet, and theorising as an intellectual and social practice.

Tauel Harper

Tauel Harper is a Lecturer in Communications Studies at the University of Western Australia. His PhD examined the effects of media upon democratic systems, with an emphasis on the influence of the Internet on the public sphere. His research has covered the relationship between technology and subjectivity and mass media and policy. He is currently researching Deleuze and fluid politics.

Timothy Murray

Timothy Murray is Professor of Comparative Literature and English at Cornell University, director of the Society for the Humanities, and curator of the Rose Goldsen Archive of New Media Art. The co-curator of CTHEORY Multimedia, his research concerns new media, film and visual studies with a strong emphasis on philosophy and psychoanalysis. He is the author of *Digital Baroque: New Media Art and Cinematic Folds* (Minnesota, 2008).

Saul Newman

Saul Newman is Reader in Political Theory at Goldsmiths College, University of London. With interests in poststructuralist thought, as well as post-Marxist and post-Anarchist theory, he is the author of *From Bakunin to Lacan* (Lexington Books, 2001), *Power and Politics in Poststructuralist Thought* (Routledge, 2005), as well as *Politics Most Unusual: Violence, Sovereignty and Democracy in the War on Terror* (with Michael Levine and Damian Cox) (Palgrave Macmillan, 2008). Forthcoming from Edinburgh University Press is his latest book, *The Politics of Postanarchism* (2009).

Patricia Pisters

Patricia Pisters is Professor of Film Studies in the Department of Media Studies at the University of Amsterdam. Her PhD concerned the work of Gilles Deleuze and its significance for film theory. She is the author of *Micropolitics of Media Culture* (Amsterdam University Press, 2001) and *The Matrix of Visual Culture* (Stanford University Press, 2003)

Mark Poster

Mark Poster is Professor of History at the University of California, Irvine. He is the author of a number of texts that share an emphasis on media and critical theory, including *The Mode of Information* (Chicago Press, 1990) and *What's the Matter with the Internet?* (Minnesota, 2001). His most recent book, *Information Please: Culture and Politics in the Age of Digital Machines*, was published in 2006 by Duke University Press.

Horst Ruthrof

Horst Ruthrof is Emeritus Professor in the Department of Philosophy at Murdoch University. The author of *The Body in Language* (Cassell, 2000) and *The Reader's Construction of Narrative* (Routledge, 1981), his research interests include film and televisual narrative and theories of interpretation from Kant to Deleuze.

David Savat

David Savat lectures in Communications Studies at the University of Western Australia. He has a background in political theory and poststructuralist thought, with an emphasis on new media and the significance of digital technologies.

Bent Meier Sorensen

Bent Meier Sorensen is an Associate Professor in the Department of Management, Politics and Philosophy at the Copenhagen Business School. Together with Martin Fuglsang, he edited *Deleuze and the Social* (Edinburgh University Press, 2006). The author of numerous articles in both Dutch and English publications, he has a background in Literature, Psychology and Sociology, Organisational Psychology and Economics and Business Administration.

Eugene Thacker

Eugene Thacker is Associate Professor in the School of Literature, Communication and Culture at the Georgia Institute of Technology.

The author of *The Exploit* (Minnesota, 2007), *The Global Genome* (MIT, 2005) and *Biomedia* (Minnesota, 2004), his research deploys continental and post-continental theory over contexts that include biotechnology, informatics and the Internet.

Index

Diagrams are given in italics.

EUP JOURNALS ONLINE
Paragraph

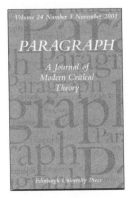

ISSN   0264-8334

eISSN   1750-0176

Three issues per year

Find *Paragraph* at
www.eupjournals.com/PARA

Founded in 1983, *Paragraph* is a leading journal in modern critical
theory. It publishes essays and review articles in English which explore critical theory in general and its application to literature, other
arts and society.

Regular special issues by guest editors highlight important themes
and figures in modern critical theory. Paragraph publishes regular
special issues by guest editors that highlight important themes
and key figures in modern critical theory. A selection of recent titles
include:
- Extending Hospitality
- Roland Barthes Retroactively
- Blanchot's Epoch
- Deleuze and Science
- Idea of the LIterary
- Jacques Rancière
- Genet
- Men's Bodies
- Practices of Hybridity
- Gender and Sexuality

Edinburgh
University Press

**Register for
Table of Contents Alerts at
www.eupjournals.com**

EUP JOURNALS
Derrida Today

ISSN   1754-8500

eISSN   1754-8519

Two issues per year

Find *Derrida Today* at
www.eupjournals.com/drt

Derrida Today focuses on what Derrida's thought offers to contemporary debates about politics, society and global affairs. Controversies about power, violence, identity, globalisation, the resurgence of religion, economics and the role of critique all agitate public policy, media dialogue and academic debate.

Derrida Today explores how Derridean thought and deconstruction make significant contributions to this debate, and reconsider the terms on which it takes place.

Derrida Today is now inviting papers that deal with the ongoing relevance of Derrida's work and deconstruction in general to contemporary issues; the way it reconfigures the academic and social protocols and languages by which such issues are defined and discussed, and innovative artistic practices that adopt a "deconstructive" approach to how our contemporary situation can be represented.

Edinburgh University Press

**Register to receive
Table of Contents Alerts at
www.eupjournals.com**

EUP JOURNALS ONLINE
Deleuze Studies

ISSN 1750-2241
eISSN 1755-1684
Two issues per year

Editor
Ian Buchanan, Cardiff University
Co-editors
Claire Colebrook, Edinburgh University
Tom Conley, Harvard University
Gary Genosko, Lakehead University
Christian Kerslake, Middlesex University
Gregg Lambert, Syracuse University

Deleuze Studies is the first paper based journal to focus exclusively on the work of Gilles Deleuze. Published twice a year, in June and December, and edited by a team of highly respected Deleuze scholars, *Deleuze Studies* is a forum for new work on the writings of Gilles Deleuze. *Deleuze Studies* is a bold journal that challenges orthodoxies, encourages debate, invites controversy, seeks new applications, proposes new interpretations, and above all make new connections between scholars and ideas in the field.

It will do this by publishing a wide variety of scholarly work on Gilles Deleuze, including articles that focus directly on his work, but also critical reviews of the field, as well as new translations and annotated bibliographies. It does not limit itself to any one field: it is neither a philosophy journal, nor a literature journal, nor a cultural studies journal, but all three and more.

Deleuze Studies is as interdisciplinary as Deleuze himself was and welcomes contributions from scholars working in all fields. Deleuze Studies is published by Edinburgh University Press with the support of the Centre for Critical and Cultural Theory at Cardiff University.
Find *Deleuze Studies* at www.eupjournals.com/DLS

Edinburgh University Press

**Register to receive
Table of Contents Alerts at
www.eupjournals.com**